THROUGH THE JINGLE JUNGLE

THROUGH THE JINGLE JUNGLE

The Art and Business of Making Music for Commercials

STEVE KARMEN

BILLBOARD BOOKS
An imprint of Watson-Guptill Publications/New York

The following have generously given permission to use extended quotations from copyrighted works: From "Twice as Much for a Nickel, Too," by Austen "Ginger" Croom-Johnson and Alan Kent. © 1940 Pepsi-Cola Company. Reprinted by permission of PepsiCo, Inc. From "Chiquita Banana," by Len Mackenzie and Garth Montgomery. © 1946, Maxwell-Wirges Publications, Inc. Copyright assigned to Shawnee Press, Inc.; Delaware Water Gap, PA 18327. U.S. Copyright renewed 1974. All Rights Reserved. Used with permission. From *Act One*, by Moss Hart. © 1959 by Catherine Carlisle Hart and Joseph Hyman, Trustees. Reprinted by permission of Random House, Inc.

Senior Editor: Tad Lathrop
Book Design: Bob Fillie
Jacket Illustration: Arnold Roth

Copyright © 1989 by Steve Karmen

First published 1989 by Billboard Books, an imprint of Watson-Guptill Publications, a division of Billboard Publications, Inc., 1515 Broadway, New York, NY 10036.

Library of Congress Cataloging-in-Publication Data
Karmen, Steve.
    Through the jingle jungle / by Steve Karmen.
        p.   cm.
    Includes index.
    ISBN 0-8230-7707-1
    1. Popular music—Writing and publishing.   2. Radio advertising.
3. Television advertising.   I. Title.
MT67.K36   1989
    780'.23'73—dc19   88-38573
                                                                CIP
                                                                MN

Manufactured in the United States of America
First printing, 1989
1 2 3 4 5 6 7 8 9 / 94 93 92 91 90 89

*To the spirit of my father, whose vision and wisdom
taught me to formulate my own rules when there were none.*

*To the constant love and support I receive from
my mother, who taught me about the rainy days.*

*And to my wife. Only a woman named Mary could
put up with what it took to write this book.*

ACKNOWLEDGMENTS

I WISH TO THANK the following professionals, friends, and colleagues for their willingness to share their expertise and talk about the things they do:

Robin Batteau, Debra K. Bedell, Ken Bichel, Dick and April Capri, Suzanne Ciani, Kacey Cisyk, Bill Cotton, Steve Cowles, Lee Davis, Jules Delgado, Bernie Dreighton, Wally Dunbar, Gerry Edelstein, Jean Thomas Fox, Jack Garten, Gary Geyer, Moe Goldstein, Jake Holmes, David Horowitz, Susan Kamil, Kenny Karen, Mary Karmen, Gary Klaff, Joey Levine, Mary Little, Rich Look, Dick Lord, David Lucas, Bonnie Malen, Burt Manning, Helen Mikkelsen, Charlie Moss, Hunter Murtaugh, Faith Norwick, Ted Pettus, Marion Preston, Ed Rak, Anne Ranta, Roger Rhodes, Joanne Rodgers, Elliot Schrager, Dick Schwaeber, Gerry Schwartz, Billy Slapin, Lynn and Jeffrey Slutsky, and Sid Woloshin.

I offer special thanks to my editor, Tad Lathrop, whose talent, guidance, and understanding during the process were a constant reminder that everyone needs to be edited.

CONTENTS

INTRODUCTION *1*

1 AN OVERVIEW *3*

2 JINGOLOGY 101 *27*

3 A FOOT IN THE DOOR *55*

4 THE CREATIVE PROCESS *79*

5 MAKING YOUR PRESENTATION *100*

6 THE TALENT AND THOSE WHO BOOK THEM *109*

7 THE PRODUCTION BUDGET *133*

8 TALENT PAYMENT *175*

9 MAKING THE DEAL *184*

10 THE DAY OF THE RECORDING SESSION *217*

11 POSTPRODUCTION *234*

12 YOU'RE ON THE AIR! *238*

13 FINDING OUT WHERE THE "HITS" ARE *243*

APPENDIX *252*

INDEX *258*

INTRODUCTION

I LOVE MY WORK.

I compose in the comfort of my own home, then go to a state-of-the-art recording studio where I spend a few hours with the best musicians and singers in town, who bring my music to life. My clients mostly leave me alone to do what they hired me to do. We eat a good on-the-job lunch, and when I come home there's money in the mailbox.

It's not too shabby.

Sometimes there's *no* money in the mailbox. This is one of the "fringe benefits" of self-employment.

When people ask what sort of work I do, my response invariably evokes surprise followed by a sudden knowing smile, as if I'd let them in on a little personal secret. They've never met anyone who does *that* for a living. Then comes the inevitable: "Anything I know?"

Whenever I talk about my profession, people's reactions never cease to amaze. Their eyes light up and their interests are kindled; they're fascinated about the way the process works.

And everyone has questions.

And, without exception, an opinion.

And a relative who sings.

It's become obvious to me that there is a lot of curiosity and more than a little misinformation about what really goes on in the business—among the general public as well as those who are or would like to become actively involved. So to clear up a few popular misconceptions and provide some understanding of the beginner traps that start the sleepless nights, I offer this work.

If you are someone interested in the influence, creation, production, and execution of advertising music; a student or teacher concerned with techniques of effective product promotion; a musician or singer who wants to perform on jingles; an advertising professional (producer, copywriter, art director, business manager, or account person) seeking a practical reference about one of the most important and communicative segments of your industry; a publisher of popular music who wants to participate in the huge license fees that are available when advertisers use your songs; or just a civilian who wants to know more about the inner workings of those inescapable melodies—perchance to take a shot at making money in America's newest musical art form—then, as the song says, This Book's for You!

Whether you are a novice bursting with enthusiasm to write the next great hamburger song, or a creative director trying to find it, or a client desperately in need of it to refurbish his sagging image, it is my hope that this work will provide some insight into the methodology of musical advertising.

And while this is about music and the very personal techniques of composing, it is also about the craft of doing business in the trenches of Madison Avenue. It has been written from the perspective of someone who does it full-time, a composer working for himself, running a one-man shop for his entire career. In some cases this leads to opinions that may be contrary to established industry policy, or in conflict with guidelines accepted by those who are sheltered on someone else's payroll.

I have attempted to present the issues impartially. But if some discussions seem to favor one side, kindly remember that self-employed people in the arts are motivated by the basics of survival, and that the very nature of creative work demands that everyone does it his own special way.

The composer with the most realistic chance of making it is the one who can most uniquely express his or her own point of view.

In the jargon of the trade, this is the person who comes up with the best hook.

1
AN OVERVIEW

"BEFORE WE BEGIN," suggested the moderator of the Big Apple Advertising Awards judging session, "let's go around the table and introduce ourselves, by name and occupation. Please tell us who you are and what you do."

And when it came to his turn, he said, "I write jingles."

And they all laughed.

Jingles? Jingles are a Rodneyism: they don't get no respect. Aren't they those cute little ditties that people hum on their way to the refrigerator? And yet, as the distant notes joggle your memory and stimulate last-minute additions to your shopping list (though you can't quite make out the words while you're chewing), advertising music is working its inescapable influence on your life and on the buying patterns of TV watchers and radio listeners all over the world.

Jingles (the industry) is one of the very few remaining businesses where someone with a little courage, daring, talent, imagination, sense of adventure, and not necessarily a lot of formal musical training can have a few hits, earn big bucks over the short term, and develop an intimate relationship with anxiety and insecurity.

The public perception is that any work in musical advertising generates unbelievable ongoing wealth via residual payments, and that a jingle composer enjoys a cushy life of fun and games (a little louder on

3

the strings), where everyone lives happily ever after.

America, it just ain't so.

There are two sides to the story of the jingle business: the fun side of invention and creativity, which brings with it that exhilarating feeling of accomplishment when a pleasing melody is born or a lyric works; and the business side, where the client wants everything—in some cases unjustly—and the wrong people reap the big rewards because they have a union, while composers do not.

Although composers in the other branches of the music business (records, theater, TV film scores, and movies) regard jingles as a stop-gap source of income between their regular jobs, there is an entire industry of specialists—composers, arrangers, producers, jingle houses—who work full-time creating custom-made music specifically for advertising.

Never before have so many people expended so much personal energy, worked so many long hours, been late for so many appointments, and missed so many birthdays and anniversaries, all for the aggrandizement of inanimate objects (which include politicians, who are always packaged and sold like inanimate objects). Measured in dedication and dollars, the effort is monumental.

In advertising, the product rules, and the goal is to get you, the consumer, to buy something because it fits your image, the image created by the ads. And though no one likes a salesman, music is a part of the sales team that is welcome. A strong, unique, musical statement can add much to the success of a product. Within the daily deluge of broadcast advertising, a good music track can cut through the clutter and get attention. Sometimes the music in a commercial is the one saving element, changing mediocrity to magic. For a big-budget client, one who produces many spots during each year, a good musical image means that the agency doesn't have to reinvent the wheel each time a commercial is made. Music keeps the ads fresh with friendly nonoffensive repetition.

Yet the jingle writer, unlike composers of other kinds of music, earns only a one-time fee in return for the ongoing contribution of his work.

So please rid yourself of any preconceived notions about jingles, as we begin to examine and dissect the whys and wherefores of advertising's most persuasive tool in the fight to infiltrate and conquer the American mind.

Welcome to the world of the jingle, the tag, the hook, the musical logo, the background score, and the donut.

THE CURRENT STATE OF THE INDUSTRY

The jingle industry today is like frontier life in the 1800s, right out of John Wayne: freewheeling, no rules, intensely competitive, with constant excitement, an oscillating synthesizer in the next apartment, an occasional gunfight at the Saatchi Corral, and everyone trying everything to keep up with changing times.

And the times and ways of doing business are changing rapidly as a direct result of the rampant onslaught of digital and MIDI technology.

At one time the industry was concentrated in the big cities: when agencies needed music, they usually went to New York, Chicago, Los Angeles, or Dallas. Now almost anyone anywhere with a synthesizer and a recording machine can become a one-man band and produce jingles, creating more competition for the available jobs.

The quality of advertising music has suffered accordingly. These days, cheap tracks are easy to come by, and their appeal has given the budget-conscious advertiser a brand-new argument when making production decisions: "Can the public really tell the difference between a live drummer and a machine? A real brass section and a button?" When close enough is good enough, does it matter?

The jingle business is not like other music businesses. Few non-jingle composers are required to crank out the poundage and variety of sounds needed to satisfy the frequency of the twenty-house cattle call, that wild orgy of musical glut produced to appease a client who isn't sure what he wants for his product, except that he wants to use music to sell more of it. Sadly, it is rare today for an agency to commit itself to a single composer without holding a creative competition for a job, even though this simple statement of artistic confidence would add immeasurably to the energy brought into the effort and invariably produce a better product.

No other industry is as public as advertising. While business failures appear on the financial pages and are casually noticed and soon forgotten, advertising failures appear in the living room, unavoidably there for everyone's comment.

If an agency loses an account, it affects all the suppliers who service that account. And when one jingle house's work replaces that of another, everyone knows it. The industry then waits attentively for the arrival of the new agency's campaign, poised like envious cats, ready to pounce on the new creative, veins pumped with venom, conjuring spirits that will cause the new music house and winning agency to turn out lousy work (and contract leprosy—and that goes for the dumb client, too!).

But for a composer, outweighing all the negatives is the opportunity that advertising provides to write many different kinds of music and have them produced under the best possible conditions. A busy jingle house might be working on a high-tech electronic corporate spot, a bouncy cola tune, a symphonic airline chart, an operatic rip-off, and a hard-rock car commercial, all at the same time. And while songwriters often wait a year or more for recordings to come out, advertising composers enjoy the instant gratification of being on the air in days, and sometimes literally overnight.

The demands of changing tastes and technologies make the musical advertising industry potentially one of the most rewarding businesses imaginable.

And everyone needs it by tomorrow.

THE CLIENT IS KING

America's economy communicates with the consumer through advertising and is constantly in need of new and innovative selling ideas. The relentless impact of advertising cannot be overstated or underestimated. The tone of commercials often reflects the economic mood of the land and in turn influences popular culture, with ad slogans providing a constantly fresh source of the catchphrases that pepper our conversations. "Try it, you'll like it!," "I can't believe I ate the whole thing!," and "Where's the beef?" all began as part of product advertising.

Nothing happens without advertising. Every event, every entertainment program, every triumph and tragedy, is brought to you by someone. And almost all advertising is paid advertising, paid for by a sponsor with something to sell. The singular exceptions are the small number of commercials called "public service messages," which stations are required by law to broadcast free. Some public service ads are the most imaginative and inventive ads on the air, requiring the ultimate in creativity when there is not the clout of a large production budget or the advantage of paid-for repetition. But these announcements—about diseases, health, charities, education, current local events, and other issues of vital personal and social import—are usually aired in the middle of the night when there are few people watching. After all, prime time is a marketplace, not a charity.

But for the rest of television and radio, the business of broadcasting, advertising is king, paying for everything, and sitting in final judgment over what America watches. If an advertiser pulls his support from a show, it goes off the air, and it's a rare public outcry that can create enough pressure to influence a network to save a program once it has demonstrated an inability to attract a large audience. Television's job is to provide an audience for advertising, because the stations with the most-watched programs can charge the most when they sell their airtime to sponsors.

Nothing is presented in its entirety anymore. Even "with limited commercial interruption" is a rarity. And advertising is everywhere. We rent video cassettes for home use only to discover that they, too, begin with commercials, sometimes more than one, if not for specific products, then for the sequel of the film we are about to watch or for other films from that particular production company. Some viewers zap the ads, but those who don't have paid to be advertised to. Think about that power: advertising is so strong that it can reach you even when you have expressed your freedom of choice and paid to watch a videotape in the privacy of your own home. Whose choice, Big Brother?

People are used to commercials. They accept them as the way things are. At one time movie theaters never showed advertising, but today a theater owner has no choice but to do so—somewhere up the line a deal was made to include a commercial at the head of each first-run film. Because of the intense competition to show the few money-making movies, exhibitors have to take what they can get. And they can't delete the commercials even if they want to—tampering with the print could result in the possible loss of a distributor. But since theater owners make most of their money from concessions anyway—popcorn and soda are advertised on the screen before the picture begins—what does it matter if there has to be a car commercial or a plug for the local shoestore? Nobody objects; it's all in the family.

But all of this was inevitable—simply a case of advertisers discovering a way to take advantage of a captive audience.

Music is major part of the ad blitz: over 70 percent of all commercials use music in some form or another, and over 40 percent of all music on television is advertising music (see Appendix: "The Bruskin Report"). That astounding amount of daily exposure translates to power and big bucks for the music industry.

Music is advertising's most easily recognized messenger, the universal communicator that crosses over the cultural boundaries and volume settings of every generation.

Sound like an interesting place to start a business?

A LITTLE BACKGROUND

History and accepted lore have it that the jingle revolution began on December 24, 1928, on a local radio broadcast in Minnesota, when "Have You Tried Wheaties?" was performed for the first time. Advertisers had discovered a new and unique way of delivering their messages, with little songs that the public could hum or recall when they were not listening to the radio. As jingles became new tools for mind stimulation, they began to be recognized as a foundation upon which to build a long-term advertising image. As the popularity of ad music grew, many sponsors turned to jingles to help serve their advertising needs.

The art of successful advertising is understanding what the sponsor wants to say, and then finding a unique way to make the consumer remember it. Early jingles told the whole story with lyrics—everything you ever wanted to know about the product, and more!

> Pepsi-Cola hits the spot.
> Twelve full ounces, that's a lot!
> Twice as much just a nickel, too.
> Pepsi-Cola is the drink for you. *

At that time Coke also cost a nickel, but Pepsi was telling listeners that they could have twice the quantity of drink for the same price as

---

* From "Twice as Much for a Nickel, Too" by Austen "Ginger" Croom-Johnson and Alan Kent. © 1940 Pepsi-Cola Company. Reprinted by permission of PepsiCo, Inc.

the other guy. And to underline the message, part of the rhythm figure was sung, "Nickel, nickel, nickel, nickel . . . ," making an indelible mark on the memory.

It was the beginning of the cola wars.

Let's imagine what might have happened when the Chiquita Banana Company came to their advertising agency for help.

The account supervisor, having just returned from a lengthy briefing with the president of Chiquita Banana, is leading the meeting. On the table in front of each person is the strategy paper outlining what the problems are, along with some recommended solutions.

"I'll sum it up: people are just not buying curved fruit. This year *round* is in. Look at apples. Look at plums. Skyrocketing! Round. That's what people want. People perceive curved as passé. Look at pears—in a nose dive. Look at pineapples—ugh! They have that thick-skin problem. We need to do something great for curved fruit, something unique and original to make the public aware of the benefits of *bananas*!"

The creative director: "Okay, let's examine the good things about bananas."

Copywriter One: "They taste great."

Copywriter Two: "They're less filling."

"Taste great!"

"Less filling!"

The creative director: "No, that approach doesn't seem right for this product category. Besides, apples and plums are doing taste campaigns, and we don't have the budget to out-clout them. We've got to develop something different, something original! Let's go easy on the taste angle. Everyone knows what bananas taste like anyway. Let's tackle the storage problem. I think there's a different direction here. Nobody is talking about fruit storage. Bananas spoil quickly. What can we say about that?"

"Keep them in the refrigerator."

"Bananas don't do well in the cold."

"Neither do I, Norman."

"I've got it! Suppose that instead of telling people about how a banana tastes, we tell them how to make bananas last longer when they get them home."

The account supervisor: "Great!"

Copywriter One: "I can write something about how bananas taste better as they ripen, with a warning not to put them in the fridge. That'll make good copy. And it'll please the legal department—they like commercials with warnings. Maybe we can get some canned music. How about something African—bananas sound African, don't they? Let's get some African library music. I can write scary copy warning people not to put their bananas in the refrigerator."

The creative director: "No, we need something friendly, and something more distinctive than library music. We have to sound *different*, with our *own* sound that's not like anyone else's."

"Wait! Suppose we do it with a jingle. That's right—with a jingle! I'll build the sets, you get the band and . . ."

"And I'll write the words."

"Why not invent a character to be the spokesman for the product? We can call her Chiquita Banana. She can be like Carmen Miranda—we'll make her turban out of bananas."

Copywriter Two: "How about this for a lyrical direction:

"I'm Chiquita Banana, and I've come to say,
Bananas have to ripen in a certain way.
When they are fleck'd with brown
And have a golden hue,
Bananas taste best
And are the best for you.

You can put them in a salad.
You can bake them in a pie—aye!
Any way you want to eat them,
It's impossible to beat them.

But bananas like the climate
Of the very very tropical equator,
So you must never put bananas
In the refrigerator.
No no no no!"*

*From "Chiquita Banana" by Len Mackenzie and Garth Montgomery. © 1946, Maxwell-Wirges Publications, Inc. Copyright assigned to Shawnee Press, Inc.; Delaware Water Gap, PA 18327. U.S. Copyright renewed 1974. All Rights Reserved. Used with permission.

The account supervisor: "That's great guys, just great! You have my go-ahead to contact some jingle houses and get a few demos. But keep the costs down, okay? You're not apples and plums yet!"

This dialogue is hypothetical, of course, though not improbable. In the old days, jingles like the great Chiquita Banana song were usually created from within the agency infrastructure—the lyrics, certainly, and probably the music, too, which was often composed by someone whose payment for the job would have been nothing over and above his regular salary. It was the style then, in the old days, to keep things in-house, since in the beginning there was no out-of-house.

But later on, as more and more advertisers began to use music to color the mood of their messages, independent jingle companies started to pop up, companies who specialized in creating custom-made music and background scores specifically designed for advertising.

Today's advertising problems are approached from essentially a similar, standard direction:

1. The client communicates his goals to the agency account team ("the suits").

2. The account team, in conjunction with the research department, develops a position paper, sometimes called the strategy paper, detailing as much history and marketing information as necessary to begin seeking a creative solution.

3. Creative types (long hair, hip clothes, often cranky and depressed) are brought into the process, and ideas are proposed and rejected based upon current market conditions and knowledge about what others in the product category are doing.

4. Ways are discussed to make the message preemptive in its field.

5. A creative theme is agreed upon and approved for development.

STEPS IN THE JINGLE-MAKING PROCESS

Here is the usual order of events that take place before a successful jingle reaches the American living room:

1. The agency producer or the agency music department contacts jingle suppliers (typically four or five, though in some cases as many as twenty), requesting demos of a musical direction they want to develop.

2. After reviewing submissions, the agency chooses a winner.

3. The winning jingle house hires an arranger (usually not the same person as the composer), and a recording session takes place.

4. Either before the session or immediately thereafter, the jingle composer and/or the jingle house sign the agency standard form contract wherein they give away—forever—all rights to their song, including the right to provide future rearrangements of their music.

5. If the jingle composer or jingle house remains in favor at the advertising agency, they will be permitted to produce future tracks that use their song. But the agency has no legal obligation to hire them ever again.

SOURCES OF INCOME

Income in the jingle business can be earned from the following:

1. demo fees
2. creative fees
3. arranging fees
4. musician's (AF of M) session fees and residuals
5. vocal (AFTRA/SAG) session fees and residuals
6. performance royalties (ASCAP/BMI)
7. continuance fees (dreamt of, but mostly unattainable)
8. publishing (sheet music) royalties and other possible ancillary income
9. payroll handling fees

Most often agencies will pay for demos. Sometimes they won't. The decision about whether to work for nothing at the demo stage is up to the jingle supplier (discussed further in Chapter Three). Typical demo fees range from zero to $1,500, averaging $500 to $1,000. These are either spent on production costs (studios, singers, musicians to augment machines, and so on) or are allocated for ongoing operation costs (rent, telephone, electricity, the cost of equipment).

During the demo stage, though he completes his creative assignment and writes an entire jingle, the composer receives nothing for the investment of his time.

After winning a competition, the composer/jingle house is paid a creative fee, currently ranging from $2,500 to $10,000, averaging $7,500, depending on whether the client is a big national advertiser or a smaller regional one.

If the composer is working for a jingle house, and not for his own company, the usual creative-fee split is 75 percent to the jingle house and 25 percent to the composer (sometimes 70/30, occasionally 60/40, rarely 50/50).

If the composer works for himself or in a partnership, he gets to keep more.

When production begins, the winning jingle house receives an ar-ranging fee, normally between $1,500 and $3,500 per spot, averaging $2,000. The arranger usually receives 40 percent of the total arranging fee from the hiring jingle house.

If the arranger works directly for the ad agency, and not for a jingle house, he gets to keep more.

After the recording session, the names of the composer and arranger are listed on the musicians' union (AF of M) contract in one of the four double-scale categories—orchestra leader, contractor, arranger, or or-chestrator—thereby qualifying for *musician's* residuals (ongoing tal-ent payments), modest amounts won by the weakest of the trade unions.

But most importantly, now the composer and arranger will each have the opportunity to sing on the final track (or appear to sing), either as soloist or more often as part of the background vocal group, qualifying them for union *singer* residuals, which can be enormous. In some not-so-rare cases, vocal residuals can run as high as $100,000 per year for a *single national campaign*, with the average in the $20,000 to $50,000 range for network advertisers. Even local and regional vocal residuals can range between $5,000 to $15,000 per year, per product.

Please note the striking difference between fees to compose and fees to sing. There are no residuals for composers who just compose.

When the composer/jingle house signs the agency contract, as men-tioned earlier, they give up all rights to their song. But unlike popular songwriter contracts or TV/film scoring contracts, in which the composer retains his right to collect fees for broadcast performances of his music (see Chapter Nine), agency music contract language is usually not acceptable to the societies that dispense these royalties (ASCAP and BMI). Therefore the jingle composer usually receives no performance income.

If involvement with the ad agency and account continues after the initial recording, the jingle house can earn rearranging fees, again divided between the arranger and the jingle house—not the composer. But unquestionably the biggest plus of being able to provide rearrangements is that the jingle house will again have the all-important right to select the vocalists for the new tracks (usually the composer and arranger, as well as other members of the jingle house), thereby permitting everyone to requalify for the rich rewards of the vocal residual. If, for any reason, the composer is unavailable to sing, then he receives nothing for the new versions of his song (and may want to kill himself).

In the event that the agency decides to hire a different jingle house to provide rearrangements, the original composer and jingle house receive nothing. If the agency decides to *continue* reworking the original jingle with other music suppliers for the life of the campaign, the original composer and jingle house receive nothing. Ever again. Even though the music goes on and on.

So for the composer, the real money in the jingle business is not made from composing, but from the ability to be counted among those who qualify for vocal residuals. (Note that I did not say anything about vocal *talent*.) For everyone, the driving financial force, second to none, is to maintain and retain the ability to sing on the final tracks and appear on the AFTRA/SAG vocal reports. It is often the creative force as well, with composers ever inventing musical ways to justify the uses of a background vocal group. *80 to 85 percent of a top composer's income is earned via the vocal residual.*

Through the years, attempts have been made to achieve residual status for composers, or at least a similar equity with composers of other kinds of music. Being able to negotiate a *continuance fee* (the industry term for any type of ongoing payments for ongoing uses of compositions) would eliminate the need for jingle writers, arrangers, and producers to continue the sham of running from one side of the glass to the other to sing, when they have really been hired to compose and produce. But the addiction to the vocal residual continues to choke any progress. The income it generates vastly colors how business is done by all participants: the composer, the jingle company, the agency, and the client.

The enormity of the vocal residual relative to total income is illustrated in figures 1 and 3 below. Figure 2 shows the sources of income for the jingle house—most of which is absorbed by operating costs.

FIGURE 1. INCOME FOR THE JINGLE WRITER

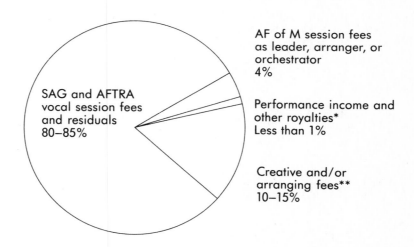

SAG and AFTRA vocal session fees and residuals 80–85%

AF of M session fees as leader, arranger, or orchestrator 4%

Performance income and other royalties* Less than 1%

Creative and/or arranging fees** 10–15%

*Includes sheet music, licensed band arrangements, and phonograph records.
**This is the composer portion of the 75/25% split.

FIGURE 2. INCOME FOR THE JINGLE HOUSE

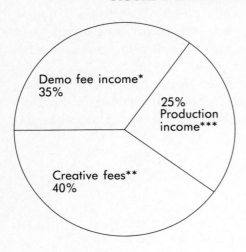

Demo fee income*
35%

25%
Production
income***

Creative fees**
40%

*Demo fees paid by agencies (typically $500–1,500 per demo) are usually exceeded by production costs. At best, the jingle house will break even.

**This is the jingle house portion of the 75/25% split. Creative fee income varies depending on the number of successful compositions. On average, 10% of demos become "finals," qualifying for payment of creative fees.

***Includes studio rental, markup on billable musicians and singers, and other fees, earned when a jingle is produced as a final in the jingle house or home/office studio.

FIGURE 3. INCOME FOR THE JINGLE HOUSE OWNER

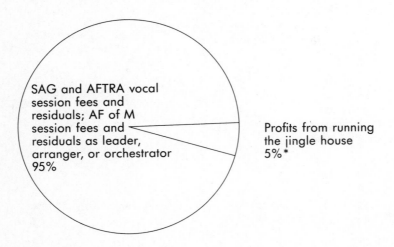

SAG and AFTRA vocal session fees and residuals; AF of M session fees and residuals as leader, arranger, or orchestrator
95%

Profits from running the jingle house
5%*

*Increases to 10% when creative fee income is especially large. The assets that might be considered if the jingle house were for sale would include recording equipment, any copyrights owned by the jingle house, and the creative good will of the principals. In the current competitive atmosphere, the "good will" factor is "as good as your last hit."

A summary of the possible income generated from one jingle during the first year it was created is shown in tables 1, 2, and 3. The jingle (designated Spot 1) is broadcast in four consecutive thirteen-week cycles by a sponsor who ordinarily buys air time on regional radio and TV, with an occasional network use. A rearrangement (Spot 2) is created for use during the third and fourth cycles, and it runs in addition to the original version rather than replacing it. For this example we assume the composer and arranger are working for a jingle house (instead of on their own). Both composer and arranger are singing in a group of three to five (a union wage category) with other jingle house staff members. The creative fee is $10,000; the arranging fee is $3,000.

TABLE 1. COMPOSER ONE-YEAR INCOME FOR ONE JINGLE	1st Cycle	2nd Cycle	3rd Cycle	4th Cycle	Year Total
Spot 1: 25% of creative fee	$2,500.00	—	—	—	$2,500.00
AF of M session fee as orchestra leader (double scale)	156.00	—	—	—	156.00
AF of M residuals as orchestra leader (double scale)*	—	117.00	117.00	117.00	351.00
SAG session fee as vocalist (including 50% overdub)	233.18	—	—	—	233.18
SAG vocal residuals	5,000.00	5,000.00	5,000,00	5,000.00	20,000.00
Spot 2: AF of M session fee as orchestra leader (double scale)	—	—	156.00	—	156.00
AF of M residuals as orchestra leader (double scale)*	—	—	—	117.00	117.00
SAG session fee as vocalist (including 50% overdub)	—	—	233.18	—	233.18
SAG vocal residuals	—	—	5,000.00	5,000.00	10,000.00
Total	7,889.18	5,117.00	10,506.18	10,234.00	$33,746.36

*First cycle residuals are included in session fee, based on 1989 wage scales.

TABLE 2. ARRANGER ONE-YEAR INCOME FOR ONE JINGLE

	1st Cycle	2nd Cycle	3rd Cycle	4th Cycle	Year Total
Spot 1:					
40% of arranging fee	$1,200.00	—	—	—	$1,200.00
AF of M session fee as arranger (double scale)	156.00	—	—	—	156.00
AF of M residuals as arranger (double scale)*	—	117.00	117.00	117.00	351.00
SAG session fee as vocalist (including 50% overdub)	233.18	—	—	—	233.18
SAG vocal residuals	5,000.00	5,000.00	5,000,00	5,000.00	20,000.00
Spot 2:					
40% of arranging fee	—	—	1,200.00	—	1,200.00
AF of M session fee as arranger leader (double scale)	—	—	156.00	—	156.00
AF of M residuals as arranger (double scale)*	—	—	—	117.00	117.00
SAG session fee as vocalist (including 50% overdub)	—	—	233.18	—	233.18
SAG vocal residuals	—	—	5,000.00	5,000.00	10,000.00
Total	6,589.18	5,117.00	11,706.18	10,234.00	$33,646.36

*First cycle residuals are included in session fee.

TABLE 3. JINGLE HOUSE ONE-YEAR INCOME FOR ONE JINGLE

	1st Cycle	2nd Cycle	3rd Cycle	4th Cycle	Year Total
Spot 1:					
75% of creative fee	$7,500.00	—	—	—	$7,500.00
60% of arranging fee	1,800.00	—	—	—	1,800.00
AF of M session fee as contractor or orchestrator (double scale)	156.00	—	—	—	156.00
AF of M residuals as contractor or orchestrator (double scale)*	—	117.00	117.00	117.00	351.00
SAG session fee as vocalist (including 50% overdub)	233.18	—	—	—	233.18
SAG vocal residuals	5,000.00	5,000.00	5,000,00	5,000.00	20,000.00
Spot 2:					
60% of arranging fee	—	—	1,800.00	—	1,800.00
AF of M session fee as contractor or orchestrator (double scale)	—	—	156.00	—	156.00
AF of M residuals as contractor or orchestrator (double scale)*	—	—	—	117.00	117.00
SAG session fee as vocalist (including 50% overdub)	—	—	233.18	—	233.18
SAG vocal residuals	—	—	5,000.00	5,000.00	10,000.00
Total	14,689.18	5,117.00	12,306.18	10,234.00	$42,346.36

*First cycle residuals are included in session fee.

It should be noted that, while it is traditional for the composer to be included in the vocal group on rearrangements, the jingle house is under no obligation to also place his name on the musicians contract. Instead, a jingle house principal may serve as the orchestra leader, and may only occasionally allow the composer to qualify as an AF of M sideman. Sometimes the composer's name will not appear on the AF of M contract at all.

Also, in contrast to the example above, a rearrangement might *replace* the one on the air, and limit the income accordingly. Conversely, if an advertiser has the broadcast budget to run more than two spots (as is often done by insurance, auto, and beverage advertisers), it becomes clear how important vocal residuals are on the composer's road to Mercedesville.

How sad if the composer is unable to, or chooses not to sing.

THE FORMS OF ADVERTISING MUSIC

Back to the fun part: let's get familiar with the terms for different types of ad music.

The Jingle

A jingle, the flagship of the musical advertising industry, is the advertiser's message delivered in its most memorable form: music and lyrics. Jingles evoke an emotional response that can't be articulated by an announcer. No spoken word, no visual image communicates with the instant recognition of a catchy jingle.

The Tag, or Hook

A musical tag, or *hook*, is the key line of the jingle, the sponsor's audio banner. Although sometimes used at the beginning of a spot, this ultimate musical climax is usually the last thing the consumer hears. "America Believes in Liberty—Liberty Mutual Insurance," "Fly the Friendly Skies," "At Beneficial (Toot, Toot), You're Good for More," "Trust the Midas Touch," "Have You Driven a Ford Lately?," "Nationwide Is on Your Side," and "I Love New York" are examples of tags that sum up the sponsor's message in one fell swoop.

Sometimes a musical tag is developed separately from a jingle. An advertiser may wish to have his key line sung and nothing more.

The most effective use of a tag is to provide long-term continuity in campaigns that generate many different types of commercials for a single product. The tag becomes the single unifying theme, the common connector. A beer commercial's story line may vary from spot to spot: from the machismo of sports participation—baseball, football, hockey, basketball, nutcracking—to patriotism and special product imagery; from the brewer's heritage to the most recent six-pack sale. But while each commercial has its own mood and flavor supported by the background track, all the spots end with the delivery of the musical tag, "For All You Do, This Bud's for You."

McDonald's commercials, from McNuggets to old folks; from hamburgers to fries; from breakfast to salads, for any kind of promotion (each with it's own custom-tailored musical score), are all tagged "Good Times, Great Taste, McDonald's," making each spot a part of a greater whole, part of the campaign.

Having a memorable tag provides an advertiser with the ability to communicate all kinds of secondary information under one umbrella, yet always return to the central theme that America has come to know and love. "G.E.—We Bring Good Things to Life" and "There's More for Your Life at Sears" are musical tags that have supported many different kinds of messages for their advertisers.

The Logo

A musical logo is the same as a tag, except without the lyrics. Most often the logo represents an instrumental repeat of what had been sung in earlier commercials.

Logos, or *mnemonics*, can be derived from jingles, but are also created independently. A series of notes or sounds used consistently over time can establish a long-range product identity. The three famous notes for "N-B-C" or the two door chimes used by "A-von" are musical logos.

Background Scores

The background score provides the invaluable underlying mood for commercials that present their messages with announcer or live action, *sans* lyric. Background tracks are wall-to-wall musical themes, scored to match the film visuals or radio copy. Sometimes there are only music and sound effects in a spot, with no announcer at all.

A score may also be an instrumental rearrangement of a jingle melody, or completely original music leading up to an established vocal tag. Those who specialize in scoring often complain that they do not receive sufficient credit for their creativity when all the public remembers is the hook that someone else wrote.

The Donut

The donut, indispensable for those who earn their living as announcers, is exactly what it sounds like: something with a hole in it. It is the space left between lyric sections of the jingle for the voice-over copy. Donuts are constructed by dropping out the lyrics and replacing them with an instrumental melody, played softly so it won't fight the announcer. (Some advertisers use the background track *without* a melody as the rug for the announcer. It's a matter of taste and style.)

While jingles can tell much of the story on their own, donuts are inevitable, constructed to accommodate the nuts-and-bolts copy about dates of sale or other points that couldn't be effectively stated in a lyric. Sometimes the spot might be constructed vocal-donut-vocal-donut-tag. Voilà! The *double* donut.

Putting It Together

At the end of a typical session you're going to wind up with several *mixes*, or versions, of the jingle you've recorded, each one tailored to a specific use. The titles might be:

1. *Generic :60 Full Instrumental* (no words at all). The word *generic* refers back to the first arrangement, the original sound, sometimes called the *anthem*. Later versions might be called "Hard Rock," "Easy Rock," "Heavy Metal," "Latin," or "Motown." Still later versions might be titled "Son of Hard Rock" (no kidding), "Son of Latin," "Son of Motown," and so on. But the first spot is usually called the generic version.

2. *Generic :60 Full Vocal* (the complete lyric version of the jingle).

3. *Generic :60 Short Donut* (one hole in the jingle, usually somewhere in the middle, leading up to the tag).

4. *Generic :60 Long Donut* (typically just the opening lyrics or the hook lyrics followed by a long instrumental rug until the end, when the vocal tag takes over).

5. *Generic :60 Instrumental with Vocal Tag* (the complete instrumental from the top until the key line is sung at the end).

Since these mixes have to be completely reconstructed for the thirty and fifteen second versions, it shouldn't be surprising to learn that studio costs are inevitably the highest production budget item. More and more, to keep costs down, advertisers want to work with someone who can produce all of the above without also producing a killer studio invoice. Enter the home/office studio operator, with synths, sequencers and other machines, and perceived unlimited time-without-payment-for-production.

Adaptations of Music from Other Sources

"What a great-sounding record."
  "That's not a record; that's a commercial."
  "Oh? What's the product?"
  "I don't know. I couldn't tell. But I sure love that old song."

Advertising uses of songs from the fifties and sixties, Broadway show tunes, top 40 hits, motion picture themes, and classical and opera works, all come under the heading of adaptations of music from other sources.

An advertiser may purchase the rights to a particular song because he believes that the message is exactly what his product needs. "Can't Live Without You," the Barry Manilow song, serves the telephone company with great effectiveness (along with "Reach Out and Touch Someone," a custom-made jingle).

Often the original lyrics of a pop song are reworked to deliver a product message. The Trump Plaza Hotel and Casino in Atlantic City uses a rewritten lyric version of the fifties song "Boy from New York City." Sometimes, if the original lyric is appropriate, an advertiser will not only license the right to use the composition, but also the right to use the hit recording of it. Automobile makers, beer and cola companies, and other sponsors with deep pockets will often pay the necessary high license fees because they believe that it's worth the investment to be able to show off their products with the most current, with-it musical sounds.

But the use of adaptations has its drawbacks. Often the mood and feeling for which the big bucks were paid suffers because a substantial truncation was required to make that great four-minute epic work in thirty seconds. Money might have been spent for not much more than a tag or logo. And if, during that fleeting burst of a thirty second spot, a listener hears an adaptation of a pop song and remembers it with fond recognition, his mind was probably on the song, and not on the product. This is the kind of familarity that can *hurt* a campaign. Taking away the impact of originality gives the consumer yet another reason to tune out the message.

The first and foremost job of advertising music is to attract the listener's attention. While adaptations of music from other sources will inevitably be used (perhaps because it is easier to be creative when a big part of the work is already done), they are less effective in the long run than the custom-made jingle. Music and lyrics that have been conceived, nurtured, and designed specifically for one purpose give a product its own identity without trading on something that was born elsewhere. (This is obviously not the point of view of popular music publishers, who stand to make big money whenever their songs are used in advertising.)

Library Music

Hidden among the jingles, background scores, and music adaptations is a segment of the jingle business that provides up to 20 percent of all music used in advertising. Libraries of prerecorded music offer an alternative for a client who doesn't have the budget or the time to produce an original custom-made track.

If a radio spot about a certain sale has to be on the air overnight, library music can provide a quickie rug under sixty seconds of copy. If a TV spot calls for a stand-up announcer and he sounds deadly just spouting words, a needle drop (the term for one use of one hunk of library music) goes a long way toward making the message tolerable and interesting. Using canned music (the libraries hate this term) is both fast and cheap.

A good library will have thousands of hours of music available. There will be knowledgable professionals, both librarians and sound engineers, who are familiar with the contents of the numerous music catalogs. Their expertise can create scores for.television spots that, in some cases, rival the custom-made stuff. A talented editor's razor blade can make segues between various tracks to create a rainbow of sounds for one commercial.

Being able to clearly describe musical needs can help a librarian locate the suitable tracks. Often, if the agency notifies a studio beforehand that they are looking for a certain type of sound, the session engineer can have choices waiting.

In addition to offering instant tracks for tight deadlines, sound libraries provide access to nearly every type and style of music. And a library will often have a small MIDI studio, where a track of a synthesizer or drum machine can be overdubbed on to an existing library selection, making even the most mundane prerecorded music sound interesting.

Every voice-over recording studio has library music available on compact disks to accommodate the client who decides in the middle of a session that his commercial needs more than just an announcer. Most studios have comparable libraries and charge $200 to $600 per spot, out of which they pay a percentage (depending on the areas of use— local, regional, national, network, or cable) to the owner of the library as a license fee. This amount provides non-exclusive use of the music in one specific commercial for an unlimited period of time. If the commercial is changed or altered in any way, or if the music is reused in other commercials for the same product, the purchaser is obligated to pay an additional license fee for each new spot.

Rarely does an advertiser negotiate an exclusivity for library music. The "rug factor" (the innocuous fuzz under the announcer) makes this unnecessary.

Music libraries also provide sound effects, having infinite choices available of every aural shape and texture.

Library soundtracks are usually created and recorded in Europe under buy-out conditions (where both the composer and musicians receive one-time fees and nothing more), making this budget item attractive to the advertiser who only wants music to be an incidental mood and not an expensive part of his message.

The use of library music does not require payment of residuals to musicians.

But our story is about *original* music.

Influential advertising music, whatever its form or style, is supposed to sound *different* from other types of music, different from everything that surrounds it on the airwaves. Jingles should jump out at you and stand on their own. (That's one of the reasons that commercials are always louder than the programming—to break the consumer's lull so he'll pay attention to the sell.) In some TV sporting events, for example, when the station is getting set to go to a commercial at the end of a half inning, they usually play some sort of dramatic, pulsating sports music while the commentator signs off. If the same kind of music supports the first commercial, the beginning of the spot will probably be lost in the transition. Of course, some similarity is inevitable: when one style of music becomes popular everyone wants to use it.

Sounding different and original, a theme I will often repeat in this book, is the only unchangeable requirement for successful product identification with music. Seeking and achieving an original musical identity is vital in establishing a lasting image of the product in the mind of the consumer.

2
JINGOLOGY 101

MOST PEOPLE start out wanting to be something else . . . anything and everything else. But no one starts out saying, "I want to be in the jingle business."

Perhaps you grew up practicing piano or guitar, playing in your high school band where you scribbled out a few tunes to impress your first heartthrob. Maybe you're a singer on the fringes of the record business, hoping for a hit, but not yet connecting with the right chemistry—and you need extra money. You might be a talented musician, Juilliard trained, trying to make a living in an industry where players have been replaced by computer chips, and your ability to arrange and orchestrate has led to consideration by a jingle house. Or you have only passing musical skills, and are intrigued by the business or sales aspect of advertising (with a little doo-wop thrown in), and you would like to hire *other* people to perform the musical chores for your company. Possibly, you can carry a tune (everyone says you can) and have a special ability to remember an entire melody after hearing it only once, and though you don't read music, you want the chance to translate this talent into something that pays the rent. Perhaps you just lust after money, and have heard that for ten minutes' work on the right product a union jingle singer can earn $50,000 or more over a year, amounts which increase with each newly negotiated contract. Maybe you're just plain tired of working under the direction of someone else, contributing what you feel is *more* than anyone else, and getting less for it (that's what your mother says, anyway). Perhaps you've drifted into ad music through the back door by working for an advertising agency as a copywriter, and now you've teamed up with a composer to form your own jingle house. Or possibly you're just plain tired of medical school—stranger things have happened. (Medical school is my metaphor for everything else: the civilian world, the non-musical world, the world of nine-to-five.)

Whatever your background, you have decided to reach out and embrace the world of musical advertising. All roads lead to the Land of Ads, and the ones to the Palace of the Great and Magnificent Residuals (where all spots run Class-A forever) have been mined at the crossroads, booby-trapped with questions about technique and policy and morality (heavy stuff) to which only you can provide answers.

For purposes of this narrative, the reader is designated as a beginning composer, brimming with talent, bursting with energy and enthusiasm, with time for nothing else, and blessed with a willingness to learn and experiment. Any use of gender implies both sexes, or any combination thereof.

THE NEED FOR MUSICAL TRAINING

You may not need to know how to read music at first, but if you don't, you'll have to know someone who can. It is to your benefit to be able to read notes and carry a tune, at least well enough to present your songs to other musicians and singers. You should also have some ability to play an instrument, preferably a keyboard or a guitar. A basic knowledge of synthesizer/drum machine operation is indispensable for making your own demos, an important economic factor in getting jobs.

Somewhere in the process you will have to work with an arranger, or, at the very least, provide a lead sheet of your work for copyright purposes. So if you don't already know how, it pays to learn to read and write music. You don't have to be trained to conduct or compose symphonies—you've been hired to produce unique musical messages—but it looks nicer to the neighbors when you can speak the language.

If you can't read music, play an instrument, or carry a tune, and if on top of that your time is bad, Jingles is not a good business for you.

IF YOU ONLY WRITE LYRICS

What if you're a wizard with words and want to pursue employment solely as a writer of jingle lyrics? The problem with being a great independent wordsmith is that you are often in direct competition with the agency copywriter. Unless you have another talent to add, no matter how brilliant you are, you will have difficulty finding work. To move up the ladder you will have to affiliate yourself with a composer or become a principal in a jingle house. There are no jobs for someone who just writes lyrics (except at agencies under the title of copywriter).

SETTING UP YOUR BUSINESS

Before committing yourself to serious jingle activity you'll have to decide what sort of work situation makes you most comfortable: (1) working for a big jingle house, (2) working in a partnership, or (3) working completely on your own.

Working for a Big Jingle House

Self-employment is not suitable for every temperament. Some people need the protection and comfort of knowing that they are following someone else's instructions, and are not making unsupported decisions. They are drawn to the security of that other person who will give the orders and provide a partner for bouncing around creative ideas and sharing opinions—the more people bouncing and sharing, the easier it is to bounce and share.

To be considered by a jingle house you must have a tape. People at jingle houses constantly listen to new reels in the hope of finding the next musical genius who can help their company. Names of jingle houses can be found in the trade directories, *The Madison Avenue Handbook*, *The Motion Picture and Theater Directory*, and by asking around to learn who is busy. Jingle houses take ads in the yearly music editions of *Back Stage* and the *Clio Awards* program book to tell the world what they are doing (a form of selling). For the beginner, these publications are a good place to start.

Becoming a writer at a jingle house is one of the most expedient ways to break in and learn the business. You will have a place to go each day to use the phone, where the bills and rent are paid by someone else. You will benefit from the "team" concept and from the feedback and advice of someone with more experience (which you should always take with a grain of creative salt—originality requires its own fuel). When you don't yet have a reputation to trade on, or when you're cool and out-of-vogue, as happens to every artist at some point, it's nice when the company carries the financial ball.

At a jingle house the responsibility for finding work will not rest on your tender artistic shoulders because the procedures for getting jobs are already in place. Work will come in based on the reputation of the house and the expertise of their sales people. Your opportunities to compose will result from the good taste and benevolence of the head of the jingle house. All you will have to do is be brilliant.

Musical equipment will be in-house and readily available. Chances are there will be at least one home/office MIDI studio, and probably several, each with its own sound engineer. These studios will be equipped to produce demos and often final recordings.

In the beginning it will seem as if you've joined a dancing chorus with a hundred tapping feet, and you, the jingle writer, only have two of them. Until you have a hit, or have at least proven your abilities, you'll just be one of the bunch, picking up whatever bones are left after the regulars have had their chance. Everyone wants to compose the big national campaigns that generate the Class-A singer residuals, rather than the local spots that qualify for the lowest AFTRA/SAG vocal scales. House composers with seniority will be given first shot at the plum jobs. You would insist on this, too, if you were one of them.

Working at a jingle house is not like working for General Motors. There is no weekly salary for composing. Composers do not share in demo fees, which are retained by the jingle houses for demo production or as operating income. You will earn money only from successful jingles, and you won't get paid anything until your work is sold. In the old days, a composer might have been able to negotiate a weekly advance from the jingle house against his potential creative fees. But today, high operating costs and the large number of available writers have made every nonstockholder an independent contractor. In every sense, a jingle composer is free-lance.

There are no employment contracts at jingle houses, but when a composer gets established at a particular house it is understood that he is working exclusively for that house. Sometimes, to keep a hot writer happy (so he won't leave to form his own company and steal away the business), the jingle house will allow him to sing on compositions other than his own. As we have seen, this can be a pretty potent inducement.

Composing for a jingle house will not entitle you to company employee-type benefits such as medical insurance, a pension plan, and so on. But such benefits are provided by the craft unions for singers or musicians when they earn their required minimums. As a jingle house regular you will not get a paid vacation. In fact, if you're on vacation when a major new assignment comes in and you miss it, you may become paranoid about ever taking a vacation again. And if an emergency new session of one of your own hits must take place while you're away, you will miss the opportunity to sing on the track—your only chance at continuing income—and you might become suicidal. Ocean cruises are not for jingle writers, unless you happen to be a very fast swimmer. When you are sick, someone might cover for you, but don't count on it. (If you die, some other young smiler will replace you immediately. But look at the positive side: you won't have to worry about residuals anymore.)

Jingle houses may have five or six writers on their team and several favorite arrangers on nonexclusive call, along with salaried secretaries, bookkeepers, sales reps, and reception people. But it is usually impractical for *every* composer to work on *every* job, although this does happen at times when the house is trying to win a biggie.

For each job, there can only be one winning composer, and if your composition was not accepted to represent your jingle house, you will have worked for nothing. Even if you win the mini-competition in your own jingle house, the first money you see will be the creative fee percentage that is awarded to the winner of the overall competition. If one of your in-house colleagues wins the job, you may be given the opportunity to sing on his track. But don't count on that either. At every level, your ability to accept rejection will be tested and retested.

The artist, by nature, is not a sharing person. It takes a healthy ego and a certain amount of self-centeredness to be a writer. When you work for someone else and are lucky enough to have a hit or two, you may become unhappy about sharing the glory with the jingle house (which you begin to perceive as having done nothing more than provide you with an air-conditioned place to work).

When a writer gets hot, which is something every composer hopes will happen, it's not unusual to feel a creeping sense of dissatisfaction about the division of money. Artistic success is often accompanied by an attack of why-shouldn't-I-be-keeping-more-for-myself-itis. One of the symptoms of this malaise is the feeling that you are carrying others who have contributed less. It is at moments like these that new jingle companies pop up.

Working in a Partnership

Although the essential operating procedures will not change when you open your own store, the advantages and rewards of an ownership interest in a business far outweigh the downside.

Foremost is the fulfilling sense that you really did it yourself, in your own style, making your own choices, participating in the harvest of the opportunities of the American Dream. In your own company you are your own master, as much as any person can be his own master. When you have a hit, it will be *you* who helps to decide what happens to it rather than someone else whose needs and goals might be different than your own.

And instead of earning just a percentage of the creative fee, you'll now be able to split with your partner(s) all of the income generated by a project, minus costs. You're a self-motivated participant in the free enterprise system, and the only limit to your ultimate success will be your own imagination. You can charge whatever you can get, whatever you think your product is worth, regardless of what others in the industry are charging, based solely on your ability to compete in the marketplace. (Of course, you'll have to find a client who thinks your music is special enough to justify any imaginative demands.)

Now, in addition to composing, either you or your partner will have to handle business affairs, pay the bills, send out reels, and worry about keeping clients happy. You will also be responsible for all operating expenses—items that were taken care of when you worked for someone else.

People usually form companies with those whose abilities complement, rather than duplicate, their own. A company of two composers without a business or sales person is less likely to cover all the bases necessary to compete in the big time.

Writer/producer relationships are the most common collaborations, with each partner having a creative say. (In advertising, there is an expert for every subject.) The producer sells, then the composer writes. When they get to the recording session, each has his own role: the producer stays in the booth producing, supervising from the inside, holding the client's hand, making jokes at appropriate times, and ordering lunch; the composer stays in the studio, away from the fray on the other side of the glass, conducting the band, listening on headphones, being the artistic genius. The producer doesn't have to be a musical expert, but the writer/arranger, of course, does.

If you have decided to team up with another person—a composer or lyricist or sales rep or businessman—it is essential that each partner set out his view of his responsibilities beforehand, and that you agree on how you intend to divide any income. Even though you may see yourself as a creator who doesn't deign to think about the dirty green stuff, at some point you will have to sit down and take care of business. Don't fall into the trap of thinking, "We'll talk about it later." "Later" could be as adversaries in a courtroom. You don't have to rush out before your first job and hire a lawyer to draw up partnership papers; at this stage it's more important that you devote your energy to the job. But it is smart to reach a simple spoken agreement at the outset, with the mutual intention of writing down the terms of the partnership as soon as you have the opportunity.

"I'll write the music."

"I'll write the lyrics."

"We'll both sing whenever we can."

"If one sings and the other doesn't (or can't), the one who sings will split the fee with the one who doesn't."

"I'll act as music contractor."

"I'll act as orchestra leader."

"We'll both own the stock of our company."

"We'll split all profits fifty-fifty."

The possibilities are limited only by your business clout.

Collaboration is like a marriage. Are you flexible and willing to listen to criticism? Is it worth the aggravation of a partner just to have another person to share the load?

The One-Man Shop

If you fancy yourself able to write both music and lyrics, do arrangements, produce sessions, supervise bookkeeping and payroll handling, act as your own sales force, change the light bulbs, *and* leap tall buildings in a single bound, then you should form your own jingle company.

Working entirely on your own offers the security that you can never be fired. There is a special pleasure in the knowledge that you answer only to yourself.

Again, all the standard rules about business procedures and self-employment apply here, except that under your own shingle there is no one else to share the load. You will sink or swim based upon your own decisions.

Conversely, any income will be yours alone, the reward for taking the risk.

The composer who runs his own business wears many hats and needs a head big enough for all of them. Knowing how to share and schedule time is important. As your company grows, and you hope it will, you may have to hire employees of your own, in some capacity. Each additional person, whether creative or administrative or clerical, will come with his own baggage and problems, which will further demand your attention and take away from your time as composer. Hollywood producer Jerry Weintraub, on a CNN interview, recalled two bits of fatherly advice about running your own business: "At the end of the day always know how much you have in the bank and how much you owe, and when you come to work in the morning, don't ask your employees how their lives are—they may tell you."

With self-employment comes the reality that when there are no jobs the only income may be from vocal residuals for some earlier ongoing composition. And when that particular music track is no longer broadcast as part of a campaign, the income from it stops completely. It is not easy to support two (or more) people from demo fee income only.

And the rent will still have to be paid on the first of the month.

Income fluctuation in the jingle business can be as wild as in the stock market. Running a company requires that you know how to stretch the bucks from the fat times to cushion the lean ones. Successes in the music industry are often meteoric, and all too many hit composers alter their life-styles so drastically as to be only realistically afford-able during peak employment. Beware: every artist has lulls. It's part of creative recharging. In your own shop you must become your own cushion.

If, for these reasons, plus others that are known only to you in your heart of hearts, you have decided to form your own jingle operation, a new title will now appear after your name: vendor.

How does it feel to be a vendor?

TO INCORPORATE OR NOT TO INCORPORATE

Until you're rolling, you should do business in your own name. Initially there is no need to form a corporation. If the local clothing store asks you to provide a simple background track for their once-a-week radio commercial, you can send them a simple invoice, keep simple records of what you have disbursed, and put the rest of the simple money in your simple pocket.

If you are not incorporated, you should at least establish a separate business bank account and keep business records separate from your personal records. If you use a fictitious name, you must apply for an ID number with the IRS, and register the name with the state.

If you intend to pursue advertising music as a serious profession, however, it is to your advantage to hire an attorney and form a corpo-ration. Whether it should be a Subchapter-S corporation (which files tax returns but pays no taxes itself, where profits and losses are passed directly on to the stockholders) or a C corporation (a regular corpora-tion like General Motors) is a decision that should be made by you and your accountant. There are advantages to incorporating, which change with the mood of the U.S. Congress. Becoming a corporation provides the availability of pension and retirement plans (though this is also available to individuals through Keough plans), the ability to deduct certain business and medical expenses, and the protection of limited liability when you do business under a corporate name. These are all subjects to be discussed with your advisors.

How does it feel to have advisors?

BECOMING A UNION SIGNATORY

When you open your own jingle company—either by yourself or in partnership—as far as the unions are concerned you are now considered a "music producer." In order to compete in the big-time world of advertising, your company, Greatest Jingles, Inc., will have to become a signatory to the various union codes that govern advertising: the AFTRA Radio Recorded Commercials Contract, the Screen Actors Guild Commercials Contract, and the American Federation of Musicians Television and Radio Commercial Announcements Agreement. Becoming a signatory is easy, and free—just call or write to the unions (see Appendix), advising them that you have formed a company to do business in the jingle industry and would like to become a signatory to the codes. They will provide the necessary paperwork.

Right-to-Work States

There are certain right-to-work states (Alabama, Arizona, Arkansas, Florida, Georgia, Idaho, Iowa, Kansas, Louisiana, Mississippi, Nebraska, Nevada, North Carolina, South Carolina, North Dakota, South Dakota, Tennessee, Texas, Utah, Virginia, and Wyoming) where the ability to hire *nonunion* talent is guaranteed by law. In a right-to-work state, a person does not have to belong to a particular craft union to be eligible for employment on a union job. The provisions of union security do not apply. In English, "union security" means that only union members are eligible for jobs. But all other provisions of the union codes remain in full force, meaning that in a right-to-work state, a union signatory company may employ nonunion talent as long as it pays them union-scale wages, union residuals, and all other union benefits.

The Facts about Nonunion

Big-time advertising is a union business, and all the major advertising agencies are signatories to the union talent codes. If your jingle house is not a signatory company, a major advertiser will not hire you because of its own union affiliations. (Some advertisers might want to work nonunion but can't because they are heavily involved with trade unions at their manufacturing plants.) Every independent jingle house, with rare exceptions, is a signatory to the codes.

As a beginning company, you may work on whatever side of the street you wish. But once you have signed the codes, you are honor-bound to comply with all the conditions and provide all the benefits that the unions have won for their members through the years (including minimum pay scales and residuals, as well as pension, welfare, and disability payments). Singers, musicians, and actors all aspire to union membership because it means recognition as professional craftsmen of their trade. It would seem crazy for anyone to want to work under any other system.

Yet, for the jingle house, the pressure to produce buy-out work grows as each client's yearly advertising budget shrinks. (Even President Reagan's second inauguration committee advertised for nonunion talent to perform at the ceremony, but backed off after a storm of protest from America's labor unions.)

Too often, cheap has supplanted quality on the production budget. With nonunion work there are no talent residuals, even if the track runs forever. Advertisers would like to purchase their music this way, but the strength of the craft unions has been that top talent will not work under nonunion conditions.

But what if a sponsor can't afford or, for whatever reason, does not wish to allocate money for union scale wages or residuals? Suppose he is willing to pay you, his jingle supplier, your full creative and arranging fees, but asks that you produce his tracks nonunion. Are you prepared to work that way? Will you be able to sit in the confines of your living room and hear your music, knowing that you will never earn anything more from it than that one-time payment—not only for your work as composer, but also for your contribution as musician or singer? Will you throw up during every broadcast when your theme enters its ninth year?

Only a nonsignatory company may legally produce buy-out work. If you are not yet a signatory and you intend to compete for these types of jobs, it is a prudent policy to notify the performers in advance that you are producing nonunion. Some may not work. Others will. Union musicians and singers are not permitted to accept nonunion commercials, but obviously the talent comes from somewhere—it is not unreasonable to assume that some folks are AC/DC.

At times when there are lots of jobs, and everyone is making money, and musicians, singers, and composers are busily zipping from studio to studio, there is always great support for union principles. But when economic pressures demand that jingle houses (and therefore the talent they hire) take whatever work is offered, under whatever conditions, the system is weakened. During poor business cycles, working nonunion is often more a matter of survival than choice.

Jingle houses are not permitted to participate in the biannual contract negotiations between the advertisers (represented by the Four As: the Advertising Agency Association of America) and the unions, even though it is the jingle house that actually chooses and books the talent and controls the working conditions.

But when jingle house budgets go up as a direct result of a new labor contract, the heat is on to cut costs. "Keep the band small—and don't use too many singers" becomes the cry of the agency whose client has just given the unions a big raise. (In the history of advertising unions, no meaningful scale has ever been reduced. But when jingle houses give estimates based on union budgets, they are told to come in low or they will not get the job.) And what costs are left after talent? Studio costs? Maintaining an on-air-quality studio today is more expensive than it has ever been, and there is not much room to strike the kind of studio deal that would have a positive impact on a production budget.

No, the only area for cutting is in creative and arranging fees. Running a jingle company is guaranteed to challenge your basic belief in business ethics.

Today, across America, there are nonsignatory jingle companies producing first-rate music under nonunion conditions, competing effectively against signatory houses because they are able to charge lower production costs.

And across America there are signatory companies that will produce buy-out work, in violation of their commitment to the union codes. In some cases a jingle house may have a separate corporation for non-union work. In most instances, however, the work is done under a house's main banner—but no one talks about it. Signatory jingle houses don't like to admit that they do nonunion work. But, as the old expression goes, "It has to come from someplace." It's a matter of economics. Often, that "for-a-favor" job promised to an out-of-town client is produced nonunion, along with that synth-track background score, where only a guitar and bass player were brought in and paid directly, with no union contract filed (and therefore no residuals required).

Generally, however, the big advertiser still wants the best talent, and has accepted the union system as a part of the expense of doing business. Residuals are the glue that keeps the system together, and are conceptually the only hope of fairness for creative talent.

Each individual should decide where his best long-term interests lie when choosing to work union or nonunion.

OUTSIDE REPRESENTATION

"How does a rep work?"

"Hard."

"What does a rep do?"

"When the rep says your price for the package is twenty-five thousand dollars, and the agency producer says he only has six thousand, the rep is the one who says yes."

As a composer, either alone or in partnership, you might prefer to stay in your ivory tower creating while someone else beats the bushes to get the jobs. You may feel that you don't have the personality—or the desire—to represent yourself or negotiate effectively on your own behalf. Maybe the client-relationship part, the business part, talking about ugly subjects like money and contractual terms, and why you are *so* expensive, turns you off. (At every level of your career you will be considered "too expensive." People always want it cheaper.) It may be more palatable to have someone else do it for you. The amount of interest you take in selling yourself is a guide to determining whether you need a rep.

A rep is someone with whom you should be able to get along, who will take your reel around to agencies and do all of the selling that is necessary to get you a job. Your rep can tell a prospective client that your music is the greatest thing since chopped liver, and coming from him it won't sound bad. (It would sound less than modest if you said it about yourself, even though you and your mother know it's true.) A rep is a salesman selling you.

Servicing a client takes many forms: sending out reels, making lots of phone calls to keep in touch, following up to see that the tapes arrived, making the "What-did-they-think?" calls, wining and dining (as much as it is in your style to wine and dine), and all the other nonmusical chores that go into client relations.

The range of services that a rep can provide may be as limited as simply taking around your wares and directing any business-type talk to you or your partner, or as extensive as doing everything short of the creative work. Some production houses have several reps spreading the good word, often in different cities.

Reps earn their money in various ways, depending on the level of their repping. The rep will expect either a weekly salary ($200 to $400) plus commission, or a weekly draw against commission, plus expenses. He will charge 10 to 15 percent of your creative and arranging fees. If the jingle house has its own home/office studio, the rep may charge a similar commission on studio time jobs that he brings in. Some charge a lesser percentage (5 percent), but figure it on the *entire* production cost of a job—this depends on the deal made with the jingle company. A good rep, one who brings in business, can often make a strong deal for himself. The terms of agreement between composer and rep depend on the negotiating skills of each.

The rep works for the moment, not for the future. When striking terms you should consider questions like: What happens if the rep provides an introduction to an agency where you have never previously worked, after which you and he have a parting of the ways? Is the rep entitled to his commission for *all* the jobs you ever get from that agency or merely a smaller percentage (3 to 5 percent) of fees earned for perhaps a year on a specific account? The latter is the standard.

The down side of repping is that some reps work at the whim of the jingle house, and are often just fired and get financially screwed. So to protect both parties, as much detail as possible should be discussed before you hire the rep. There are no standards except what the participants judge as fair.

You should agree with your rep about whether he can rep other jingle people. In Hollywood, many film composers have the same agent, operating under the assumption that each writer in the stable (a cruel, but accurate term) creates differently. For advertising, you may want your rep to be exclusive to you, and you may have to pay for his exclusivity with a higher percentage.

Some jingle houses pay their reps by putting them on the AF of M contract in one of the Big Four jobs: leader, contractor, arranger, or orchestrator. This approach falls under terms-to-be-negotiated. A rep may even get to sing on the jobs. This is "hallelujah" time for the rep (and for the person who hired him: the rep's salary may be indirectly covered, perhaps paid for completely, by the sponsor).

Are you getting the impression that more and more people are taking singing lessons?

THE INVESTMENT IN EQUIPMENT

They used to be my clients; now they're my competition.
—RECORDING STUDIO OWNER

The days when all a writer needed were piano, pencil, paper, and songs in his heart, are gone. Today, inspiration has taken on a whole new form. Without a plug and an outlet, you can't get a job. The business of recording has moved from the professional big-time studio into the home/office studio, where sounds can be produced that are equally as professional and big-time, at considerably less cost (at least as far as talent payments are concerned).

Initially, you will require a simple recording setup, at home or in your office, to produce demo tapes of your work. Demos rule the business because every client wants to hear, as cheaply as possible, the direction his music will take before committing the big bucks for full production.

At the very minimum, you should be able to plug a synthesizer keyboard and drum machine into your stereo amplifier, record the results, and then overdub a vocal. A very basic system, including a portable multitrack recorder (four-track on a standard audio cassette), a programmable keyboard with a built-in digital recorder, and a basic drum machine, can be purchased at a price in the $2,000 range. The sounds will certainly be good enough for a demo. You might even produce recordings that could be considered on-air-quality. (From the accounting point of view, when it comes to electronic music, on-air-quality often means "the public can't tell the difference, anyway.")

Your demo-producing ability will be limited only by the amount of money you are willing to invest in equipment. For composers with ten thumbs, modern technology makes a Van Cliburn out of the Incredible Hulk. Sequencers and computer sequencing programs, either built in to your synthesizer or available as separate equipment, allow even the most modest pianist to perform difficult technical runs by simply slowing down the tempo, or programming in the notes one at a time (a process called step recording). Rhythm patterns are played to perfection by drum machines, and the drummer never gets tired!

Having the ability to generate a tempo with an accurate metronome is essential. This is the only sure way to guarantee that the spot comes in at the right length. It is too late if you wait until you are in the recording studio and paying musicians to figure out exactly how many bars and beats will make up the :30 or :60. The length can only be guaranteed when it is governed by a guaranteed time source. Digital metronomes that produce clicks in metronome settings or in film-frame clicks are available as outboard equipment for your home/office studio. Don't settle for a cheaper electric piano-top clicker or anything that is hand-wound—after two bars you'll find the time drifting. A computer-driven sequencer has its own built-in metronome.

You will need a good stopwatch. A ten-second sweep or one of the many racing watches available will serve well. The bigger the face, the better. Don't waste energy squinting at your electric wristwatch—get something that you can see easily.

As a matter of personal choice, I've found that the most valuable piece of equipment for a writer (other than his talent) is a little hand-held tape recorder. One of these mini-dictating machines, widely available, costing $50 and up, can be the instrument of your genius, providing the ability to remember a flash of inspiration that might come to you at an inopportune time when you have nothing to write on. An investment in several recorders, left in strategic places—next to your bed, in your car, in your bathroom, in your kitchen, in your briefcase—will pay for itself quickly. A midnight inspiration remembered could be the difference between success and failure on a project. If brilliance comes at odd times, you need the ability to recall it later.

Once a musical idea has been born, the home/office studio provides the ability to create without the restrictions of time and budget (or so it will seem to your clients).

The Technology Trap

At one time, a demo could be produced simply as a demo, an approximation of the final product, and agencies paid demo fees on that assumption. But today, because of the profusion of electronic equipment (with quality improving daily), clients expect their demos to be close to on-air-quality tracks, including all the embellishments that might go into a final recording. Agencies may claim that they are only paying for a demo, but a jingle company knows that the better the demo, the higher their chances are of winning the job. If pushing a few more buttons (to add strings or horns or flutes) is all it takes to make the music sound better, then why not do it? The theory is that it's worth the effort even though you're not getting paid for it.

To produce competitive demos, jingle companies, regardless of their size, have been forced to be in the recording-studio business. The expense of MIDIing up into a multi-track studio has lead to a substantial increase in funds necessary to operate a jingle house—even though demo fees have not risen accordingly and remain in the $500 to $1,500 range. Home/office studios require additional space at higher rent, and additional maintenance personnel, all to accommodate an industry that wants to pay less and less for music.

However, if the studio has better equipment, a demo can become a final, or at least the basis for a final. If and when this happens, the jingle house can bill out studio time costs at whatever hourly rate they feel they can charge. But until that time, and certainly throughout the demo process, the use of your studio is considered to be part of the demo fee.

Free.

For the agency.

For the client.

But not for the jingle company who wrote the check to pay for the equipment, often in the $100,000-plus category. In fact and effect, every jingle house studio is in competition with the independent studio.

SCHEDULING YOUR TIME

Time for working as a composer, for writing the melody and lyrics, should be estimated separately from the time needed to produce the demo. The simple piano/voice tape is practically obsolete, especially if you are competing with others who will be presenting with as finished a product as their home/office studio will allow. So you will have to allocate hours *after* creative time to the detailed recording of the song. And then more time to mix it. And the more equipment you have, the more time you'll be spending as an engineer trying to speed up the process of recording and programming (unless you hire another body, thereby increasing your costs).

Achieving the technical perfection necessary to be competitive will test your patience. You should schedule your time so that you can devote enough attention to each step in the process.

The use of computers to record MIDI music has created its own problems: until they have mastered the techniques, composers sometimes spend more time and energy operating the machinery than they do working on their creation. Losing sight of the original task is one of the pitfalls of computers. The most frustrating thing for a composer is to come up with a great idea, and then have to struggle for five minutes to find a way of recording it while waiting for a computer program to boot up. Sometimes it's quicker the old-fashioned way.

At times like these, those little hand-held tape recorders are worth their weight in platinum.

PUTTING YOUR REEL TOGETHER

Eventually you'll have to put together a demonstration reel of some music. A reel is the most essential tool for getting a job. Without it there will be no consideration for work. Even if your dear uncle owns an agency, someone is going to want to judge your ability to compose and hear something that you've written. Believing the protestations of your mother is no longer enough.

Starting from Scratch

Record something you've written, either a song or a sample jingle, that shows off your ability as a composer. A sample jingle might be your original invention, music and lyrics, of a campaign for any real or imagined product. It might be an arrangement of an existing campaign that you've heard on the air, but *in a style that you could represent as your own*. Don't duplicate something that has already been done—the world is filled with that. When you make your presentation, be sure to tell the listener that the music they are hearing is a composition demo. You are attempting to demonstrate your skills as a composer, not your ability to arrange for the New York Philharmonic.

How Long a Reel?

For a beginner with no track record, a few short samples, meaning not more than ninety seconds each, totaling not more than five or six minutes tops, should be sufficient to let someone know if you are worth taking a chance on. You can always carry another reel of additional material in case you are asked for more, but usually this won't be necessary. If you are composing sample jingles specifically for your reel, try to work in lengths that are practical for advertising, usually :60 and :30. While that wonderful two-minute spot that you saw on the Olympics was a tour de force for the composer, the fact is that to have any real usability, advertising music *must* work in a :30. (We'll tackle this later in the chapter on creativity.) Try not to present songs with long intros, because in advertising there *are* no long intros, just enough lead-in to grab the consumer's attention.

Keep in mind that you are writing music for the *advertising* business, not for two-hour movies in Hollywood. Get to the point, quickly, in the most original and unique way you can, but *quickly*. Know your audience. Know your market. And make the music work in a short format.

What Styles of Music Should You Put on Your Reel?

The more variety you can demonstrate, the more varied the work for which you will be considered. A top 40 sound, a hard rock sound, an emotional ballad, a twangy country tune, something zany with sound effects, something for kids—try to cover them all. You know what kind of music you are best at writing. Include two of these, but not placed back-to-back.

Lately, advertising has been screaming out at the consumer with hard rock vocals and heavy metal tracks. Being different from the rest will be your key to recognition. *Unique* and *original* will always triumph over the convenience of imitation.

Someone is muttering, "Nobody can write in every style," and that's true. But you are trying to show your potential at creating advertising music, and that means variety. The worst thing that can happen to a jingle composer is to be relegated in someone's mind to a narrow category of ability: "Oh, he's only good for scoring," or "He can only write hard rock," or "He's a good arranger, but he can't compose a strong melody." You are in the selling business. Variety of presentation, done well, increases the chances of success.

The Order and Form of Music on Your Reel

Your reel is your meal ticket. It should say, "This is what I do."

Some jingle companies present full :60s and :30s in all their glory, before they were buried under the announcer saying, "Open Friday night 'til nine! Free parking! Bring the kiddies! Toys and games for everyone! Member FDIC." Other companies like to present with key lines only, blasting away with hit tags linked together via musical segues.

Don't be afraid to present your work at its full length, especially when it's familiar. While everyone will recognize the hook, there is a tremendous amount of unheard creativity buried under all those announcer words. An agency professional knows that there is more to a track than just the hook. So play the entire jingle. If you only present the ending you may miss the opportunity to make an impression.

You should not present a tape that contains an announcer. Your music will be less audible under the voice and won't be shown off properly. Your business is music. That's what the client should hear.

Jingles and tags should be placed before instrumentals except when you are seeking scoring work.

Sometimes a client will request a "scoring reel" from a jingle house. This is one that shows how good the composer/arrangers are at creating instrumental melodies and moods that work with visuals. If your main jingle reel does not contain background scores, and you are able to do this kind of work, you might want to consider keeping a special scoring reel on file, adding to it after each new session. Or you could make up a special scoring reel whenever one is requested. If scoring is your main objective, you might consider making a "video reel" with the spots that you've done. Nothing sells scoring like actually seeing it. For jingles, however, the music is the message. It's best not to let anything—soap, pouring beer, bathing beauties, or a 440 V-8 overhead cam engine—distract from your creation.

I have always believed that the first-ever arrangement of a jingle, the one from the first session that made the campaign a hit before all the spin-off versions, is the track that sounds the most original. Here, creativity is shown off at its best: the first song and its first sound. You might also include some rearrangements to show how a musical campaign developed, but people in advertising always respect that first sound.

Speed of recognition is the name of the game. Place commercials that are heard in the area where you want to do business near the top of the tape, rather than somewhere toward the end. It helps your case immeasurably if a jingle has been broadcast in the area where the agency listener is located. While you might have created a fabulous jingle for the Savings and Loan Association in Hawaii, the recognition factor won't do you much good in Boston. Nothing beats the familiarity of something heard on the way to work in the morning, or on the network news. This also shows that someone else thought enough of your work to hire you.

For the beginner, your first *real* commercial should take the number one slot on your reel. There is a school of thought that believes in holding the hits until later, but in advertising there's no time for the long build. Get to the point. Always put your best spot first.

How Many Copies Will You Need?

Once you have finished putting together your reel you will need copies to give out. Fifty is a good starting number. But before spending the bucks to duplicate it at a professional studio, it is wise to get someone in the business to listen to it. There is nothing as valuable as the opinion of a professional, even if you don't agree with it.

Your reel should be in audio-cassette form. Having it available on a reel-to-reel 7½ ips tape may offer a convenient alternative, but most listeners will want to hear cassettes.

Somewhere down the line you may wish to have special labels printed, or artwork designed for your tape box. Initially, a simple typed label will do.

FINDING SOMEONE WHO WILL LISTEN

Imagine that you have decided to become a baseball player. Without knowing anyone connected with the Yankees, you take the subway up to the Bronx and walk into the locker room at Yankee Stadium, where they hand you a uniform and send you out to play in place of Don Mattingly.

Unfortunately, it just doesn't work that way.

Once you have a reel in hand, you'll have to begin the most difficult part of your adventure in advertising: getting that first job. The process begins with finding someone who will listen. Everyone makes contact differently, and *everything* works. The way you approach the task will be largely a matter of style and what feels comfortable for you.

Where to Find the Names

Don't be bashful. Getting started calls for remembering and using every possible contact you can. If you know someone who knows someone who knows someone, beg favors. The world was built on favors. Call anyone you know in the business: musicians, singers, people who might have worked for other jingle houses, even relatives who live next door to advertising people. Call them all.

Read the trade papers that talk about spots that are going into production. *Back Stage*, *Advertising Age*, and *Adweek* are all directed toward advertising people and report on what's happening in the industry. The *New York Times* has an advertising column each weekday and is a good place to learn the names of people with current action. The *Agency Redbook* lists names of advertising agencies and the accounts they represent, even the names of the account people and production staff. But be forewarned: trying to send a reel to everyone at every agency will be prohibitively expensive and will probably be unproductive.

Once someone has given you a name, the next step is up to you. And again, how you do it is a matter of personal style. It is a good idea to start the introduction by mentioning the person who referred the name: "Henry Smith gave me your name and suggested that I call. I'm a jingle writer, and I'd like to ask if you would take a few minutes to listen to my reel." (Of course, if he has never heard of Henry Smith, or if Henry Smith owes him money, you'll have to scramble. Try not to spend too much time explaining your relationship with Henry Smith.)

Starting an Address Book

Keep a record of people to whom you've spoken and sent reels. It never hurts to jot down any personal information you think might be helpful in the future: a spouse's name, kids, sports, or any tidbit of information that might help to place you in a more memorable spot in the producer's mindfile.

To Mail or Not to Mail

Rarely will you luck out and reach a producer out-of-the-blue who will invite you to come in that very afternoon and wait while he listens to your reel, riveted to every note. If you get through to someone who asks that you mail the tape, do it. At least you've gotten it to an agency. You might include a short note of introduction naming the person who referred you. Deal with getting the reel heard in the follow-up call. (Don't forget that you are in the "short" music business—long letters end up in the circular file.)

The Follow-Up Call

After a week or ten days you should call the mailee "just to make sure that my reel arrived." It's a good way of making contact. Everyone recognizes this as a way of saying, "Hey, I'm the greatest! Why haven't I heard from you?" or "I'm starving to death and need a job desperately. You'll save my life if you listen to my reel."

You may be able to glean information from the secretary or receptionist about the lay of the land. Is your target producing at the moment? Is he on vacation? In conference? (When you can't reach someone, they are always "in a meeting.")

Call once a week, once every two weeks, once a month—whatever it takes to get a reaction. To some you will be an awful pest, and you'll hear it in their voices; to others, a mild annoyance to be dealt with as part of the job. But in time you'll find someone with whom you will establish a rapport, and they may talk to you every time you call.

Others may keep your reel without ever listening to it. This is all part of getting the job.

There is no pleasant way of calling to seek employment. If you're not great with the gift of gab, you might consider sending a postcard every once in a while. Remember the adage, "The squeaky door gets the oil."

Start a tickler list (accounting language) of calls to make every few weeks. These calls will establish you as very persistent, aggressive, and a pain in the ass.

But all it takes is for one person to remember your name at the right moment, and before long you'll be sending out invoices. Isn't that what advertising is all about? Getting that reel out is advertising yourself.

"It's that jingle guy again."

"Tell him I'm in a meeting."

When the world has you on hold, smile.

And prepare yourself: not everyone will like you or your music. This doesn't make you a bad person.

Should You Leave Your Reel?

It is always more satisfying to be present when someone listens to your music, but if this is not possible, leave it. When it is added to the pile on their desk—not the pile on the floor (which are film director reels waiting to be viewed) or the pile on the windowsill (which are announcers looking for work) or the pile on the chair (which are singers)—don't take it personally. No one can listen to all of the reels they receive, at least not immediately. They wouldn't have time for anything else.

Don't expect to get your reel back unless you ask for it. This is part of the investment you must make in your craft. You should have enough copies to go around.

How Long Should You Expect
an Agency Producer to Listen?

A good agency producer listens to reels during his spare time, or when he is looking for a specific sound for a specific job. At times when he's busy, you might get fluffed. Some producers will play the whole reel. Others will pick and choose and fast-forward through things that don't interest them. When a producer has a specific job in mind, he may tune out something wonderful because he is not looking for that particular style of music, only for that certain sound that might help his current spot. The time a producer spends with you is not necessarily a comment on your reel. It is up to you to be patient and accept the time you are given.

Keeping Your Reel Up to Date

Your reel should grow longer with your ability to add new and interesting things to it. Ten or twelve minutes of your latest hits, varied and staggered into an exciting presentation order, should be sufficient for a client screening reels. Resumés are not necessary. Nor are pictures. In the phonograph-record industry, they have an expression that "the hit has to be in the grooves, and no amount of conversation can fix what's not on the record." The same is true for your tape. After a few minutes, people will have enough information to judge whether they like your work or not. After all, the world makes its judgments in thirty seconds. Or less.

Staying in Touch

When I began in business, I used to draw a music stave in the center of my letterhead containing the tag of my latest jingle (see page 52). Under it I would put my credits—and nothing else. By sending it to everyone in my address book, I had found a simple, inexpensive, and distinctive way of letting potential clients know what I was doing. Finding inventive methods of placing your name and credits in front of prospective employers is part of the craft of successful creativity.

How It Really Happens

If you decide to call the copywriter who was touted in last week's *Advertising Age* as the hot, creative talent responsible for thirty million dollars' worth of new business at his agency, be prepared for stonewalling.

You ask for the target by name.

"What is this regarding?," asks his secretary, guarding her boss from the vendors of the world.

"I'm a jingle writer, and I'd like him to hear my reel."

She gives you stock answer number eight: "Mr. Gordon is at a client presentation."

"When will he be free?"

"I don't know. Please hold."

You hold.

She comes back, dripping ice. "May I help you?"

"I'm trying to reach Mr. Gordon. I'm the jingle writer."

"Oh, yes. Well, he won't be available until tomorrow. Please hold."

You hold more.

When she comes back she says snappily that she's all alone at the phone, and would you mind calling back later? You hang up feeling frustrated.

When you finally get a hearing at an agency with a music room, it's

STEVE
KARMEN
PRODUCTIONS,
INC.

35 ROXBURY ROAD • ROCKVILLE CENTRE • NEW YORK 11570 • TELEPHONE 212-889-3424 OR 516-536-5577-8

You can take SA-LEM out of the coun - try , but.....!

You can't take the coun-try out of SA - LEM !

Composed, arranged, and produced by
STEVE KARMEN

possible that your tape will be heard on equipment that comes close to studio quality. It's equally possible that it will be reviewed in someone's office, and you should be emotionally prepared to listen to your creations on the first rip-off of Edison's original invention. Agency audio equipment is rarely in the same top condition as the machinery you might have at home or in your car: a channel may be out of whack; the "play" mechanism may run slow or fast; a speaker may distort every bass note that you were convinced would boom-boom you to success. Beyond that, your meticulously prepared melodies may have to compete with nonstop telephones and the clatter of typewriters.

This is another moment to show your pearlies, and to avoid making any excuses for your work. Now may be the time to ask yourself: Are you certain you're in the right business, or should you reapply to medical school?

RULES AND REMINDERS

1. The advantages of working for a big jingle house boil down to expedience: the equipment is there, the jobs are there, and all you have to do is write. The down side is that you will earn less in the long run because fees will be divided between you and the jingle house on the 75/25 split. (The house keeps the bigger number; if you thought it was the other way around, you are a dreamer and probably very creative.)

2. The owner of the jingle house always turns out the lights when he leaves. The employee leaves them on—to him they are someone else's problem.

3. When you're looking for work, one contact can be turned into several simply by asking, "Can you suggest anyone else who might give my reel a hearing?"

4. When you find a rep who is productive and compatible, try to negotiate an agreement that is equitable for both sides.

5. A drum machine, a synthesizer, one outboard echo unit, a recording machine and microphone, and a guaranteed time source are the minimum basic tools necessary to make you competitive. (The key phrase today is "Everything costs $1,995.")

6. Learning the techniques of electronic music is an essential part of competing in the jingle jungle, if for no other reason than to provide you with the ability to make a cheap demo.

7. Getting the job is the art of selling yourself. Follow your instinct; it is the most reliable tool you have.

8. For your first job (and many of the rest) take whatever money is offered. Money is not important in the beginning (at least that's what Donald Trump says). Building a reel is. Your ability to raise your price will only come as a direct result of your ability to provide a competitive product.

3
A FOOT IN THE DOOR

YOUR REEL IS READY. You know the lingo. Let's see what happens when you get your first job.

A friend of a friend has begged a favor from a man who works as an elevator operator in a building that houses a small advertising agency. He has pestered a kindly producer into listening to a tape of some songs that you wrote three years ago, recorded at a band rehearsal where the drummer was too close to the microphone and all you can hear are the drums and very little melody (except for your mother, who hears only *you*). It turns out that this particular producer has a quickie project that needs "something different," and he remembers your reel because he used to play the drums. He calls you, declaring that he has no money but if you'd like the opportunity to do a free demo, he needs a :60 and :30 in two days. Or sooner. You'll be competing against four other houses, also doing free demos (or so he says; until you know for whom you are working, this is something to confirm through other sources).

It's time to begin dealing with the ad agency.

During the creative process you'll attend meetings and be working with people who know and are intimate with each other on a daily basis (creatively and intellectually, of course). Try to remember names. I always have difficulty with names until I associate the person with a function in the job. The names of the suits (the account executives) are usually farthest from my mind because they are the most removed from the creative process, acting only as overseers, giving approval at various steps along the way. You might casually jot each person's name on your note pad in the order they are seated around you. (Don't let them see you do this. If you do it right, you can speak to everyone by name. For all the right reasons, this helps.)

Now, let's meet everyone.

THE AGENCY MUSIC DEPARTMENT

Many major advertising agencies have in-house music departments, whose function is to coordinate the production of music with the needs and schedules of the creative teams. Agencies that produce large amounts of music often have several people who work only in the music department. These music producers work under the direction of the music director (everyone please rise), and are there to guide their assigned accounts through the complex production of any needed music. A large music department is usually staffed with assistants and secretaries to do budgets and other music-related paperwork.

Other agencies, also in the major category, function without a music department, leaving each creative team to research, contact, and negotiate directly with the composer of their choice. The philosophy here is that a freer, less channeled approach to finding music will lead to a less restricted product.

Each way works well. It's strictly a matter of style.

At a big agency that does a lot of music, there are often several full productions taking place at the same time—expensive and complicated commercials of which music is only one element—all facing air dates. As the vendor finds out when he calls, people are always "on location," "filming," "doing on-line and off-line editing," "recording voice-overs," "mixing," "making transfers to video tape," all activities that you should not be concerned with since they are completely out of your sphere. Just know what they are and file them. When contact has to be made, music departments become a point of coordination between the scattered agency teams and their composers.

Music departments also provide expertise in seeking the correct library music for low-budget spots or assisting with sound effects. Anything audio-related usually goes through the music department.

When music is one of the principal elements in the commercial, involving a jingle or at least a score and a tag, the music department helps the creative team find the right composer and/or arranger for the job, often becoming involved early in the process to understand what kind of music is needed.

The music department also acts to protect the composer from receiving too many conflicting musical instructions from the nonmusical members of the creative team. In the world of continuous audio, everyone knows everything about music. People on every level of advertising, especially younger ones fresh out of college, know all the top songs and all the "in" groups, as well as all the obscure ones. For a jingle composer, there is nothing quite as dangerous as an account exec with a ghetto blaster. It is often the role of the music department to act as go-between, translating any confusing agency directions into music-ese.

Although agency music departments like to deny it, most jobs are awarded through the process of competitive demos. Music departments would like to be thought of as autonomous and decisive when it comes to choosing a composer, but more and more people from the account and client level are venturing into creative territory. Clients know about synthesizers and cheap music and the willingness of the jingle houses to do inexpensive demos in order to qualify for vocal residuals. Today's expertise demands *lots* of demos.

While jingle houses usually compete for *jingle* jobs, the trend lately is for agencies to ask for competitive demos for lower paying *scoring* jobs, traditionally awarded on the basis of the composer's reputation and reel. Here again, the quality and detail of the demo can have a direct affect on winning the job. For a film scorer to provide a demo means not only computing the timing of the images on the film, but also producing the score on tape—the days of presenting ideas on the piano are gone. MIDI has made it possible to provide an extremely detailed track in the demo stage. In the highly skilled world of film scorers, those who provide *free* scoring demos in competitive situations are in need of psychiatric assistance. It is up to the individual jingle house to decide whether to enter this type of competition.

The Agency Music Director

The head of the music department, the person who assigns the accounts to the individual music producers, the one who supervises and is ultimately responsible for all the music department's work, the *capo di tutti capo*, is called the music director. This person is also called other things by the jingle houses he does not hire.

A music director who can dole out work obviously wields great power in the jingle industry. Especially at major agencies with network clients. (Picture the dock boss in *On the Waterfront*: "You, you, you, *not* you, you. . . . ")

A good music director will keep an open mind and not fall into the trap of assigning too much work to one jingle house. Yet no matter how ethical or fair they may try to be, there is always in-agency and out-of-agency gossip accusing music directors of favoritism, with all its attendant benefits.

Some agencies follow the policy that all music shall go only through the music department. This tends to cause grumbling from creative teams when they aren't happy with the music director's choice of composer. A strong music director can have a big influence on the creative color of his agency's commercials.

The music director's job usually carries one of the top agency salaries, and is often filled by someone who has experience as a writer, player, or producer. He is knowledgable about recording-studio techniques, and also has the social skills to be a mediator and a guide through the process. It is the music director's diplomacy as the person-in-the-middle that insures, both technically and creatively, that the music recorded is what everyone agreed it would be.

The music director is a sought-after friend, and a much-maligned entity. It comes with the territory. No one in the jingle industry is spoken of with more emotion.

The Agency Music Producer

While the music director oversees all the agency music, individual accounts are handled by music producers, who deal more with the day-to-day needs of their creative teams. Much the same professional qualifications are required for this position. When agencies search for producers for their music departments they often interview people who have worked as assistants in recording studios, because these individuals are technically versed in how to get the sounds and have also been first-hand yet silent witnesses to the politics of many recording sessions.

The agency music producer carries a heavy load of responsibility, sometimes covering several sessions each day for different clients. This requires the ability to switch musical heads in the taxi between the rock-track session for the car client and the jingle bells spot for the cheese client. When music producers are busy, their time is taken up with preproduction meetings and overseeing sessions, and when sessions run long into the night, it is the music producer who remains to the end. In the studio he or she will pass judgment on each stage of the production, and will discuss with you, the composer/arranger/jingle-house producer, any variances from the agency-approved direction. Music producers are often unmarried, and if they are socially or emotionally involved, it is with someone who understands the crazy hours required by the job.

THE AGENCY CREATIVE TEAM

Inside the agency, the creation of advertising is a collaborative effort, usually between the art director and the copywriter. There is a growing tendency in some agencies, however, for producers to contribute equally in the birth of a spot. Though there is often an overlapping of functions, these three entities—the art director, the copywriter, and the producer—each have distinct, specialized responsibilities apart from coming up with ideas.

The Art Director

Advertising is the art of sending messages to the public. Art directors are visual message senders, responsible for the look of everything: the color (or black and white), the impact, readability, gestures, style (whether an actor should wear a jeans or a tuxedo), movement (to run or not to run)—whatever falls under the category of visuals.

The Copywriter

Copywriters are the verbal message senders. The story, content, words, facts, accents, pauses, breaths, laughs, cries, and shouts, are all the domain of the copywriter.

The Agency Producer

This person is a combination of roles: creative type, administrator, secretary, and mother and father to all the people on the production. The agency producer is the great facilitator, the conduit, the one who makes it happen the way everyone else wants it to happen: on time, within budget, and true to the original creative concept. This person holds the entire production together and is the liaison between the creative team and the outside world. An agency producer works the long, thankless hours after everyone else has gone home, and is the one who ultimately gets the job done.

A good producer will be knowledgable about the current fee structure of suppliers (that's you), and will deal with matters of cost control (which means keeping the price of music down). The producer knows the technical and political aspects of what's going on at his agency. When a commercial needs music, the agency producer will collect reels—independently, or from the music department—for presentation to everyone on the creative team. He will schedule the meetings and coordinate demo and session dates, and will usually be the direct contact for the music supplier during the production.

The Creative Director

Much as the music director rides herd over his music producers, the creative director is responsible for the overall creative product of his agency. He manages the creative department. A good creative director will recognize good ideas, and protect and nurture them as they flow through the murky waters of agency and client approvals. He is the team leader, and if he hires good people he can help his agency break new creative ground. CDs attend high-level client meetings and are the creative people closest to management.

Creative group heads are also creative directors who report to an executive creative director. The group head directly supervises the work of the individual creative teams in his charge.

THE AGENCY ACCOUNT TEAM

On another floor of the agency (far above where the creatives sweat and toil over their coffee-stained desks, in dark poster-covered cubicles with broken tape recorders, breathing air thick with the acrid odor of inspiration) works the account team. This exclusive group of impeccably coiffed individuals represents the agency's work to (please rise again) THE CLIENT. Here, in the rarefied atmosphere of elegant plushness, deep carpets, mahogany furniture, and private washrooms, "the suits" hold forth. (It has been rumored that from an account person's office it is possible to see daylight, and in some cases even a view of the street, although this has never been confirmed.)

Keeping in mind that advertising isn't all art, that it's a business, let's meet the account team.

The Account Executive

An account executive is the full-time link between the agency and the client. The AE will deliver anything needed by the creative team from the client. Account execs are the infantry, the guys who slug it out every day for the benefit of their client. The AE is the one who makes sure all the details are covered: script and budget approvals, air date confirmations, network clearances, and so on.

The amount of an AE's authority—from grunt to God—varies from agency to agency, but for the jingle house, it is important to remember that no matter how loud they bark, the account execs are not responsible for the final finished creative product. Ninety-nine times out of a hundred, creative decisions are made by the creative department. If the spot doesn't turn out well, it is ultimately the creative team that takes the blame.

But the AE gets to explain it to the client, something they hate to do. If the spot turns out great, the AE can only smile and watch while the creatives get the praise. Most account executives will tell you it's a thankless job, a hellish servitude they must pay before they can proceed to the next rung up the ladder.

The Account Supervisor

The account supervisor is someone who has real reasons to get ulcers. With anywhere from five to ten years of experience in advertising, and usually seven years in whatever product category they service (packaged goods, credit cards, autos, beers, and onward) the account supervisor is expected to have a thorough knowledge of what he is doing. He is the person held responsible by the agency for the success or failure of an account. Often account supervisors aren't involved in the day-to-day affairs of the account, but they certainly keep close tabs on their account execs. It is the account supervisor who makes the important decisions about the account.

The Management Supervisor

The management supervisor is the top agency representative on the account. He negotiates the fees, spends weekends with the client, and signs the contracts on behalf of the agency. An account executive's client and a management supervisor's client are usually two different people with two separate agendas. The former is a brand manager, the latter a marketing VP.

He does not deal with numbers, go to casting sessions, voice-over recordings, or edits (although sometimes he will fly to a shoot to pose with Bob Hope, Michael Jackson, or Spuds McKenzie).

The management supervisor sees the production budgets and approves the finished commercials. (Sometimes they don't approve; that's when they make their positions felt.)

When your music finally reaches this level in the glass tower, it's best just to smile and say thank you.

The Business Affairs Manager

One of the many roles of the agency business manager is to oversee the legal aspects of obtaining the necessary rights from composers and publishers to use their music in advertising. He may not be a lawyer, but will often act like one. The business manager is the voice of the agency on all business affairs. He is used to sitting opposite those who make demands, and is definitely part of agency management and not on your side (although this doesn't make him a bad person). Sometimes, the business manager serves as part of the agency management team that negotiates the SAG, AFTRA, and AF of M contracts, updating industry conditions and scales.

Whether you, the composer, end up signing the agency contract as written, without any changes, will be determined by your bargaining power and ability to convince the business manager of the rightness of your positions on issues of principle (in the face of the very real possibility of losing the job). Sometimes the business manager must pass along your comments to the agency attorneys. Then you will really find out about people who are not on your side.

(You'll meet the business manager again when you make the deal, discussed in Chapter Nine.)

THE AGENCY RESEARCH, MEDIA, AND BROADCAST DEPARTMENTS

The research department, which provides the invaluable background information for the creative team; the media department, which handles the highly skilled and competitive job of planning and buying air time; and the broadcast department, which, among other things, insures that the spots get to the stations on time, are all indispensable cogs in the great wheel of sell. But since they have little direct impact on the jingle person, who has most of his agency contact with the creative and music departments, we salute them and move along.

YOUR AUNT IN TOPEKA

Now that you've been introduced to the agency cast of characters, you may begin to understand why that great idea your Aunt in Topeka has for Coca-Cola will never reach the air. Quality advertising is a business of professionals, who do it all day long. The bigger the account, the more people there are who work on it in every capacity. Some agencies employ hundreds of people to service a single client. Sorry, Auntie Em; it's impossible to take that brilliant idea you had in your kitchen in Kansas and expect it to get anywhere unless you are prepared to play the game out in the real world.

DOING BUSINESS BEFORE THE CREATIVE MEETING

The business part of jingles falls into two categories: (1) the agreement reached in the first phone contact with the agency, either with the agency producer or the music producer, and (2) the contract and all the legal things that go with it—usually not finalized until after you've won the job, but always discussed beforehand (see Chapter Nine).

When an agency representative calls, he will say, "We are working on a new campaign and would like to know your availability, your demo fee, your creative and arranging fees, and how you work."

We know you're available, so let's look at the other items.

The Demo Fee

A demo fee is the amount an agency will pay to a jingle supplier (with the client's approval) to hear a presentation of music for possible use in a commercial. For example, an agency might allocate $750 to each of four competing music houses as demo fees.

What Happens to the Demo Money. From the agency point of view, the demo fee covers everything: musicians, singers, the studio—whatever the jingle company has to spend to provide a realistic demonstration of how the music will sound before the big bucks are spent on a full production.

From the jingle company's point of view, the demo fee doesn't even cover production costs.

At a big jingle house, demo income pays for whatever live musicians and singers are needed to complement the machines. The composer receives no compensation at all for his creative time at this stage. The jingle house justification for not paying creative "think fees" out of demo money is that they have borne the expense of building the office studio(s), and the continuing costs of running the business. The money has to come from somewhere. Therefore, at the big jingle houses, composers do not participate in demo fees.

Smaller houses have the same studio-rent-cost problems, but partnerships (or the one-man shop) may sometimes set aside $100 or so for the composer as a basic think fee.

When you present your demo, you, the jingle writer, will have written an entire jingle, solved an advertising problem, and provided a competent demonstration of your ideas, all without any payment for your time and effort. Therefore, it would not seem unreasonable for a composer to expect some compensation at this important early stage, above and beyond any payment for demo production costs. But current industry practice doesn't allow for it.

For an advertising composer, a think fee—payment for time and energy beyond demo production costs—is an unrealized dream. Advertising agencies have come to expect composers to work for nothing. Agencies have been able to take advantage of the jingle houses' willingness to provide demos without creative compensation because they know that every jingle house is anxious to qualify for the vocal residual if the work is approved.

Free Demos. A jingle maker will occasionally be asked to do a demo for free, without even receiving payment for production costs. It could happen during an agency pitch for new business.

When an agency pitches an account, they usually do so "on spec"—without receiving any compensation from the prospective client. Creative materials such as print, film, or music are usually financed out of the agency's new-business budget. A sponsor will occasionally provide a minimal payment to each competing agency during the pitch stage, but generally the behemoths never do. If an agency is graced with the opportunity to enter a competition for a big account, the sponsor expects them to finance the pitch themselves. To win the business of a monster account—a car or cola or beer or hamburger—agencies have been known to invest over a million dollars of their own money.

During a new business pitch, people at the agency continue to receive their weekly salaries; no one works for free. The creative teams who invest their time are compensated for their work. The expenses of new-business presentations—man hours and production costs—are simply taken from agency operating capital, as a cost of doing business. And if the agency doesn't win, the employees wipe their eyes and get on with their jobs.

Yet, when an agency finances its own pitch, especially a smaller agency, the jingle house is often asked to spec the job, meaning no demo production fee whatsoever. ("Do us a favor . . . you have a studio and . . . ") It's one of the curses of the home/office studio.

And if a pitch requires fully produced on-air-quality music tracks, the agency will pay for production costs but will often expect the jingle house to defer their arranging fees until after the account is won and the work is approved for broadcast.

At various times in my career I have participated in new business pitches where the agency has hired a top film director, at his going rate, and sent him off to a distant location with a full crew to shoot commercials of, say, a plane taking off into the sunset. Yet when it came time for the music session, invariably someone said, "Keep it cheap. Remember, it's agency money."

Even if the agency is doing work for an existing account, they occasionally ask jingle houses to spec demos, especially for clients who are always screaming about the high cost of production.

Try not to do free demos. You shouldn't have to bear the burden of financing the research and development of a client's advertising. Film houses won't shoot film for free, yet music houses are routinely expected to work on spec. At the very minimum, you should charge something to cover production costs.

Crediting the Demo Fee. When a project becomes a reality, the music is usually rerecorded from scratch, and the demo fee is regarded as spent money. The amount the agency has paid for demo development should not be applicable against any future fees or costs.

But if the actual demo track (not a later rerecording) is selected to be used as the final broadcast-quality track, the standard procedure is for the jingle house to prepare the appropriate paperwork so the musicians (if any) and singers will be repaid through the unions "on the contract." The talent who accepted a "demo payment" (an underscale, strictly union-prohibited practice that happens every day), now earns a double fee—one legit, one not. These repayments are made by the agency and billed to their clients as production costs, separate from demo costs. Also, the home/office studio may now submit a bill for the time it actually took to do the job.

If an amount has been paid to the composer by the agency as a think fee, above and beyond the demo production cost, the agency may correctly request that it be credited against the ultimate creative fee when the work is approved.

The Creative Fee

The fee you earn for your work as composer after it has been accepted by the client is called your creative fee. It is a one-time fee, never, never, ever, ever to be repeated. Never. Ever. This fact bears remembering in every discussion of payment for your creativity.

As we have seen, the division of the creative fee at the big jingle house is usually 75/25. Regardless of how the split works, you should attempt to receive your portion at the time the composition has been accepted for use.

Agencies, however, have been known to try to spread out the payments, tying them in to a number of contingencies:

1. *Use in test commercials.* If a commercial is going to be placed "in test" before being broadcast on the air, to prove the credibility of its creative content, the agency may want to pay you only a *partial* creative fee until the test results are in (even though you've done *all* your creative work).

Testing can take several forms. Some agencies use focus groups, in which a small number of people are gathered in a room, shown a selection of commercials (including the one that uses your work), and are then asked a series of well-planned, skillfully devised questions about the spot. Memorability, impact, and product recognition are all measured. Some clients do their testing "on-air," measuring a spot's impact via next-day phone calls to consumers. The spot is given a score, and high scores make it "out of test." Low test scores are frowned upon as an indication of weak creative work.

Since there is a possibility (unheard-of if they used *your* music) that the spot won't score well, indicating to the advertiser that the creative direction is incorrect, your music may never see the light of day. Some advertisers place inordinate faith in testing, and your frustration will not be unfounded if you learn that a small group of people don't like the commercial.

Some testing seems to go on forever, literally years, especially with new product development. If the agency wants to defer your fee until after the test period, you might limit testing rights to a thirteen-week cycle, after which you will receive the balance of your creative fee, or at least an additional test fee.

You also might claim that since you did your part, you should be paid the total amount now. Though your unwillingness to defer compensation might occasionally cost you a job, it is not unreasonable to expect full payment at the time of delivery. Don't ever forget—you did your part, and if the client is using your product for his benefit, you deserve to be paid for it.

2. *Local, regional, and national spots.* If your commercial survives the testing process, the advertiser may want to begin his broadcasting schedules with a few local areas in different parts of the country. This time, instead of judging the spot by committee, the effectiveness of the ad will be measured by consumer sales.

Again, the agency may want to defer part of your payment until it has broadened the area of advertising into regional or national levels. (National use is different from network use. Don't confuse them when negotiating your fee deferrals. Some spots go national and are seen all over the country on a spot-buy basis, but are never broadcast on the network.)

3. *Fees for separate media.* The agency may wish to pay a portion of your fee for radio, and the balance for television. In making the decision, you should be prepared to accept that the music you write for one media may never get to the other.

Setting Your Creative Fee. When deciding what to charge, bear in mind that your work will take as long to execute for a local advertiser as it will for a national advertiser. With that as justification, some jingle houses keep their total creative fees constant regardless of whether the product is local, regional, or national. On the other hand, a local advertiser may feel that he should not be paying, or cannot afford to pay, the same fees as the big guys. The fact that you are expending the same amount of time and effort will have no weight with him.

Winning jobs will be determined in part by your understanding of what to charge. A breakdown of a partially deferred ten-thousand-dollar creative fee might be as follows:

Test rights	$ 1,500.00
Out-of-test single media (radio or TV) rights	1,000.00
Second media rights	2,500.00
Regional use	2,500.00
National use	2,500.00
Total	**$10,000.00**

This example spreads out the money far beyond what will normally be called for (especially if you only earn 25 percent of it). Keeping up on current industry standards and practices will help you make the right decisions about whether to defer part of your fee.

Creative Fees for Scoring Jobs. One fee, a combination creative/arranging fee (usually $2,500 to $3,500 per spot plus production costs), has been the standard for scoring jobs where original background music is developed for a non-jingle commercial. Recently, however, jingle houses that specialize in this type of work have begun to charge a separate creative fee (up to $5,000 per spot) in addition to their standard arranging fees. This new creative fee does not apply in cases where a background score is developed from an existing jingle theme.

Arranging Fees

If your jingle is to be part of a long-running campaign, new versions and rearrangements will eventually be needed. Whatever arranging fee is negotiated should be enough to hire a real expert to do this most important work.

An arranger is the person who paints the musical portrait of your song so all the instruments of the orchestra can play it. If you have the ability to arrange and orchestrate your own music, you will have a decided advantage in the fight to maintain a financial and artistic interest in the life of your music. In addition to selecting the musical colors, you'll also be able to hire yourself as a vocalist (unless you have worked out another form of ongoing compensation for the uses of your music).

If you are a composer who doesn't arrange, you'll have no financial interest in rearrangements unless you qualify for a vocal residual, or are given a line on the AF of M contract.

An arranging fee, like a creative fee, is a one-time fee. Often the arranger will include permission to sing on the track in his negotiated terms. (Arrangers are not stupid.)

Continuance Fees

As we have seen, the only way that a composer can receive ongoing income for the uses of his work is to latch on as a union vocalist or musician. On rare occasions, however, a composer can secure a per/cycle or semi-annual or yearly continuance fee for the uses of his composition. Since this is not unfair, it never hurts to ask.

Sometimes it's possible to negotiate fees that will pay amounts equivalent to those paid to singers, actors, or announcers under the union contracts. This method is by far the most satisfying for the composer because it provides the same type of ongoing compensation that the vocalist receives—he gets paid when his work is used—and also provides payment for all instrumental uses of his jingle as well as for tracks produced by others.

The concept of continuance fees—residuals for composers—is not yet industry practice. They are available only to those who are willing to risk losing the job when their requests are denied.

Seeking the Right of First Refusal

Often jingle houses will attempt to negotiate the right to produce future arrangements of their work, which, in addition to providing rearranging fees, guarantees their ability to hire themselves as vocalists. This is the right of first refusal, which essentially means that if the agency wants future rearrangements of the jingle, they have to offer the work to the original jingle house before going to someone else.

Be forewarned: most agencies won't grant it.

While the right of first refusal that binds the agency into hiring you might seem advantageous, it often creates a restrictive atmosphere at the agency, which could lead to the diminishing of the jingle house/agency relationship.

Agency creatives will want and need the freedom to choose whomever they wish to produce their music. If you can supply it, that's great; often an agency will be loyal to the original jingle company. But many times they won't, and they should not be forced into rehiring you.

Your primary concern as a composer should be achieving ongoing income for the ongoing uses of your composition. It's better to earn your continuance fee through a negotiated composer residual than by restricting the agency into hiring you so you can sing on the session.

The Standard Agency Contract

Agency producers are often told to have the composer sign the agency's music rights contract before the job. You might be handed a form, or bid sheet, with terms and conditions printed on it, and be expected to sign without comment or discussion and without reservation or hesitancy. In fact, any resistance might immediately remove you from job consideration. One major agency requires that all suppliers, including music houses, sign an agreement containing wording that insures that their one-sided client-protecting terms will continue *forever.* This one-time document covers all future work done at that agency by the supplier, regardless of product. You might question the morality of such a practice, but of course they have the right to run their agency any way they please. And under the free enterprise system, the American way, no one is twisting your arm to work there. But if you want to, bring your pen.

I have always liked to believe that there is no such thing as a standard form contract, at least not if a negotiation is to take place. Industry attorneys have at times convinced me otherwise. Most agencies have their own music-rights contract that can be categorized as a standard form.

But if you can't change the terms, be aware that the contract has been prepared for the benefit of the party that paid the preparer. And that was not you.

Risking the wrath of a music director, who will have to refer any nonstandard terms and requests to the account team and legal department, is not a path often traveled in the jingle industy. But if you do wish to introduce a wrinkle that is not a standard agency practice (such as owning your work, or seeking composer residuals, or retaining your performing rights, or limiting your indemnification—all discussed later), it is best that you present these details before you start your creative effort. The agency may not let you begin work before ironing out any contractual details.

Also, your efforts to provide fairness and equity for your composition might label you a troublemaker. Such is the price, Oliver Twist, of seeking more. But at the very minimum, you should never be afraid of trying to amend terms of an agreement that you are not happy with. You will have to honor what you sign.

A good rule to follow is: Never sign anything without understanding what it contains.

THE CREATIVE MEETING BEGINS

At the agency, you gather around the conference table and someone, probably the copywriter, hands you a storyboard (a cartoonlike series of drawings that depict the visual action and dialogue of the commercial), and explains the assignment. Ideally, you should come out of this meeting with the sense that everyone is working toward the same goal.

Your main task during the discussion is to find out all the essential information about the product and the advertising direction desired by the agency.

Questions You Should Ask the Agency
(If They Haven't Told You Already)

Before delving into the details of the campaign, you'll want to establish some basic parameters. These are matters that may have been discussed on the telephone prior to the meeting, but are worth nailing down again, just to be certain.

1. *Will the spot be radio or TV or both?*

2. *What kind of demo is required?* Piano/voice or something more finished? (We know the answer to that one, don't we boys and girls?)

3. *When must the demo be ready to present?*

4. *Is this a competition?* You should establish whether you are competing against other jingle houses for the job. You might ask who they are. If this knowledge pumps you up, then seek it. Ask if everyone else is receiving the same demo fee. Whether the agency tells you, or refuses to tell you, will teach you something about the agency. Learning what others charge will help you set your own price structure, and the only factual place to learn is at the agency. (Most jingle houses have a tiny tendency to exaggerate when discussing the deals they make.)

Questions to Ask about Product Background

Until you have been working on an account for a while, all participants will be versed in the history of the product except you. Now's the time to pick up any background information you can.

1. *What kind of advertising has been done in the past?* You should have a knowledge of what was done before, and why it isn't working now. Clients rarely change campaigns for the sake of change—there's always a pretty good reason (like the current approach didn't test well, or sales are in a nosedive). Find out what isn't working so you don't duplicate it. If you don't already know, you should ask about the kind of advertising that is running for other brands in the same product category.

2. *Why are they changing campaigns?* The answers to this will vary from "to save the account" to "we need to freshen up a good idea gone stale," with all the stops in between.

3. *Is the account in trouble?* This is tough to ask when you don't know everyone, but important to find out. Here you'll notice an added touch of desperation in everyone's attitude.

4. *Who is the target audience?* Male? Female? Kids? What is their age level? If you'll be writing for a candy product that is advertised mainly on Saturday morning cartoon shows, you will compose differently than you would for a beer advertised on NFL broadcasts. Is the consumer affluent? Upscale? Downscale? White-collar? Blue-collar? ("Hi, Ma, I'm writing blue-collar downscale music." "That's nice, son. Wash your hands before you come to the table.")

5. *Where will the media budget be spent?* Will more money be spent in one part of the country than another? This might have an influence on the style of music you choose. Or even on your attitude while composing.

Questions to Ask about the Fine Points of the Job

Now it's time to establish the details of demo preparation.

1. *If you want to, can you invest your own money in the demo?* (And should you?) This question has roots in the presynthesizer era.

In the days when it was necessary to hire musicians to produce a demo, some agencies considered it unfair if one jingle house brought in a piano/voice tape—as requested for the demo fee—while another presented with a full orchestra version at their own expense. This put extra pressure on the smaller suppliers to invest money they might not have.

Some agencies made it a policy not to accept more than a piano/voice demo in a competition, seeking to judge only the composition, the music and lyrics, and not production values. Of course, other agencies encouraged composers to make their demos as complete as possible, regardless of any personal expense involved. After all, "The client is going to hear this tape. The client is a businessman and a great manufacturer, but not a judge of music. The better it sounds, the better the chances he might like it and buy it. Right?" (It's always easier to spend someone else's money.)

The electronic revolution has settled the issue. Now sophisticated demos are made in the home/office studio at minimal cost (at least to the agency and the client), while the jingle house has the continuing expense of their studio and equipment.

Therefore, you should not feel obligated to spend more than you are earning.

2. *What form of presentation do they expect?* Most agencies will want only a tape delivered by a specified time. Sometimes, however, the agency may want to listen to the composition "live," in raw form, played only on a piano in their conference room. Agencies know that any song sounds better when performed by professional musicians (or professional buttons), and they might want the freedom to talk about the basic composition without the distraction of fancy accompaniment.

But even if you are making a live presentation, you should prepare a demo tape to leave at the agency for those unfortunate few who can't attend the meeting (thereby missing your effervescent performance).

Along with your presentation (live or tape) you should provide typed copies of the lyrics. You might take the time to find out how many people will be attending the meeting, so you can prepare enough lyric sheets for everyone.

3. *Will the agency allow you to present more than one idea?* Since they are looking for the best possible creative material to show their client, certainly no one will be opposed to hearing more than one approach. Jingle houses will often present several creative solutions, especially when they have several in-house composers to work on the same project. The individual composer must make up his own mind whether to put in the time and effort needed to develop multiple solutions.

Analogies about creativity are never satisfactory, but try to imagine that you are a physician treating a patient with an arm problem. Your professional education, experience, and knowledge lead you to suspect a broken bone. The X-ray confirms the diagnosis. The treatment is a cast.

In jingles, once you've pinpointed the problem, based on research and an understanding of product background, you will begin to develop a solution drawn from your professional expertise. But not all broken bones require a cast (or the same kind of cast), and in music there are potential solutions as numerous as there are styles to compose. And each creative problem will inspire a different solution from each different person asked to compose.

It has been my experience that the presentation of a single idea shows that you have attempted to solve the advertising problem, not just deliver several songs that might work. If you are unsure of your creative direction, you may wish to present an alternative. But initially it is best to work toward a single solution, rooted in an understanding of the problem.

4. *What time lengths will be required for the final spots?* Will the advertiser use more :30s than :60s, or more :15s than :30s? The answer to this may have an impact on your creativity.

5. *Should you do a long version?* Sometimes the agency will request a full-blown epic to impress the client. For a presentation (especially in a new business pitch, or for an account in trouble), nothing sounds quite as uplifting as a ninety second or two-minute track. It might have a four- or eight-bar musical intro that sets the groove and allows everyone to settle in, without concern for the fact that the intro takes ten or fifteen seconds, or half of a :30. The long version allows the music to breathe and establish itself, giving everyone the opportunity to hear the work at its grandest and to absorb the depth and nuances of the arrangement. If the agency is willing to pay for a long version, have a good time. It will sound great on your reel even though it will probably never reach the air.

But while you may have occasion to prepare a long version, your genius must work at its best effectiveness in a :30. In jingles, the world turns in thirty seconds. Long versions might end up being played somewhere (in movie theaters as part of the inevitable commercial-before-the-film, or on MTV, where length is not critical and air time less expensive), but these versions can be recorded later, after the demo stage, when your idea has been accepted in real-world length. Only when a sponsor buys an entire program can commercials be produced in out-of-the-ordinary lengths.

Creatively it's easier to expand a work built to perfection in a :30 by adding a musical verse or bridge or repeat, than to have to eliminate something from a longer version that was essential to the delivery of the message (or a part that everyone falls in love with that just won't work in a :30).

If you want to write long music, try the record business.

6. *Does the advertiser want a hit record?* What a silly question! Every advertiser has a secret desire to have his jingle become a hit record, rising to the top of the pop charts, thereby receiving lots of free air time and free product publicity. Once in a very rare while this happens ("The Girl-Watcher's Theme," "The Coffee Council Song," "I'd Like to Teach the World to Sing"). But because radio stations resist giving free air time to one product's music, while charging full advertising rates for a competitor, getting the initial airplay to establish a song-length version can be difficult. Usually energies aimed in this direction are wasted. You, the jingle genius, should be working toward the creation of effective advertising music, and not worrying about the ancillary events that may or may not become realities.

7. *Who owns the unused material?* There is the ridiculous, very re-mote, isolated, near-impossible chance that, because the moon was in a funny place, the sponsor will reject your work (and risk the loss of your mother's business!). If this happens, you should have the right to salvage the jingle for your own future use. So before you begin, you should establish who owns the material if it is not accepted.

Musical folklore is filled with tales of great Broadway songs that were originally composed for one specific show, then were deleted, only to be revived and included in another show years later, becoming the hit the composer had hoped for in the first place.

An agency that has paid you a demo fee might want an option to purchase your composition for an agreed amount of time. They might want to cover themselves in case the client changes his mind someday and recalls your Herculean jingle and can't imagine why some idiot rejected it in the first place. In this case, you should insist on setting a portion of your creative fee as their price for the option fee.

But this kind of agreement is actually extremely rare. For all prac-tical purposes, your work is dead with this client. You should have no hesitation about seeking to retain unconditional ownership of the demo music, meaning the composition as well as the recording of it.

If the project has gone beyond the demo stage into full production, paid for by the agency, they might ask that you not use the actual music tapes again without reimbursing them for the money they spent. This is not an unrealistic compromise. Nor is it unrealistic to think that with the addition of a few synthesizer overdubs, a new melody tailored to fit, and new lyrics sung by different singers, you could rework the track so that even your mother would not recognize it. And having done so, you could then resell it to someone else. You'd be astounded at how easily three-syllable car names become three-syllable cola slogans.

A life-after-rejection is the flame of vindication that glows in the hearts of all composers. But for the health of your creative juices, it's best to think of each job as a problem unto itself requiring a fresh start. That is what your client is expecting of you, not a shoe-horned adaptation of someone else's throw-aways. It's a better approach to channel your energies into new efforts, instead of trying to bring Frankenstein back to life.

To some people, however, Frankenstein was charming.

DURING THE MEETING

As you digest the creative requirements, don't hesitate to ask as many questions as you feel necessary, even to the point of repetition. If you don't understand something, chances are that they didn't say it right. There should be no doubt in your mind about the direction of the campaign. If there is, keep asking questions. Soon, your work will be on the line, and you are entitled to as much input as is necessary to help you in the creative process.

You should also find out who to call if you have creative questions. And who to call about business questions. (For creative matters it might be the copywriter or music producer, and for all business matters the agency producer or music department.)

Never talk business during the creative meeting unless someone at the agency brings up the subject. And then keep it short, deferring details until later. It is not productive to wave your deal in front of the entire creative team. Most will already know it, and a few will be jealous that you have the potential for big bucks (via vocal residuals), while they only earn their never-enough salaries. Some people may resent your role, failing to understand that you are working for a one-time fee. Keep the flow creative.

AFTER THE MEETING

If you have never worked with this agency before, at the end of the meeting you should request a purchase order and payment information from the producer. If agency policy is to pay all production invoices thirty days after receipt, or on the first or fifteenth of the month, it is to your advantage to know it so you can get your paperwork in early.

ON YOUR WAY HOME

Now, as you leave the meeting behind and confront the task that lies ahead, you begin to think about the crucial issue: Did you make a favorable impression, at least on the music director's secretary, the all-important life line to the person who hires?

It's Friday evening, and even though you were planning to go away for the weekend to celebrate your wedding anniversary, you've been instructed to deliver on Monday morning at 10:00 A.M. Can you do it?

RULES AND REMINDERS

1. Bring your own pad and pencil to the agency meeting. Nothing is as tacky as arriving with nothing to write on.

2. Never do free demos.

3. Try not to break your creative fee into too many deferred pieces.

4. When you negotiate, remember that agencies will automatically keep whatever you do not try to retain.

5. Ask lots of questions.

6. Beware of the copywriter who taps his foot to Muzak.

4
THE CREATIVE PROCESS

YOU ARE AT HOME. You are a night person who does his best thinking when the world slows and allows a breath to search for an idea. It is 9:00 P.M. The kids are in bed or on their way. Dinner is done. Your time is coming. Your mate is involved in something else, purposely leaving you alone to concentrate. From odd places around the house, you have gathered up all your first scribbles of ideas, those shards, rippings, and scraps of paper containing your midnight jottings. You pour a cup of coffee and dim the lights until the only visible area is your workbench. You ease in at the piano, and review the scraps. You begin . . .

No.

You are at home. It is 5:00 A.M. You are one of those who likes to work early, to jump in before the fury of the world has reached ramming speed. The automatic coffee pot has clicked on at 4:55, and a quick shower has rendered your body alert. Your thoughts are singular, focused, unclouded, directed at the task before you. Outside, the sun has yet to show its face. Everything is still—too early for chirps, too late for crickets. Last night you tossed and turned, questioning if you really have the ability to live up to the faith and trust that the agency has placed in you to write their music. You roiled on sleep's surface, with disconnected melodies and rhythm patterns racing through your brain, lyrics and phrases dueling for the attention of your subconscious. Now you tip-toe down to your basement studio/office, your creative sanctuary, the place where you'll make it happen. You smell the coffee, and flick on the light over the piano. Somewhere in another room a refrigerator motor starts, a quiet hum interrupting the perfect silence of dawn. Last night, before going to bed, you off-loaded your inspirations, your hummings and mutterings, from all those little tape recorders you have strategically placed throughout your life. You spread out the notes and regard them with the eye of the commander of a great vessel ready to chart his course.

You pour the coffee and sit down. You begin . . .

No.

You think best while on your feet, in the midst of a crowd. You are on the midtown bus, in rush hour, in July. The press of the throng has jammed you into the rear doorwell, one step down, your favorite vantage point for watching the mob. You have been shopping, which is your way of taking your mind off everything else and putting it into the job (when the going gets tough, the tough go shopping). You hang on for dear life as the big bus lumbers over the potholes. Suddenly, a bicycle-messenger type, wearing skin-fitting racing tights and a beret, darts out from between two cars. Your driver curses and swerves to avoid hitting the oblivious kid. That's it! The rhythm of his words— what he says and how he says it—is exactly the cadence of the tune you have been searching for! Frantically you twist around, contorting, fearful of forgetting the gem, finally managing to reach the pencil in your pocket. At last you are able to scribble on the side of the Bloomie's bag . . .

LOOK OUT—HERE COMES A GOOD ONE!

Ideas come to fertile minds anywhere and everywhere. They happen when you are willing to let them happen. Certainly the physical setup might be more conducive to creativity in surroundings that you can control (like someplace cozy with the right lighting and coffee perking; *not* on a midtown bus), but the location is not important. What is important is understanding what goes on when the process begins. Something keys a message to your mind that you are ready to receive at that moment. Call it what you like—an inspiration, a brainstorm, a bolt from the blue. The point is that you get an idea.

Being inspired is that wonderful feeling when the right thought pops into your head and gives you the solution to your creative problem. But being consistently creative—enough to earn a living from it—requires more than just inspiration. No one is inspired all the time. Creative success comes from understanding what happens during that blinding flash of brilliance when the idea is born, and then knowing how to recall and repeat the process when the inspirations don't come.

"Writers write to eat," many have said. The art of composing is the *business* of composing: learning how, on a regular basis, to keep turning out a product that is saleable.

One great idea is simply that: *one* great idea. It's possible, of course, to have a single hit that will be successful enough to provide a living for a lifetime. *Gone with the Wind* was Margaret Mitchell's only book; nearly fifteen years passed between *Catch-22* and Joseph Heller's next book. But these are examples of the miracle few, and we mere mortals are not among them. The standard genius needs more than one idea to survive.

Talent is God-given and can't be bought or taught. But personal techniques of talent development and the disciplines of the creative process can be learned and mastered.

ONE WRITER'S TECHNIQUE

When I started as a jingle writer (a pup fresh from the nudie movie scoring business) there was no such thing as a weekend. I would work for endless stretches at any hour, day or night. Fortunately, I was lucky enough to be able to minimize my distractions because my young world was less complicated. In a recent Masters Golf Tournament interview, the legendary Sam Snead offered this advice to a beginner: "If you want to play good golf, don't get married, don't have children, don't buy a house with a mortgage and crabgrass. Pretty soon your mind starts worrying about taking the wife for dinner and paying the mortgage and curing the crabgrass—and there goes your golf game."

As a creator matures, his priorities change along with his life-style. To remain productive he knows that he must rely less on raw inspiration and more on the techniques of his craft.

In order to sustain creative growth, the professional writer must, at one time or another during his career, recognize that talent is more than the ability to produce during flashes of genius. I have always believed that everyone, to some degree, has the potential ability to create or write or compose—certainly to come up with a good idea. What most civilian "idea makers" lack are the techniques needed to carry their ideas through to completion. They don't know how to write it down or what to do next. A professional writer is someone who knows what his business is all about and has mastered the technique of making his inspirations grow into marketable product.

Personally, I have found that a set writing schedule works best. I compose on Monday, with Tuesday as a backup (in case I haven't been brilliant on Monday); on Wednesday I arrange and orchestrate the job, sending it to my copyist late in the day; on Thursday we record; and on Friday I try to take care of all the business aspects of my business—billing, correspondence, office stuff, and so on. The weekends are my own, except on the occasions when work is required and I remind myself that I'm self-employed. Sometimes the client's schedule will dictate a different starting day, but the pattern is the same.

When you work for yourself, the allocation of your time is crucial. I prefer to begin early in the morning, in a quiet, dim corner of my office, curtains drawn, room lighting only, without the distractions of weather and daylight. On composing days, I reach my piano at 5:00 A.M., aiming to get in as many hours as possible before the world wakes up and the phone starts to ring. Much can be accomplished between 5:00 and 10:00 A.M.—half a day's work and more—because it is uninterrupted.

On Sunday night, before a writing Monday, I try to get to bed early, reading, watching TV, relaxing, shutting out the crabgrass, tuning my mind to the task ahead of me. I have already completed the night-before ritual of setting up my workbench and preparing the coffee for brewing. I've found that this is necessary *for me*—getting details out of the way sets the process in motion before I go to sleep.

During my working day, I eat lightly or not at all. Nutritionists say that this is not healthy. But my experience is that eating saps my energy. I used to drink coffee with caffeine, but f..found that it m..m..made me t..t..too j..j..jumpy. The distractions of alcohol or other substances are counterproductive. (A composer should try to adhere to a moderate life-style. If you think you can live like Ernest Hemingway, drinking, carousing, staying out all night, killing lions, tigers, and bears—forget it. For every Hemingway there are five thousand unproductive, soon-to-be-let-go drunks.)

One summer, to try something different, I rented a house on the beach, mainly because it had a grand piano in a room that faced the ocean. I had images of spinning out magical melodies as I composed at sunset, accompanied by the wind and crashing waves. But I soon learned that others also had a fondness for the beach at sunset, and each night as I pounded and composed, groups would gather under my window and sing the choruses of the jingle I was writing. This loss of creative privacy completely killed any thought I had of working in that place that summer. The midtown bus technique is not for me.

If all this sounds a little silly or weird, please remember that the few moments a prizefighter is in the ring represent the culmination of months and months of disciplined preparation. Pulling a melody out of your subconscious deserves no less an amount of dedication. Other composers will work differently, but they certainly have their own creative rituals and methods that prepare them for the job.

I have often been asked how I know that I will be able to compose on Monday morning, rain or shine, winter or summer, when on Sunday I may have had no hint of inspiration. How do I know the ideas will be there on Monday, exactly as planned? Where will they come from?

Scheduled self-discipline is the first technique for inspiration.

SOUNDING ORIGINAL

Inspiration begins with the desire to be original. On every level of the advertising industry, people are being paid to serve one basic function: to provide the client with a continuing unique and original image that will set his product apart from the competition.

Initially, you should remember that you are not in the record business—you are in the *advertising-music* business. Your music is supposed to sound like advertising, not like a hit record. Unhappily, a lot of advertising music has started to sound like FM radio, with one song melting into another similar one.

To further appreciate the impact of original musical motifs, try watching commercials without the sound. See if you can identify the product before you spot the name. Car commercials have one type of look, colas another, beers another. But within each category there is very little visual difference. Not only do cars themselves look alike, especially the American imitations of foreign designs, but in their commercials they all come barreling over that same hill and sweep around that same curve.

(I'm convinced that all automobile commercials are filmed on the same location, in a little town called Running Shot Village, where car companies rent the streets to shoot their commercials. Oh, they change the set decoration once in a while, and use different camera angles, but everything is filmed on Running Shot Lane, right next to Running Shot Hill and Running Shot Valley. You've seen the place a thousand times—the only thing that changes is the car, and from year to year there's not even too much difference in *that*. That's why car spots all look alike.)

When the visual is not unique, then the sound must be.

But even with an audio track, it is often difficult to tell one car spot from another. In recent years, almost all automobile advertising has been using either hard-rock/heavy-metal sounds, with similar Joe Cocker-esque voices growling out the lyrics, or futuristic electronic tracks with long, dramatic synth tones that make the spots sound very much alike. The same kind of audio grouping happens in other product categories. Colas try to out-rock each other, beers to out-sock each other, detergents to out-cute each other.

When commercials look and sound the same, America tunes out.

The look is not your department, but the sound is. If your product's competition has been using a certain style of music, you should use a different one. Being aware of competitive advertising is an important tool for successful jingle composition.

Approach your subject matter from an unexpected angle. As outrageous and wacky as you think your musical idea may be, it could be that much of a success in an industry constantly searching for originality.

In the early days of my company I was asked to write a jingle for the Beneficial Finance Company, using the slogan, "At Beneficial, You're Good for More." But instead of using the line as given, I chose to break it up with a mnemonic "toot toot," to try to make it sound different. The musical tag "At Beneficial, Toot Toot, You're Good for More" was retained for over twenty years as part of Beneficial's advertising, mostly due to the recognition provided by the "toot toot." In fact, for a while people were calling Beneficial the "toot toot" company. Those two little notes made all the difference between ordinary and special.

Every product should have a sound of its own. Seeking originality is the first requirement for finding it. You won't always succeed, but when you do your work will be outstanding.

KNOWING THE PRODUCT

If the product is not already a part of your life, whenever practical you should try it out. Examine your own reaction to the advertising claims. Only from first-hand use will you be able to decide whether the things the agency wants to say are credible. (You'll say them anyway, won't you?)

In addition to personal experience, your main source of product information will be the research provided by the agency. You should always ask for as much background as possible to confirm your creative approach to the assignment. If you live in the geographical area where the product is advertised, you will be familiar with what they have been saying and with the claims of competing products.

If you are writing for a product sold elsewhere, request to see and hear a year's worth of earlier commercials. Your awareness of how the product was positioned before is invaluable; it tells you where *not* to go. Review the spots to see what kind of image the client accepted before. Then try to figure out where you can go for a departure. Sometimes the agency will have a reel of spots for other products in the same category. Auto agency creatives are always looking at other agencies' car spots. It teaches them what not to do in the search for originality. Taking the time to learn about your product will add depth to your creative direction.

DO YOU HAVE TO BELIEVE IN THE PRODUCT?

First you must have an opinion.

In 1970, after much government pressure, the advertising agencies agreed to discontinue cigarette advertising on radio and television. For many years prior to that time, the amount of money spent on the production of cigarette commercials had been among the highest in the industry. The ads were big business for the agencies as well, because the cigarette companies were big network spenders.

Today there is no broadcast advertising for cigarettes, although many agencies still receive huge fees for producing print ads for tobacco products. And even though the entire world is aware of the hazards of smoking, many talented people work to create the ads that glorify the use of this potential killer. Aren't these people concerned that cigarettes cause cancer?

As Don Corleone said, "It's a business."

Every election year we see political commercials trumpeting images created for candidates by advertising agencies. Actually, the first thing a person wishing to serve the public does is seek out an agency to "package" his image. Presidential candidates attract ultra-heavy-weight creatives who are given leaves of absence (paid, of course) to go forth into the land and work on the national campaign-of-campaigns electing President Right-for-You.

The outcome of an election is no longer determined by political positions and viewpoints, but instead by the public profile molded by a copywriter and an art director. And composer. Do the people at the agency believe everything they write about a candidate? Does the composer have to believe in the man when he provides the patriotic background score that helps elect our next President Bubblegum or Senator Cola? "If we didn't do it, then someone else would," is the most often heard justification.

People who trust political advertising are being duped. To paraphrase P.T. Barnum, "There's a sucker born every thirty seconds."

After all, it's a business.

Should you say something is "the best" when you think it is not? Does honesty matter, at least from the creators of the ads? (Don't worry; the agency legal department will have cleared any possible conflicting copy points that might be challenged by a competitor, who is also claiming to be "the best.")

The fact is that the commercial will say that the product is "the best" with or without you simply because people are being paid to say it. They are not being paid to pass morality judgments—just to help sell the product. In *Aurora Dawn*, Herman Wouk described advertising as a means for inducing people to want things that they don't want.

The legal debate continues about whether an on-camera spokesman (or star presenter) should bear a responsibility for the words that he says, even though they were written by the agency copywriter. People believe stars. That's why they get big money for appearing in commercials.

"Let the buyer beware," is never truer than when someone is being paid to create a pleasing image for something that might not be so pleasing.

Are these thoughts disturbing? All you wanted to do was write music for toothpaste, right?

Composing jingles really *is* a business, isn't it?

STARTING WITH THE LYRICS

In jingles, perhaps more than in other types of songwriting, the lyrics are of crucial importance. The words provide a jumping-off point for your creativity.

The Slogan

We are all victims of sloganism. Everything from a presidential candidate to toilet paper has a slogan. In Jingleland, the words rule. A melody can be set to nearly anything. How many times have you been to a party where people sat around inventing musical executions for the most outrageous phraseology? "Here comes Mary with the hot dogs!" "Is there any more guacamole dip, dearie?" (Guacamole is a wonderful word for a lyric—you can do so much with it!)

The roots of what *not* to do are here. The fact that something is singable doesn't make it a jingle. But in your quest to be original you will need a landmark, a signpost to point the way. So lean first upon the slogan, the umbrella theme for all the commercials. Recent slogans that have translated into strong musical messages include "Weekends Were Made for Michelob," "Maxwell House Coffee—Good to the Last Drop," and "Kentucky Fried Chicken—We Do Chicken Right."

The Sponsor's Name

How often you sing the name of the product will depend on your psychological background: If you came from a secure family (like most jingle writers), once will be adequate. If you needed lots of reinforcing (like clients or suits), you'll have to sing it often.

But no matter how many times you are inspired to sing it, place the sponsor's name in the most memorable musical setting that you can. This is the most important part of your effort. The purpose of the jingle is to make the product name memorable. All the other words are secondary: don't forget the name!

Your Lyrics or the Agency's?

If the agency has given you the freedom to write your own lyrics, and you're staring at that first blank piece of paper, ask yourself these questions:

Should you begin with the slogan? (You already know that you have to *end* with the slogan.)

Should you begin with unrelated lyrical imagery that gets married to the slogan later on?

Should your lyrics be factual, hard-hitting copy points, completely product-oriented, extolling consumer benefits?

Should your lyrics not mention the product at all, but merely create parallels that are left to the listener to understand? (Cosmetics use this approach with great effectiveness.)

Because there are so many commercials on the air, all sponsors recognize the difficulty of making an impact. For this reason you will sometimes get an unimaginative script that begins with three repetitions of the slogan, then allows for an announcer-copy section and concludes with the slogan as a tag. The theory here is that if you simply repeat a thought enough, it will be retained. It's like the army: first they tell you what they're going to tell you; then they tell you; then they tell you what they told you. This boring structure leads to music of limited interest.

If the agency has given you an unchangeable script, you're stuck. The words may be wonderful—and they may not be. If the directions provided are conflicting with the ideas that are developing in your head, you might consider asking if you can make changes in their unchangeable structure. The agency's response could be the first test of your ability to be flexible.

Internal Lyrics

Internal lyrics should define and support the message of the slogan, building up to it logically and clearly.

In 1970, I was given the assignment to create a sixty second jingle that would support the slogan "When You Say Budweiser, You've Said It All."

I had composed the Budweiser Beer advertising music for the two previous years, and was familiar with the various directions that the advertising had taken. The previous campaign was "Bud Is the King of Beers, But You Know That . . . ," and the new line was in keeping with the preemptive position that Budweiser wanted to maintain in its industry.

By beginning with the first half of the slogan as my key lyric ("When you say Bud"), I discovered a structure that allowed for descriptive internal lyrics that supported the main theme. ("When you say Bud," *this* happens, "When you say Bud," *that* happens.) The rest of my thoughts developed from this starting point.

When you say Bud, you've said a lot of things nobody else can say.
(You're special, Mr. Beer Drinker! So's our beer!)

When you say Bud, you've gone as far as you can go to get the very best.
(You have great taste, pal. We're the best and you know it!)

When you say Bud, you've said the word that means you like to do it all.
(You and me—we're the greatest. And we know what's good in life!)

When you say Bud, it means you want the beer that's got a taste that's number one.
(You know what you like—and we've got it!)

When you say Bud, you tell the world you know what makes it all the way.
(You're a leader in the crowd!)

When you say Bud, you say you care enough to only want the King of Beers.
(It's your choice and you know what you're doing.)

The use of the client's trademark, "The King of Beers," somewhere in the song was mandatory.

At this point, there was a change in lyrical rhythm:

There is no other one,
There's only second best,
Because the King of Beers
Is leading all the rest.

And finally the slogan, wrapping up all the lyrics before it, sung in its entirety. The legal requirement here was that the full product name, rather than the shortened version, be used at least once in each spot.

When you say Budweiser, you've said it all.*

The client later required that the words "second best" be changed to "something less." They felt that "second best" was too hard and aggressive, especially since they manufactured other beers—Michelob and Busch—that were certainly not "second best."

For the next eight years all Budweiser Beer commercials began and ended with some form of delivery of the slogan, "When you say Budweiser, you've said it all."

BUDWEISER—"YOU'VE SAID IT ALL"

Music and Lyrics by
Steve Karmen

far   as   you can go ____ to   get   the   ve - ry best.
want the   beer that's got ____ a   taste that's num - ber one.

When you   say   When you   say   Bud,

you tell   the   world you know ___ what   makes it ___ all   the way.

When you   say   Bud,

you   say   you   care e-nough ___ to   on - ly want ___ the

king   of beers. _____ There   is   no   oth - er one. ___

___ There's on - ly   sec-ond   best. _____ be - cause the
     There's on - ly   some - thing less. _____

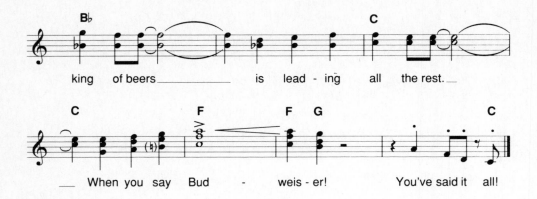

king of beers_____ is lead - ing all the rest.__

__ When you say Bud - weis - er! You've said it all!

In 1978, to update the advertising, the agency rewrote the lyrics using the same well-established melody:

> This Bud's for you
> For working hard all day just like you always do.
> So here's to you.
> You know it isn't only what you say,
> It's what you do.
> This Bud's for you.
> For all you do, the King of Beers is comin' through.
> This Bud's for you.
> You know there's no one else that does it
> Quite the way you do.

This time, however, because of the new world of the :30, the change in lyrical rhythm was not required. At the ending was the new slogan:

> For all you do, this Bud's for you.*

"When You Say Budweiser, You've Said It All" told the whole advertising story with words. Its children continue to be used in the advertising for Budweiser beer.

SETTING THE WORDS TO MUSIC

No matter how inventive the lyric, it must be presented with unique audio.

For the first arrangement of "When You Say Budweiser, You've Said It All," I sought a new musical sound, at least one that was not being used by other beers of the day. In 1970, Schlitz (with Gusto!) was using big outdoor-type sounds, with macho visuals of mountain climbing and sailing. Miller was being presented with lush music as the Champagne of Bottled Beers. Pabst was banjo-ing "What'll Ya Have? Pabst Blue Ribbon!"

To try and stand out in this crowd, I chose to begin my Budweiser song with a rhythm section of a tuba (playing downbeats) and three trumpets (playing offbeats). The tuba is a traditional beer-hall instrument, but it is used infrequently because of its Germanic um-pah-pah sound (not hip for the hip beer drinker). But as the basis for a rock and roll track, the tuba proved to be a unique and perfect bottom for the orchestra. As soon as the commercials began, even before the lyric, the consumer recognized it as the sound of Budweiser.

The musical setting provides yet another opportunity for the composer/arranger to be original.

Matching the Style with the Product

A big part of your job as composer will be to establish the style of music that is appropriate for the product. Your efforts should be directed toward creating something original within that musical product category.

Suppose you are writing for an airline. The agency wants the music to say "flying," to establish a floaty yet secure feeling. Airlines should never sound small. Small implies unsafe, like a toy plane with a rubber band. Big and majestic suggests confidence and security, like a 747. Maybe your song needs a violin sweep as the plane takes off. You might hear French horns in your head. French horns are very prominent in airline music—their long floating tones recall and suggest the feeling of flying in comfort. Today, every airline is trying to out-French-horn every other airline. Your musical skills have become a weapon in the battle for supremacy in the skies!

Car commercials mirror their potential buyers. If the desired image is speed, power, and performance, this might translate into musical motion, such as a rhythm figure that continues to build excitement with a hot drum track. If the car is in the luxury category, an appropriate sound might be lush strings, or the dignity of a classical piano, or the sustained elegance of certain synth patches.

Cola songs bounce along with a feeling of effervescence, matching the active, youthful image of the drinker-as-portrayed-by-Madison-Avenue. Cola-type visuals—outdoors, surfing, fun-in-the-sun—are usually accompanied by popular rock tracks with sounds like the Beach Boys, Michael Jackson, or Whitney Houston. A somber cello is not usually appropriate for a cola, at least not yet. A cello has no bubbles.

Beers like to sound big, full, not necessarily fast, but powerful, which is meant to suggest the power of the alcohol. Beer songs call for mammoth musical imagery to support the mammoth machismo of the traditional drinker (again as-portrayed-by-Madison-Avenue). Huge orchestras and the sound of blasting heavy metal are common. (Question: Which came first, the macho beer drinker, or his advertised image? Don't be too quick to answer.)

A perfume might sound fluid, romantic, sensuous, and slow, perhaps with a solo instrument: a lonely piano, a single classical guitar, an unaccompanied flute with lots of echo.

While each product category has its stereotypical sound, in the never-ending search to find originality, advertisers are beginning to mix styles. Cars are using beer sounds for their higher priced models, with a little airline thrown in for class; colas are using fast-car sounds with a little perfume thrown in for elegance.

The list is limited only by your imagination.

CREATIVE IMITATION

Imitation is the sincerest manifestation of the lack of an idea. It's the easy way. If the other cola is using girl rock groups, we'll out-rock 'em. If the other airline is using a star performer, we'll out-star 'em. Sometimes this approach works.

Sometimes, if a spot merely makes it into the "accepted sound" category, it is good enough to satisfy a small client who just wants to be out there with everybody else.

If you have been asked by an agency to imitate a specific style of music, or have even been given recorded examples of what they'd like your jingle to sound like—be on guard! You are now entering the tricky world of plagiarism, where the legal rules are well established.

When an agency purchases the rights to a particular hit song, and reworks the words for advertising, their license for the song does not include the *performance* of the song by the artist that had the hit. This requires a separate license. But if the advertiser has licensed a song, in all likelihood they also wanted the sound and the feeling of the first hit arrangement.

If you have been asked to find a singer that can imitate a particular top 40 star—*beware!* The star might involve you in a legal action for the unlawful use of their talent without compensation. Bette Midler set an important industry precedent in her suit against the Ford Motor Company, who purposely imitated her voice when she refused their offer to sing for them. If you agree to imitate someone's hit record, either musically or vocally, you are treading on dangerous ground and should consult an attorney. It's not worth the cost of having to defend yourself on behalf of a client who couldn't come up with an original idea. You may still want to take the job, but you should watch what you sign. (Be extremely aware of the indemnification clause in your contract, discussed in detail in Chapter Nine.)

CREATIVE DIPLOMACY

If your creative direction leads you to a jingle with more lyric and less announcer copy than the agency suggested, your skill as a diplomat will have a direct influence on your ability to get approval for the new format. In certain instances, coming up with lyrical changes will make for a much-improved commercial. But to be safe you should discuss your changes with the copywriter before you etch them in stone. Since you are both working together toward the same goal (you hope), try to impress on him that your lyrics deliver the same message as the copy but in a more memorable fashion. Also stress that you can drop the lyric and replace it with a copy donut if necessary.

TIME LIMITATIONS

The advent of the fifteen-second commercial has placed serious constraints on jingle creativity. We've all seen the quick spots that interrupt the one-minute nightly news updates. These are an advertiser's delight: cheaper to produce and broadcast, often scoring with the same memorability as the longer :30s.

For a composer, fifteen seconds is time for not much more than an intro to a musical tag. In this tiny time frame, the simpler the idea, the more chance for recall. Whenever my creative parameters are confined to fifteen seconds and I need a salve, I remind myself that if Beethoven, Mozart, and Bach were alive today, they would probably be writing jingles (and signing standard agency contracts). Imagine if they couldn't sing.

THE BIG ENDING

Someone once said that all jingle endings should go up; clients don't want to sound less cheery than necessary. There are relatively few minor-key jingles, except for fast-car spots where the minor mood adds mystery and excitement. Regardless of whether it goes up or down, the ending will be the main statement of the message and it demands to be special, topping the mood that preceded it.

The end might be a "button" (coming to a definite stop), or a fade-out (with a disappearing restatement of the tag, over and . . . over . . . an . . . ov . . . a . . . o . . .). But whatever the size of the tail, this is the important time to sing the product name in a manner that will be remembered.

TAILORING THE LENGTH

No matter how beautiful the melody you have created, or how much your mother likes it, it must come in on time. Sometimes your efforts might yield a sixty-five second song, or a thirty-five second song that there is just no way of shortening. And faster doesn't help. How can you make it work?

The odd-metered bar provides the most often heard musical fix. Bringing an overlength track down to time, or increasing a donut so that it has eleven seconds, not ten-and-a-half, is accomplished by creating one measure of an odd time signature, like 5/4, 6/4, or 7/4. For this miniscule difference—half a second—you may have to break up the groove of the music, but it's a compromise that is often necessary to meet the requirements of TV time—and a hard-nosed copywriter. But done correctly, and played right, it'll pass by unnoticed.

You can avoid carving up your music by maintaining a realistic awareness of time constraints. If the on-camera performer needs three-

and-a-half seconds to say his line, don't prepare a three-second hole. This may mean starting again—a possibility not to ignore or take lightly. Wonderful music is wonderful music, but this is business.

BUDGET CHANGES DURING THE CREATIVE PROCESS

When the great, original sound that you have created is too great to be produced within the budget you originally estimated, you have two options: try to get more production money approved, or limit and readjust the extent of your musical hunger.

Building flexibility into a budget is a must, because no one can accurately predict how long it will take for an orchestra to execute a piece of music. If your initial inspirations involve the possibility of a larger number of musicians and singers than you have previously discussed, you should let the agency producer know so he can get an approval from the client and figure the extra costs into his production and residual estimate.

FIGHTING CREATIVE BLOCK

It's never as easy as your raw talent might trick you into thinking it is.

There comes a time in every creative undertaking when you doubt your ability to finish. It happens to every successful writer on every project—you just can't seem to find a satisfactory path to the end.

And it won't come.

When you hit this wall you'll want to cop out and find an easy way. For a composer, this might manifest itself in repeating melodic phrases that fail to make the song grow, just to get the hell out of it. For a lyricist, it's falling back on trite, unimaginative, used-before words. For an arranger, it's using a first and second ending, repeating whole sections without putting in the effort to make the new parts different from what came before.

Hitting one of these dead ends is not necessarily due to laziness, or lack of ability. When you are stuck without an idea, I believe that your talent or your subconscious is sending you a message: "Hey, there's something you don't understand about this subject, something you've overlooked or haven't considered. It's there, but you're not looking in the right place."

Everyone has his own way to break out of creative block. When I'm stuck I make more coffee. I make soup (one small can in a microwave; heavy food slows me down—I'm stuck enough already). I eat a candy bar—fattening but satisfying (nobody's perfect, you know).

I don't buzz off to a movie or watch television. Both of these activities fall into the deal-with-it-later approach of goofing off and avoiding the problem. Part of working successfully is knowing how to get unstuck, and running away is never the answer. I don't leave my office. I don't talk to people, either on the phone or in person, because it's too much of a distraction. I don't read the newspaper since it's another distraction that might absorb me. But I pace around a lot. I swing a golf club (whooosh—my great four iron has me in birdie range on the sixteenth at Augusta). I putt (beating Jack Nicklaus to win the Masters). I swing a baseball bat (you guessed it—it's the bottom of the ninth in the World Series, bases loaded, two out, we're behind by three . . .) I let my mind go somewhere else. It's controlled escape. (It also lets me stretch out after an overlong session on the piano bench.)

When the block is really bad, I go outside for a short walk of no more than ten minutes, with my trusty little tape recorder tucked in my pocket, just in case.

I try to get back into the peace and calm of my own head where I feel my ability comes from. I remind myself that the people who are paying me are expecting my best effort. This always arouses my sense of pride.

And when I finally return to the piano, I search backward to the last creative landmark that pleased me, possibly an earlier section of the song, or even something that someone said during the agency meeting, captured on one of my scribble pages. I look for that first thought, that first stepping-stone toward a musical idea. And I know that I'll find it if I understand the advertising problem.

It's back to basics: What does the slogan really mean? What kind of melody will support it in an unusual way? What approach will best reach the target audience? What secondary lyrics will enhance the message? How will I pay for my next vacation if I blow the job (a major basic)?

And when all else fails, I put on my magic hat, take out my magic paper and my magic pencil, and the answers come right away.

If only it were so easy.

Music is a road to the ending. There is always a map. You just have to find it. When you're stuck, walk away, wash your face and start again. The sooner you confront the block, the quicker it will disappear.

RULES AND REMINDERS

1. Compose where you are most comfortable, but be organized and disciplined about how you approach your work.

2. A composer's job is to keep the audience's attention for thirty seconds, not lose it by sounding like everything else on the air. Always place originality above every other job requirement.

3. You should be able to defend your creative direction: the choice of words, the number of times you mention the product, the reason you chose strings instead of synthesizer. Having a creative rationale will help you avoid imitation and keep your inspirations original.

4. With experience you will be able to find a happy compromise between what you will do and won't do; which products you will write for and which you won't; which names you will or will not sing (the toughest choice).

5. Knowing what you are doing is a big part of developing self-confidence.

6. A deadline is the ultimate inspiration. How you arrive at that gem that outshines every other is dependent on your imagination and craft. The mark of a professional is getting it there on time.

5
MAKING YOUR PRESENTATION

TALENT HAS TRIUMPHED over inexperience, enthusiasm over uncertainty. You have completed, on time, a jingle that you know in your heart of hearts is the perfect solution to the agency's problem. Lyrically and musically it says everything it should say to satisfy the assignment. (As part of your research, you have learned from the weekly *Adweek* column that this account is indeed up for review, although everyone at the agency says it's only a formality.) Your music, without a doubt, will save the account from imminent disaster. The next step is to find out what others think.

ON THE PHONE

You should never begin work on the production of a demo—of any kind—until you've bounced your creative ideas off that person at the agency who has been designated as your contact.

The first exposure of your work will take place over the telephone. This is the most practical way to find out if you are on target, unless the agency happens to be next door and they're willing to come over and listen. This is not the formal presentation, or even the demo, but the beginning of the collaborative process. Anyone who is a campaign intimate can listen at this stage, but it shouldn't be a large group—the large group comes later.

Today, you are singing to the copywriter, who has asked you to hold while he finds the creative director. (The fact that a creative director will get involved at this early stage may be another sign that an account is in trouble.)

Begin by announcing that this is a "work in progress" and "an exploration of ideas" and that "nothing is frozen in yogurt." Film editors attach a leader to their rough cuts that says "Work print—work in progress—no optical effects" just in case someone thinks that this is the final spot. The same rules apply here: these are ideas only; make sure everyone knows it.

Present your lyrics first. Ask that someone write down the words before you sing them for the first time. If someone says, "just sing it," insist that they transcribe the words. This not only familiarizes them with what they are about to hear, but gives you the opportunity to describe any alternative lines and discuss them as you go. You'd be amazed at how different a lyric sounds when it is spoken to the person who has to approve it. If it doesn't make sense read in a logical sequence at this stage, you're in trouble.

When you present your melody, hum it or whistle it the first time, or play it instrumentally before you put it all together. Finding a happy balance between your voice and whatever electronic toys, drum machines, or keyboards you're using, gives you and the listener a chance to get used to how it sounds over the phone, in both volume and clarity. ("Can you hear okay?" is not inappropriate.)

Then put it all together. Sing it a few times—not just once—around and around. When you stop, wait for reactions.

You have reached the moment of truth that has faced every composer from Irving Berlin on down: Is my work good?

First-Stage Decisions

The copywriter speaks first, announcing that, in his opinion, you have created something different and exciting, suitable for presentation to everyone else. The creative director agrees quickly, and gets off the phone. (A visual of him doing a Joan Rivers throw-up flashes through your mind, but you suppress it). Your heart starts beating again.

Relieved, and now really charging ahead, you begin an in-depth discussion with the copywriter about aspects of the lyrics, such as whether to use one of your alternate lines because it makes more product sense, even though it takes away from the imagery of the song. After a few comments about the melody and musical direction, the copywriter agrees that it's time to let everyone else hear it.

At this point he will (1) ask you to produce a demo in your home/office studio and send it to him, or, as in this case, (2) that you simply record the song with piano and voice as a reference, and come to the agency to make the same phone presentation "live" to everyone. Maybe they'll even invite the client. (When the client is brought in at this early stage it is definitely an indication that the account is in trouble. This might be the agency's way of showing that they are charging ahead on his behalf.)

THE NEXT STEP

The advertising creative process is a series of presentations and re-presentations of previously presented material. The repetitions are seemingly endless, geared toward seeking approval each step of the way, through every level of the agency/client hierarchy until the job is complete. Formal music presentations can take several forms.

The Live Presentation

The advantages of making a live presentation—trial by jury—begin with the fact that your jingle can be judged for what it is, unembellished, in its raw form. This gives listeners the opportunity to be in on the ground floor of the process, invariably leading to a more directed effort. If there is a difference of opinion, you might be witness to a tense intra-agency discussion between the creatives and the suits about whose directions will ultimately triumph—a battle that you will wisely stay out of.

Today, unfortunately, clients and agencies are far less interested in the "raw" creative process than they are in the expedient, more-completed, almost-completed, all-completed demo presentation. Leaving nothing to the imagination takes less time.

But your agency is from the old school: they want to see how it happens from the beginning.

You arrive twenty minutes before the agreed hour and spend it, not rehearsing in the music room as you had hoped, getting the feel of the place, preparing to debut your work for a tough audience, but instead cooling your heels in the reception area while the secretary tries to locate the producer who hired you. At first, she can't find his name on the well-worn plastic employee list for that floor, mumbling something about being a temp on her first day.

The place is crawling with at least a half dozen seven- to nine-year-old kids, with moms, and the noise makes it sound like fifty. You have stumbled into a children's casting call. In every corner, enthusiastic mothers are coaching their offspring with copy lines. You learn, as you listen to the drills, that they are auditioning for a cereal commercial in which a little boy eats the product and gets shot out of a cannon.

The bored kid sitting next to you is nervously twitching his leg trying to placate his anxious mother. He is kicking the air absently while she runs the lines. Soon this midget is regularly brushing the crease in your pressed pants with his filthy Buster Brown, while his mother remains oblivious to the damage he is inflicting on your appearance and your concentration.

You get up, seeking respite from Romper Room, and again request that the receptionist try to locate your producer.

This time his phone line is busy. You decide to remain standing rather than endure involvement with another kicker. You swear to yourself that when you have kids of your own, you will never put them through this kind of animal casting call.

Suddenly, a wildfire whisper passes through the room: "It's a Class-A! It's a Class-A!"

One of the mothers smiles confidently at you and explains that this commercial will be broadcast on the network, qualifying for the highest residual scale. Then she eagerly confides that when her darling Henry was five, he acted in a Class-A spot and earned twenty thousand dollars from just one day's work.

You push the image of that little monster out of your mind. Crass, financial details are the enemy of art. Today, you are an *artiste*!

Finally, your producer's secretary appears and ushers you into the agency music room (quietly whispering good luck). Here are gathered the same team that you met a few days before, with a few additional folks that you've never met, including someone who is introduced as "the client." You try to take mental notes of the new names and titles, but they slip away as soon as they are introduced. Your thoughts are on your work as you pass out your typed lyric sheet, making sure you spelled the product name in CAPITAL LETTERS.

You ignore the discomfort you feel when you learn that you must present the jingle with your back to everyone. The agency upright piano is facing the wall. You toy with the idea of requesting help to turn it around so you can see their faces (Al Jolson wanted to see the faces), but decide not to make an issue of this inconvenience. You are here as a composer, not as one of the Seven Santini Brothers.

Just as you are about to begin, the phone rings. The account executive answers, tells the caller that this will only take a minute, and puts the phone on hold, motioning for you to continue.

With the hold light blinking in the background, you start by explaining the musical sounds that you have in mind, illustrating some examples on the piano. Then you turn to the keys (and to the wall) and present your complete idea.

You're nervous and your performance is stiff. You blow one of the lyrics—the name of the product, of course. Your mouth feels like cotton, your tongue sticks like flypaper.

No one speaks.

A year passes.

Another year.

Finally, someone asks you to play it again.

This time, throwing caution to the wind, you rear back and have at it, with all the energy and enthusiasm that you felt when you were composing it.

The Tape Presentation

The agency may have requested a tape, rather than a live presentation. In this case you won't have to worry about a stiff performance. You simply pass out the lyric sheets, explain any alternative lines, mention the myriad other musical styles that are possible to use with your generically-conceived composition, and then push the button.

Everyone is attentive as you start the tape. (If you haven't had a chance to check out the audio equipment before the meeting, it helps to play an instrumental version first. This will allow you a chance to adjust the volume and equalization before half your song is over.) You sit back, smiling conservatively, and bob along with the rhythm.

Don't be nervous if no one else bobs.

Mailing in Your Jingle

Some agencies will not give you the opportunity to present your work in person, wishing not to be swayed by your salesmanship: everyone knows that the ultimate judgment is made with the ear, and not the eye. Or there simply may not be time for a full-blown meeting.

When you are asked to deliver a tape by a specific date, you might enclose a brief note outlining possible instrumental and vocal styles. "I hear Billy Joel with a little Mick Jagger thrown in, and a vocal group to make the slogan stand out." (And to qualify you for vocal residuals, you little devil you!)

You are now at the mercy of Ma Bell, the condemned man awaiting word from the governor.

The Best Way

Your most effective presentation will be the one that provides the agency with as much detail and understanding about the directions you took during the creative process.

THE IMPOSSIBLE HAPPENS: THEY REJECT YOUR WORK

The worst four words a jingle writer can ever hear are "We'll let you know."

Since your back was to everyone, you could not see their expressions while you were singing. If, after your presentation, the producer politely tells you that he will call you as soon as they have had a chance to kick it around (and then everyone gets up to leave), they were probably underwhelmed.

Sometimes the kicking around takes place right in front of you.

The creative director: "It sounded much different on the phone. Did you change anything?"

"No."

The copywriter: "Well it doesn't do anything for me. We don't need all these lyrics. It's much too wordy."

"But I thought you liked . . . "

The art director: "The melody isn't special. I was expecting something along the line of . . . " and he names an obscure rock group that you've never heard of (nor has anyone else).

The music director: "Not enough punch. We need something with much more power. This is a big account. We need a *big* sound."

The agency producer: "The other presentations will be here this afternoon."

The client type has been dour, unsmiling, and silent throughout. Now the account is really in trouble.

You try in vain to explain that the jingle will sound magnificent when they hear it with the full orchestra.

But no one listens. The tense mood in the room tells you that the judges have made up their minds.

"Well," the account exec says, standing, stretching, "let's have a meeting later about this. Thanks for coming in, pal." He then picks up the phone-on-hold and makes a lunch date at Lutece.

One by one the others follow on the receiving line of failure, shaking your hand in parting, wishing you luck in a new line of work, while you try to maintain a composed visage. But the pain in your eyes and tight smile give you away, and only from the producer's secretary, powerless to help, do you see a glimmer of compassion about the massacre that has just taken place.

Expressions of rejection echo through your head:

"Don't call us, we'll call you."

"We'll call your agent."

"Leave an eight-by-ten glossy with the secretary."

"We'll get back to you."

"Dust off *Gray's Anatomy*."

Occasionally, if there is time, you may be given a chance to correct whatever you misunderstood. But in most instances, especially in a competitive situation where another jingle house's work may have been more on target, you will have taken your best shot . . . and missed.

Nothing is quite as difficult as developing a new approach after the agency tells you that they already have "something that they like."

Where did you go wrong? You study your notes again, trying to determine what you missed. You call the producer who offers polite solace, but no solutions. You ask questions: Should you have taken more of a chance creatively? Did they like *anything* about what you wrote? You press for the not-so-polite truth. Whether you agree or not, this information will be of value because it will tell you something about the attitudes at the agency, and also what not to do next time.

At this point, it pays to be philosophical: Babe Ruth only batted .347, and struck out more often than anyone in history. Being able to accept rejection, at least to the point of putting past issues out of your mind, is essential for creative success. Everyone has an opinion, and it really hurts when someone doesn't approve of your work. But again, this doesn't make you a bad person.

Failure, in many ways, is the most effective teacher. Next time, you vow, you'll be better.

THE OTHER VERDICT

Wake up! Rewind! It was all a bad dream. Just like Bobby Ewing, it never happened!

After your superlative presentation you hear the following comments:

The copywriter: "The words don't seem right in this part."

"It's all open for adjustment," you say with utmost sincerity.

Then he suggests a change in lyric that you gladly accept immediately, wondering out loud how you could have been so stupid as to have missed that point in the first place.

The account exec: "Words or no words, I like it. It's different. This approach could be the greatest thing that has ever happened to this product. It's exactly what the client's been looking for. It'll run for thirty years."

The client nods happily.

Soon everyone is agreeing that this jingle, your creation, will be nominated for inclusion in the next time capsule.

But you restrain yourself, ever modest, ever grateful to be embraced by their collective wisdom.

Whether it was your jingle, your presentation, your demo tape, your winning smile, or their incredibly good musical taste, they have accepted your work to go into production.

When you call your mother with the good news, she says that she knew it would happen anyway.

RULES AND REMINDERS

1. The first exposure of your work on the phone is critical in making sure that you are headed in the right creative direction.

2. Dress properly for a client meeting.

3. Be disappointed in losing, and humble in winning.

4. Learn from your musical mistakes.

6
THE TALENT
AND THOSE
WHO BOOK THEM

NOW THAT YOU have been awarded the job, you've been requested to provide a final recorded version of your jingle, pending the agency's approval of a budget estimate. Since this estimate will include the fees of the people you hire, let's take a look at who they are.

THE MUSICAL ARRANGER

The important choice of the person who arranges and orchestrates the spot is made by the composer or the jingle house together with the agency. At the creative meeting, the participants discuss the style and direction of the arrangement: how big a band, what type of instruments, what kind of feel, what kind of sound. Occasionally the agency will be very specific about the arranger they want.

A schooled arranger/orchestrator hears the basic, unadorned song in his head and assigns the notes to various instruments of the orchestra, transposing them into their correct keys on score paper. (The French horn is written a fifth higher than it sounds; the trumpet and clarinet are written a tone higher than they sound; the viola has its own clef designation; and so on.) This "chart" becomes the road map for everything that happens at the session.

A schooled synthesist/composer (or not so schooled) also functions as an arranger because he, too, hears the internal song in his head, even though he might not have the skills to actually write out the arrangement. But instead of developing a score and writing a chart to be performed later by others, the synthesist plays the individual parts himself—the French horn, trumpet, clarinet, and viola—simply by pressing the right buttons. A synth composer/arranger has the creative freedom to experiment with different ideas and hear them as he goes along (no transposition necessary) without having to wait for the session to confirm his musical instincts. If he wants a key change, he pushes the button marked key change. And if he does want a written score, there are plenty of computer software programs that will print out his most complicated ideas, also at the touch of a button.

An arranger might be asked to elaborate on sound directions originated by a synthesist, or to take the song in a whole different direction straight out of his own imagination (of course with the agreement of the agency).

At agencies with music departments, the arranger and the music producer usually collaborate on the choice of musicians. Sometimes the agency will suggest particular players, ones that they feel are right for the job. Agencies without music departments always allow the arranger to pick his own band.

When the composer has the musical and technical skills to orchestrate, he may also function as the arranger. For this discussion, let's assume that you, the composer, are also an arranger, thereby introducing one less person into the stew and keeping things less complicated. But the same rules would apply if the composer and arranger were two different people.

THE MUSIC COPYIST

After the arranger/orchestrator has plotted his creation on score paper, assigning each instrument the notes it will play, it becomes the task of a music copyist to transcribe them on to the individual pages that each musician will read. The more detailed the directions indicated by the arranger, the more complex the copying job.

The copyist is the last production person on the road to the studio, often receiving the score the night before the session, or even within hours of it. He is the bleary-eyed person who arrives early enough so that the parts can be passed out in time.

A good copyist has the magical ability to understand the scratches of his arranger and turn them into easily readable notes. His skills can save time and money—for an arranger it is very disconcerting to have to stand in front of an orchestra and spend the first ten minutes of a session correcting copying mistakes.

It is the keen eye and unswerving dedication to craft of the professional music copyist that brings order to the chaos of the wee-small-hour chicken scrawls that they are often given.

Copyists, however, are fast becoming an endangered species, threatened by the availability of computer software that allows a composer to electronically notate—and print out—his wildest musical fantasies.

The Lead Sheet and the Booth/Conductor Part

A single-stave part containing the melody line, lyrics, and chord symbols is called a lead sheet. (See page 113.)

A booth/conductor part is the next step up and most often what your copyist will provide. This mini-score usually contains two or three staves of lyrics, chords, some harmonic accompaniment, and the bass line. In addition, depending on how detailed, it might indicate in concert key which sections of the orchestra are to play at any given point.

The double-stave booth/conductor part provides a melody and bass line, and may also indicate where things happen in a TV spot. Listing the names of each star performer is helpful when working with a film editor or anyone else who can't read music. (See "I Love New York," page 114.)

A different double-stave booth/conductor part (see "Pontiac," page 116) might also place the lyrics on "up" stems and indicate what is happening in the score.

The triple-stave booth/conductor part (see "Liberty Mutual Insurance," page 118) is the most detailed breakdown of what is happening in the arrangement.

If you're copyrighting a jingle, either the lead sheet or the booth/conductor part would be appropriate. Both should be prepared by the copyist with utmost care as they represent the legal evidence of the composer's creation.

THE MUSIC CONTRACTOR

The musicians' union requires that there be a music contractor present on each session when there are ten players or more. He does not have to be one of the players, but he must be a member of the union.

The contractor is one who, after discussion with the arranger, calls the individual musicians and books them through their answering services. He also supervises the start time and break time, collects W-4 forms, and takes care of all the other business paperwork relating to musicians, including typing the AF of M Form B contract used to pay the players. The contractor makes life easier for the conductor/arranger by acting as second-in-command in the studio.

Unfortunately there are very few "non-affiliated" (free-lance) contractors left, at least not in the style of the old days when the contractor (always a musician) would either be part of the orchestra or standing around on the side smoking a fat cigar. In the modern jingle world, the music contractor is part of the jingle house office staff, and often the phone calls are made by a secretary or production person. Today, there is rarely an official contractor present on a session. It is the music house principal or employee whose name most often appears on the contract as "the contractor," qualifying that person for double-scale residuals. This is another way for jingle houses to earn continuing income while keeping their weekly expenses down.

THE STUDIO MUSICIAN

The studio musician is an instrumentalist who earns his living by going from one recording session to another, reading and performing music that he has never seen before, and making it sound as if he had been practicing it for this very moment all his life.

While self-contained musical groups have the luxury of being able to practice with each other over extended time periods (in symphony orchestras, road bands, and rock groups), thereby becoming familiar with the nuances of the music they play, the studio musician must be able to read and interpret exactly what appears on his part *the very first time he sees it*. Very often he sits next to a different player on each different session. The musicians' union rewards this special talent with the highest payment scales: jingles first, followed by the scales for phonograph recordings, TV, motion pictures, and industrial films.

I LOVE NEW YORK
NEW YORK STATE TOURISM

music and lyrics by
STEVE KARMEN

BOOTH/CONDUCTOR

composed & arranged by
STEVE KARMEN

I LOVE NEW YORK
"LIGHTS" :30 tv

Booth/Conductor

music and lyrics by
STEVE KARMEN

PONTIAC
We build excitement

THE TALENT

Booth/Conductor

music and lyrics by
STEVE KARMEN

LIBERTY MUTUAL INSURANCE
AMERICA BELIEVES IN LIBERTY

BOOTH/COND.

LIBERTY MUTUAL
"AMERICA BELIEVES"

MER-I-CA ___ HAS PUT ITS CON-FI-DENCE AND TRUST IN OUR EX-

PER-I-ENCE ___ WE'VE HELPED THEM ALL ___ A-

MER-I-CA ___ BE-LIEVES IN LI-BER-TY ___

LI-BER-TY MU-TU-AL IN-SUR-ANCE!

Once upon a time music was performed "live" in the studio with musicians playing together with other musicians. Now it's assembled from pieces by the sound engineer. Today, as the individual player strives to reach his level of perfect performance and blend in with the rest of the orchestra, he does it while listening through headphones to a click track and any prerecorded music. The only time he ever sees the musicians in other sections that he "plays along with" is in the hallway between overdub sessions. With this piecemeal approach, it is entirely possible that a player, after hearing a completed mix, might not even recognize his own work.

The Demise of the Studio Musician
The golden days of the jingle business are gone forever.
—OUT-OF-WORK STUDIO MUSICIAN

The synthesizer- and MIDI-equipped home/office studio has changed the face of the recording industry. The ability to produce quality sounds cheaply has altered agency thinking about the costs of music, and has had a sobering and devastating effect on how much they are willing to spend during any stage of jingle development, demo or final. The cost of musicians has always represented a significant portion of any production budget, and nowadays instrumental specialists are working less and less, having been replaced by machines.

In the world before synthesizers, the musical media—phonograph records, TV shows, movies, and jingles—all used orchestra-sized numbers of self-employed musicians who earned their income as players. For these talented people, working as a musician was the reward for years of training and practice. Sidemen (studio musicians) who played on recordings earned big money, and there was a musician available for every style. Because the union scales were the highest, and the working conditions the most pleasant, every musician wanted to play on jingles.

In pre-synth days, working in the pit orchestra of a Broadway show was considered to be "the pits"—musicians who could crack the tight circle of studio players earned more money and had better hours. Club-date musicians, who played at weddings and parties, also aimed to break into studio work, for basically the same reasons.

The synthesizer has changed all that. Today, club dates and Broadway shows are considered to be great jobs, because they are among the few remaining places where professional musicians can earn money. The potential work for a studio musician has dried up considerably.

At the push of a button, a composer can have any instrument he wants (not *almost* any instrument) without having to hire a human being. And as the clock ticks, the technology gets better, simpler to operate, and more portable.

While people can argue that a machine sounds stiff and inhuman like a machine, the incredible development of MIDI music makes it almost impossible for even the professional to tell the difference between the real thing and the real-thing-with-a-plug. And completely impossible for the agency that wants to save money. The public, of course, "won't know the difference, anyway."

Unfortunately this is not a good world in which to devote your entire life and career to the study and mastery of the flute or trumpet or trombone or French horn, unless you plan to compete for the few Broadway or symphony orchestra jobs. And teach.

"My eight-year-old daughter wants to play the harp," says the loving father. "What should I do?"

The professional musician replies, "Break her fingers."

The music industry that once provided the income for studio musicians is gone.

Depressing, isn't it?

THE JINGLE SINGER—WHERE THE MONEY IS

Advertising music may not always require live musicians or full-service recording studios, but as long as there are words to be sung, there will always be singers. The jingle singer is the only audio supplier who has survived the onslaught of the synthesizer unscathed and continues to reap healthy financial rewards. Requiring no more equipment than an answering service and an appointment book, talented jingle singers have been known to hire people to open their residual pay envelopes. (After all, who can open hundreds of envelopes each week and not have their hands hurt?)

The trade unions have established high scales of residuals for their singing members, and while a composer may receive accolades for his compositions, his only real income will come, unfortunately, from his ability to be listed on the singer contract.

The most successful jingle singers, the ones who earn incomes in *seven* figures (not a misprint), are the ones with the most discipline and dedication. Inspiration is secondary. Jingle singers are expert at subordinating their own identity and personality to the identity of the product. While a rock screamer with the ability to ad-lib and wail with distinction may have an unusual sound, he needs the ability to pronounce the client's words so everyone can understand them, including those on their way to the refrigerator.

Singers who have had a hit record and can work in the discipline of advertising often earn more (*much* more) than they did from their hits.

Becoming a Jingle Singer

The talent and studio savvy necessary for success as a jingle singer are formidable, and comparable to the expertise needed to become a successful composer. It takes hard work, the ability to sightread and take direction, the facility to consistently reproduce what has already been accepted by the producer, and the physical chops to withstand the long and arduous vocal repetition that may be necessary to complete the job.

And you must know how to smile. There is always such love and kindness and smiling and touching going on between jingle singers and the people who hire them. Why not? One job, the right job, might earn $30,000. Hiiiiii, Baby!

Preparing for the Studio

A phonograph record producer will take the time to teach microphone and studio skills to a novice with a new and unusual voice, and guide them step-by-step through a new song over a lengthy period of development. But for advertising, the recording studio is not the place to learn. It is the time to execute.

The jingle composer/producer will take a reasonable amount of time to get just the right performance from a singer he has never used before, but there are limits to what should not be a teaching process. You, the singer, have been hired as a professional, and will be expected to perform accordingly. The amount of potential income should make it completely unnecessary for a jingle singer to be coddled and coaxed through a part.

If you were provided with a tape of the song to learn prior to the session, consider yourself blessed and take advantage of the head start. If you are not a quick study, this chance to practice beforehand could win you the job. Even if you are a fat cat with an over-funded corporate retirement plan it's smart to learn the song ahead of time. Anything you can do to make your producer's task easier and smoother will win you respect and calls for other jobs.

New singers should learn by singing everywhere and anywhere to gain experience. "Paying dues" will ultimately enable you to pay your union dues.

The "Nonaffiliated" Jingle Singer

For the free-lance jingle singer who is not connected with a jingle house as a composer, producer, arranger, staff, or family member, breaking in is extremely difficult. Where an orchestra might employ thirty musicians, there are rarely groups of more than five or six singers on each jingle. Production methods and payment rules have helped to hold down the size of vocal groups. Union scale for five-in-a-group is higher than for six-in-a-group, making it advantageous for singers (and those who hire them and sing along) to keep the group small. The cost of residuals makes the use of larger groups unaffordable. And the ability to overdub voices again and again (turning a group of five into a group of forty, for a 50 percent higher overdub fee) has further limited the necessity for large vocal groups. All of this has cut back employment opportunities for free-lance singers.

The "Affiliated" Jingle Singer

Since creative and arranging fees are one-time fees, and since there are no residuals for composers, it becomes obvious why every composer must qualify as a jingle singer. That's why the most competition for singing jobs comes from the people who hire singers—the jingle composers and jingle house owners themselves.

The availability of the vocal residual has made quasi-singers out of as many people from the jingle house as the advertising agencies will tolerate on the contract. Often there will be certain free-lance singers, the strong "heavyweights" who know how to phrase and pronounce words and can hold the group together, standing next to jingle house office staff with considerably less vocal ability, but who by virtue of their association with the jingle house have managed to join the unions and qualify to be on the contract as vocalists. This internal competition for jobs makes the task of the nonaffiliated vocalist even harder.

The Need for a Reel

The guidelines for preparing and using composer reels can also be applied to singers' reels.

People who are serious about becoming jingle singers must have a reel. No one can, or will, judge your vocal ability from a live audition, or even take the time to listen. Save the physical selling for your nightclub act. The only way to judge a vocalist in advertising is by listening, not watching.

In the studio, I make a practice of never watching the singers as they work; instead I keep my eyes on the conductor score or a vocal part. Too often a smiling performance might trick you into accepting something less than perfect. Early in my career, I worked with a singer whose gyrations and body movements were so broad and funny that people in the booth were always in fits of uncontrollable laughter. In a group, I could count on him to keep things bright and gay. But on one occasion when I tried him as as a soloist he fooled us all. His pronunciation, acceptable while we were laughing as he bumped and humped along to even the most mundane advertising lyrics, was not up to snuff when it came time to mix. From that point on, I stopped watching.

How you sound on tape will be your first key to employment. Your reel should present your voice in the best possible musical settings. In the old days a potential jingle singer would have had to hire a rhythm section to make a demo; today it can be done at home. Beginner's tapes don't have to be on-air quality, but should show off your talent to best advantage. Whether the accompaniment is only a piano, or a rhythm section or synthesizer track, the musical sounds should be compatible with the vocal styles you want to demonstrate.

Always place your best efforts first, to entice the listener into hearing the next selection on your reel. You don't want to be the victim of someone who will only listen to eight bars before moving on. A variety of styles will keep you in consideration for more jobs. You don't want to be categorized as only "a screamer" or "a belter."

If your selections sound the same as other singers on the air, chances are that the producer will hire the known talent before you, the unknown clone. You, too, must sound original and unique. Welcome to the club.

Who to Call to Find Singing Work

Jingle composers and producers are constantly on the lookout for new and exciting vocal talent. Those interested in submitting their reel should do so by mail, or through any other kind of introduction that they can muster. It's that squeaky door approach again. Agency music departments, as well as independent jingle houses, listen to vocal reels all the time. New singers are much sought-after commodities; a fresh vocal sound goes a long way toward making the final track sound unique.

Finding the Right Voice

As a composer, when you wrote the jingle you had something in mind, a certain sound, a certain tone of delivery. Choosing the correct solo voice is often the difference between success and sounding like everyone else out there in the big wash.

Agencies with music departments are critically involved in the selection of all singers and will certainly pass approval on the soloist and the group you wish to use. Agencies without music departments will want to approve any recommended soloist, but will most often leave the selection of group singers to the jingle house. (Phew!)

After listening to demo reels of several singers, you (and the music producer) will pick one, or perhaps two or three, that you wish to hear against the final track. If there is going to be a vocal group (and when isn't there a group?), you should have it include your second and third solo choices. Supplying each of them with a tape of the demo and a lyric sheet helps speed the decision-making process. While most of the top jingle singers can come into a studio and sightsing, nothing beats a little pre-session preparation. Not only will this save time and production dollars, but it will give the singers advance notice of what is expected so they can do their best.

Having the option of hearing two or three people will increase the likelihood of finding the correct voice, and will please your client, who will want to have an input into the final decision.

The Vocal Contractor

The singers' unions provide that there be a vocal contractor when the vocal group has three or more singers. Under the AFTRA code, this person receives $48.80 in addition to his total session fee. For SAG the fee is $58.75. But in today's jingle business, in my opinion, there is absolutely no need for a vocal contractor. All the paperwork and handing out of contracts and W-4 forms are done by the agency producer covering the session, and the actual phone calls to singers are made by the hiring jingle house, after the agency's approval of choices. So this extra union pay becomes a gift to the jingle house's favorite person-of-the-moment, either the singing composer or more often the singing jingle house principal.

KIDS WHO SING JINGLES

Every parent knows a child, a darling cherub with a voice like an angel, who belts like Ethel Merman, and has pitch like Julie Andrews. In advertising, there is a constant need for young talent (for jingles as well as for acting parts in commercials), and most often the jobs come through talent agents and managers that specialize in young performers.

Finding Work

The same rules for adults apply to children when it comes to seeking work. The child singer needs a reel, professional pictures if they're seeking acting work, and the ability to learn quickly. It is not necessary to be able to sight-read music, but familiarity with a lead sheet is very helpful.

While girls' voices are more constant, a boy's voice changes suddenly, usually around twelve years old, and he is no longer employable as a child jingle singer. (Of course, this doesn't make him a bad person. He's just not a child anymore.)

Talent agents who handle kids are franchised by the unions, and agent lists are obtainable on request from the unions. The *Madison Avenue Handbook* has a listing of all agents, managers, and casting people for legit theater, modeling, fashion, video, photographers, and every other kind of talent.

This is a job for stage mothers.

The Rate of Pay

The union scales do not differentiate between grown-ups and children. An on-camera baby can make thousands and doesn't have to join the union until he is four. (Or go to union meetings. But at that age it's tough to get them to *sing* anything, except "goo-goo ga-ga.")

The percentage of young people who sing jingles and then go on to college is very high. Tuition, medical school, and the Mercedes-after, can be paid for by a successful career before the age of ten. The age category most often needed is eight to twelve years old, and $50,000 to $100,000 per year is not unusual for a good child jingle singer who gets the work. The jingle business is the only business in the world where a kid of eight knows how to roll over a certificate of deposit.

Working with Kids Who Sing

As a composer/producer, you'll find that using kids on jingles requires some adjustment of your usual routine. When working with younger kids, I often have my copyist prepare a words-only sheet, printed in nice large letters. The choice of musical key for children is usually higher than for grown-ups. And kids don't have the staying power that older pros do, so it's best not to rehearse too long. Your engineer should record everything, especially early-on before the kids get tired.

Sometimes the manager of young talent will help by teaching the jingle to the kid(s), and then singing along in the group to hold things together, masking his grown-up sound with a high-pitched, soft voice lost in the background. (Well, boys and girls, what's going on here? Commission *plus* residuals?)

Fox/Albert Management, headed by two former jingle singers, works with their young clients, teaching them songs and techniques of delivery, *before* they are allowed to go into the studio.

JOINING A UNION AS TALENT

The advertising union system provides the classic "Catch 22"—you can't get a job if you don't belong to the union, and you can't obtain membership in the union unless you are given a union job.

The easy way to get around this is for the jingle writer to form a company, become a union signatory employer, and then hire himself.

To join SAG (as soon as you have a union job), the initiation fee is $796.50 plus current dues.

To join AFTRA (as soon as you have a union job), the initiation fee is $600 plus current dues.

To join the AF of M, the initiation fee is $210 plus current dues. You don't need a union job to join the musicians union, just the $210. (At one time it was necessary to pass a talent audition to become a member. Today, because business is so bad, they will audition for you.)

Under the Taft-Hartley Law a performer is entitled to do one job without having to join the unions. For the second job, you must join or you cannot be hired by a union-signatory company.

PUTTING MUSICIANS AND SINGERS ON HOLD

In the world of specialization, a composer usually has first-call musicians and vocalists with whom he likes to work. But when the date is scheduled for tomorrow, it might not be possible to get them if they are already booked on other dates.

In jingles, unlike on albums, it is rare for a composer to absolutely, positively require one special drummer. Or bass player. Or whatever. Each composer will naturally have favorites—the ones he likes to work with—but in a pinch there is usually a deep well of talent for each first-chair part. You and your music contractor will have established a list of the players you want to use, and the calls will go out via the musicians' answering phone service. In major cities, sidemen all subscribe to a central answering service which will seek out a player's availability and deliver his response to the contractor. If someone is not available, the service is usually instructed to call the next person on the list. The top four or five names on each instrument will all be great players able to play anything your music requires.

There are some musicians and singers who will not accept a date until they are sure they are not going to get a better job, such as a Coke final instead of your demo for the Longhorn Lumberyard of Podunk. This can wreak havoc for the producer and the contractor who have to scramble at the last minute for the next names.

Sometimes musicians will take back-to-back sessions with overlapping time commitments, and take their chances that they will finish the first in time to make the second date. This practice is a direct result of the lack of business for players. This kind of musician is obvious in the studio: he is always looking at his watch instead of the music, creating an uncomfortable atmosphere for everyone. Especially the producer.

I always assume that if a musician or singer accepts a date with a "possible," then they are available to me for the complete "possible" and they'll finish the job. As producer, you should not have to work under the pressure of another producer's session. The other date is the other producer's problem. No player or singer is worth this kind of aggravation—the out-of-work talent list is too strong. Work is supposed to be fun, not a panic to get through.

In the case of singers, however, a particular soloist might be critical to your session, especially if you or the agency have a certain sound in mind for the product. If there is time, you should notify your choice before locking in your schedule. It may be worth it for you to be flexible in order to accommodate that special voice.

If you have a few days to spare before the date, you might consider placing key people "on hold" for the hours you will need them. If they are available, a hold will be kept until the talent advises you that they have received another job offer. At that time, you will have to confirm or release. Some musicians will not accept holds, finding the task of keeping up with time changes and cancellations too much of a bother. (But today, when business for live musicians stinks, for *you* they'll do a special favor.)

Sometimes the tables are switched around and group singers will put *you* on hold. This means that they are trying to juggle around their time schedules to accommodate you—to fit your Budweiser session in between their Miller, Pabst, and Stroh's dates.

It's an amazing business.

STAR PERFORMERS

Having a star sing your song is a big thrill.

Long ago, in the infant days of television, most actors considered working in commercials beneath their professional dignity. Today, commercials provide many actors with the majority of their income along with a high degree of professional visibility: the opportunity to be seen on camera or to serve as the spokesman for a major network advertiser has given star performers exposure that is unrivaled.

Working with a star is different than working with a studio singer. Each has his own quirks and is accustomed to having his own way.

Frank Sinatra is notorious for his unwillingness to give more than one or two takes when he deigns to sing on a commercial. The smart producer knows that it is imperative to have everything prepared, the music rehearsed, the balances correct, all technical matters covered prior to Frank's arrival. Nothing is as irritating to a star as having to wait around while you get your drum sound.

Some stars have a delicious sense of humor. When I recorded Louis Armstrong for Chrysler/Plymouth, he gave everyone a packet of Swiss-Chris laxative after the session, along with a photo of himself seated on a toilet, captioned with his favorite expression, "Leave it all behind ya."

At a session for the Great Adventure Amusement Park, Jerry Lewis arrived, stuck his chewing gum on the wall, sang the song, unstuck the gum, and chewed his way out of the studio.

Muhammad Ali once sang for the anti-drug campaign, "Get High on Yourself." The champ likes to make an insect-flying sound by rubbing his fingers together. He stands behind you and "buzzes" your ear, making you brush away what you think is an attack by a monster moth. His hands are very quick, and only after seeing him do this to other people did I realize that we didn't need a can of Raid in the room.

Again, it is important to agree beforehand about the amount of work that is to be accomplished during the session. "One more time," can be wearing when extra versions are really unnecessary. A plan for defining the desired end result will go a long way toward making a star session easier for all concerned.

Some flowers sent before the session, or a phone call or note saying that you are looking forward to working with the star, will help make your session a smooth one.

THE RECORDING ENGINEER AND STUDIO

Before you can even think of hiring singers and musicians you must have a place for them to perform. If you are not familiar with the recording studios available, the agency will be able to help. Working musicians also have favorite places where they like to record. And everyone has a favorite engineer. Your choice of studio and engineer is your choice of the "sound" of your jingle. Each studio sounds different, and each engineer has his own style of recording and mixing. Initially the recommendations of others, and ultimately your own tastes and opinions, will provide you with that place to work where you are comfortable with the facility and the personnel.

Recording studios specialize in the kind of clients they attract. A record label wanting to make an album might book a studio for a month in one hunk, or longer. They will commit to the huge cost in order to keep the studio available for their artists, who might want to work in the middle of the night, or whenever else they feel inspired and "get a groove together." (In jingles, getting the groove takes twenty minutes. Less. Ten. Eight. The second runthrough. It's a business.) This type of studio is often not set up to cope with the instant time demands of advertising, where sessions are scheduled and completed in a matter of days, sometimes hours, and tape copies are needed immediately. Other studios cater to the advertising trade, where they are staffed to accommodate the overnight demands of duplicating, packing, and shipping across America those tapes that must absolutely, positively be there for that 9 A.M. meeting. These studios have office personnel who are wise to the ways of Madison Avenue, and know how to get things done quickly.

The person to contact to set up a studio schedule is the studio manager.

Putting the Studio on Hold

If they have time available, most studios will allow you to put a certain amount "on hold," at no charge, with the understanding that if they get a firm booking, they will call and you will either commit to the time or release it. The studio manager will also help with the availability of a sound engineer, by either booking (with your permission, of course) a "house" engineer, or contacting an independent engineer on your behalf. Fees for the house engineer are included in the hourly rate. Some studios will deduct something if you are planning to bring in an outside person, and some will not, figuring that they have to pay their staff people anyway.

If a studio does not know you, they may only permit you to place them on hold for twenty-four hours before releasing the time. Explaining to the studio manager that you are waiting for a signed client estimate before "firming" can help, especially if they have done prior business with your advertising agency.

RULES AND REMINDERS

1. When a singer or musician puts you "on hold" and it's getting dark as the session approaches, have your contractor start bugging the artist's answering service for a decision. You have a right to know and not be stuck trying to find a crucial part of your production at the last minute.

2. When you book musicians and singers, and their answering service asks if the job is a "demo" or a "final," tell them that life is a demo.

3. Always hire the best available talent.

4. When they ask the name of your product, it means that your job may conflict with something better that they might have, and they need to know this in order to make their choice. This is true only in boom times. And for the nonaffiliated singer or musician, things aren't booming too much lately.

5. Try not to use the same singer as a soloist on too many jingles. It makes your work sound similar. A no-no.

6. If you need to take out a short-term loan, contact the Kids-Who-Sing-Jingles Savings and Loan Association (Member FDIC—**F**antastic **D**ividends **I**n **C**ommercials).

7. Always respect the talent of the musicians and singers you hire. Their ability could win you a vacation home.

7
THE PRODUCTION BUDGET

TOGETHER WITH the music producer you have ballparked some production figures and have been given a tentative go-ahead to put a studio and some key musicians and singers on hold, all pending the client signing the budget estimate. (Verbal approval does not apply here—the budget must be signed.)

The client has requested that his music sound big and full, and has agreed to spend the money to make it so. You are instructed to record a :60 for radio and a :30 for television. Your immediate task is to prepare a production budget for approval.

The following budgets are presented in two categories: (1) the cost of a session using an independent recording studio with union musicians and singers, and (2) the budget that would apply if the track was recorded completely or in part in the home/office studio.

BUDGETING THE INDEPENDENT STUDIO SESSION

In calculating costs for an independent studio session, you'll have to figure separate costs for musicians, singers, and the recording studio. (An independent studio is *not* affiliated in any way with a jingle house.)

The Cost of Musicians

You have decided that your rhythm section will include the following instruments:

drums

electric bass

two electric guitars

two keyboards (an acoustic piano
and a synthesizer)

After recording the rhythm you will overdub the following additional instruments:

two French horns

two woodwinds, either flutes, piccolos,
or clarinets or any combination thereof

a fifteen-piece string section

Current Union Wage Scale. The American Federation of Musicians (AF of M) requires a one-hour minimum payment to all musicians. During this hour, up to three commercials may be recorded, totaling not more than three minutes of music.

The orchestra leader receives double scale, and if there are ten or more players, a music contractor, who also receives double scale, is required.

Synthesizer players normally receive double scale, as well as special cartage fees to move their equipment ($125 to $300 per session, depending on the individual player and the equipment he carries).

Unlike phonograph record, motion picture, and television sessions, where the minimum call is three hours before overtime begins, in jingle sessions there is an additional cost, per player, for each twenty-minute segment after the first hour. Currently this rate is one third of the hourly rate. In the jingle business, the meter is always running.

Your musicians estimate will be based on 1989 jingle wage scales. If five musicians or more are used:

$78 per hour per player

$26 per player for each additional
twenty-minute segment

If two to four musicians are used:

$84.30 per player

$28.10 per player for each additional
twenty-minute segment

If a single musician (soloist) is used:

$156 (double scale) for a single player

$52 for each additional twenty-minute segment

Each player, at scale, is considered a "unit." You begin the cost breakdown for your rhythm section by listing out the personnel and the corresponding units of scale.

BASIC RHYTHM SECTION	UNITS
Orchestra leader (double scale)	2
Music contractor (double scale)	2
Drums	1
Bass	1
Two guitars	2
Piano	1
Synthesizer (double scale)	2
Total rhythm section units	**11**

You then guesstimate two hours to complete the rhythm section recording of a :60 for radio and a :30 for television. The scale units are translated into dollar amounts:

First hour minimum	$ 78
Three twenty-minute overtime segments (@ $26)	78
Total amount per unit	156
Total rhythm section session (eleven units @ $156)	**$1,716**

Next, you tabulate the cost of the horns and woodwinds. The leader and contractor are required by the union and considered part of this group, and are paid accordingly (at double scale).

HORNS AND WOODWINDS	UNITS
Two French horns	2
Two woodwinds	2
Leader	2
Contractor	2
Total horn units	**8**

You estimate one hour to overdub the horns and woodwinds.

First hour minimum	$ 78
Total overdub segment (eight units @ $78)	**$624**

Finally, you break down the cost of the string overdubs, including another hour's payment for the leader and contractor.

STRING SECTION OVERDUBS	UNITS
Nine violins	9
Three violas	3
Three cellos	3
Leader	2
Contractor	2
Total string units	**19**

You estimate one hour to overdub the strings.

Total string overdub (nineteen units @ $78)	**$1,482**

The total cost for the orchestra—rhythm section ($1,716), horn overdub ($624), and string overdub ($1,482)—is $3,822.

In addition, for this example, the copyist bill is estimated at $250, and the scale arranging fee on the AF of M contract (required by the union) is estimated at $250. (Scale arranging is officially calculated by the number of bars of music and the number of players in the orchestra. In most cases, however, a token amount of $200 to $400 is put on the contract. The arranger has made his above-scale deal separately, and this amount is really listed to qualify him for residuals.)

Total orchestra cost	$3,822
Copyist	250
Arranger	250
Total musicians cost	**$4,322**

When there is an orchestrator in addition to the arranger, the orchestrator will also appear on the contract, qualifying for double-scale residuals. Clients have come to expect to see two names, the arranger *and* the orchestrator. It's in the codes. But when one person has done both jobs (and in reality almost every jingle arranger is his own orchestrator), his name appears only once. In the big jingle house this leaves open a double-scale place on the contract for someone else. In shops of two or more, often one of the jingle house employees or principals will be listed as the orchestrator.

Pension, Welfare, and Cartage Payments. Pension and welfare payments must be tacked on to the session fee, as must the costs of equipment cartage. Pension for TV is 10 percent; for radio, 9 ½ percent. Health and welfare is calculated at $7 per person plus 1 percent of the session fee. In addition to the cartage fee paid to the synthesist, players of other large instruments are entitled to extra fees for bringing them to the session. Cartages for harp, baritone saxophone, bass saxophone, contrabass clarinet, contrabassoon, cello, percussion instruments (timpani, mallet instruments), guitar, bass, and drums are included on the AF of M Form B contract. Cartage is $6 ($36 for harp).

Total musicians costs	$4,322.00
Pension (TV—10%)	432.20
Health and welfare ($7/player, including leader, contractor, arranger, and copyist) ($7 × 29 = $203 + 1%)	246.22
Cartage ($6/player) (drums, bass, two guitars, three cellos)	42.00
Cartage, synthesizer	150.00
Grand total AF of M for TV	**$5,192.42**

The union requires that each player receive an hour minimum. In the above example, if the spot were only for television (or only for radio), the rhythm players who actually worked for two hours would receive two hours of payment on one contract, and the horns and strings would be paid for the single hour that they actually worked.

But if the same track was used for both radio and television, separate contracts would have to be filed for *each media*. The rhythm players would still receive two hours of payment, but it would be split into two contracts, showing one hour on the radio contract, and one hour on the TV contract. Since the horns and strings actually worked for only one hour, they would now be entitled to an *extra* hour payment because of the second media use, and their names would appear on the second contract.

For our session, we will split the rhythm player costs on to two contracts (TV contract 655038 and radio contract 655039—see pages 140–147), and tabulate the rest of the payments according to the method described above.

Since the contractor and the leader each worked for four hours (two hours rhythm, one hour horn overdub, one hour string overdub), you will split their additional compensation equally between the radio and TV contracts. However, if the hours were different, or uneven, it would not matter which contract they were added to as long as full payment was made.

This "split" also applies to the scale arranging and copying amounts. Cartage applies to one contract only on a "split" radio and TV session.

Instrument Rentals. Most recording studios will include a basic set of instruments in their hourly fee: a piano, a full set of drums (usually housed in a booth enclosure to minimize leakage), several guitar amplifiers, a bass amplifier, and perhaps an electric piano.

Studios do not provide instruments such as timpani, chimes, vibes, marimbas, and other percussion instruments. These can be obtained in several ways: in big metropolitan centers where driving from session to session is impossible, instrument rental companies will provide, deliver, and pick up almost every kind of instrument. (In New York City, Carroll Musical Instrument Rentals, or S.I.R. Rentals will provide anything a composer can possibly need. Plus.)

The rental cost is usually billed directly to the recording studio by the rental company and is included on the final studio bill to the agency. Most studios charge a 50 percent markup for rentals.

If desired, instruments can be rented by the producer and billed directly to the agency, thereby avoiding the studio markup. Some agencies insist on this. But no one is as equipped to deal with rental houses as the recording studios, and the expense of the markup is well-earned when the studio is responsible for the instruments arriving on time. Someone other than yourself should handle the panic when an instrument is not there and the person to play it is—and is being paid to wait.

In California (specifically Los Angeles), where everyone travels by car, percussion players provide their own equipment and move from studio to studio in vans or trucks loaded with vibes, marimbas, timpani, and chimes. Studios in L.A. provide parking, and instead of the cost of rental, the producer is responsible for a hefty cartage fee. In New York, where traffic and parking are awful, that concept is impossible.

One of the modern facts about instrument rentals is that most rental-instrument-type sounds are already duplicated by "samplers," a one-time investment for the synthesist who now often replaces the percussionist in the job market.

The Correct Number of AF of M Spots. As we have seen, the AF of M contract permits three spots to be recorded for a one-hour payment. While you have only actually recorded one :60 radio track (for which you will file a one-hour contract), and one :30 TV spot (for which you will file a one-hour contract), you should take credit on the contracts for the other spots that your payments entitle you to. You might wish to mix an instrumental (with a vocal tag) and a donut version for use with announcers. On the contract, therefore, you should list *three* as the number of commercials recorded, calling them, for example, Generic :60 Full Vocal, Generic :60 Instrumental with Vocal Tag, Generic :60 Donut.

This gives the agency the potential use of three spots during the first thirteen-week cycle because the session fee to musicians includes the first thirteen weeks of on-air use. After the first cycle, however, residuals must be paid for each individual spot that continues to be broadcast, and the three-spots-for-one-hour-payment concept no longer applies.

Television and or Radio Commercial Announcements and
Electrical Transcriptions Contract Blank

AMERICAN FEDERATION OF MUSICIANS
of the United States and Canada

This page to Pension Fund

S 655038

Kind of Payment (Check one)
X Original Session
___ Reuse
___ New Use (different medium)
___ Dubbing (same medium)

Broadcast Medium (Check one)
X TV
___ Radio
___ Foreign Use

Rates (Check one)
___ National
___ Regional
___ Local

Name of Local or Region

ADVERTISER _____
PRODUCT _____
ADVERTISING AGENCY World Wide Adv, Inc.
ADDRESS _____
NO. OF ANNOUNCEMENTS _____

IDENTIFICATION (Use, Titles, Code Nos. or both)
When Identification changes, give prior and new

Original (or Prior)   *New Identification*
Identification
A. GENERIC :30 full vocal
B. GENERIC :30 donut
C. GENERIC :30 instrumental with vocal tag
D.
E.
F.
G.

First Air Date _____
Cycle Dates Being Paid _____
Pension Contribution Rate:
Commercials produced on and after 2/7/79 .... 9%
Commercials produced on and after 2/7/82 .... TV–10%
Commercials produced on and after 2/7/82 .... Radio–9½%

THIS CONTRACT for the personal services of musicians is made this date _____ between the undersigned producer (hereinafter referred to as "the producer"), acting on behalf of the Advertising Agency and its advertiser client specified herein, and 27 musicians (hereinafter called "employees"), all being members of AFM Local _____ unless otherwise noted below.

WITNESSETH: The producer hires the employees as musicians severally on the terms and conditions of this agreement and including the terms and conditions as set forth in Paragraph One on the reverse side hereof. The employees severally agree to tender collectively to the producer services as musicians in the orchestra as follows:

EITHER (if new "live" session, fill in next four lines)

Name and _____
Address of engagement _____
Date(s) and _____
Hours of employment _____

OR (if "ReUse," "Dubbing" or "New Use," fill in next line)
Original Form B Contract No. _____ dated ___/___/___

Wages agreed upon   scale
Producer's Name and   Greatest Jingles Inc. on behalf
Authorized Signature   of World Wide Advertising, Inc.
Street Address _____

City _____ State _____ Zip _____ Phone _____

Leader's Signature _____
Street Address _____

City _____ State _____ Zip _____ Phone _____

EMPLOYEE'S NAME (AS ON SOCIAL SECURITY CARD) LAST FIRST INITIAL	LOCAL UNION NO.	SOCIAL SECURITY NUMBER	H'RS W'KED	NO. OF D'BLE PER SESSION	SPOT IB. BY LETTER ABOVE	IB. OF SPOT PER DOUBLE	SCALE WAGES	PENSION CONTRIBUTION	H & W WHERE APPLICABLE
1 Leader (LEADER)			2		all		312.00	31.20	10.12
2 Contractor			2		"		312.00	31.20	10.12
3 Synthesist(double scale) 150			1		"		156.00	15.60	8.56
4 Drums	6		1		"		78.00	7.80	7.78
5 Bass	6		1		"		78.00	7.80	7.78
6 Guitar #1	6		1		"		78.00	7.80	7.78
7 Guitar #2	6		1		"		78.00	7.80	7.78
8 Piano			1		"		78.00	7.80	7.78
9 French Horn #1			1		"		78.00	7.80	7.78
10 French Horn #2			1		"		78.00	7.80	7.78
11 Woodwind #1			1		"		78.00	7.80	7.78
12 Woodwind #2			1		"		78.00	7.80	7.78
13 Violin #1			1		"		78.00	7.80	7.78
14 Violin #2			1		"		78.00	7.80	7.78
15 Violin #3 COPYIST			1		"		78.00	7.80	7.78
16 Violin #4 ORCHESTRATOR			1		"		78.00	7.80	7.78
17 Violin #5 ARRANGER			1		"		78.00	7.80	7.78

Total Pension Contributions $ _____ Total H & W Contributions $ _____

FOR FUND USE ONLY:

Date pay't rec'd _____ Amt. paid _____ Date posted _____ By _____

*See reverse side for additional terms and conditions of this contract.
*See Health and Welfare on reverse side of this contract.

FORM B-6 REV. 8-81   PRINTED IN U.S.A. 22

CONTINUATION SHEET

EMPLOYEE'S NAME (AS ON SOCIAL SECURITY CARD) LAST FIRST INITIAL	CARTAGE	LOCAL UNION NO.	SOCIAL SECURITY NUMBER	H'RS W'KED	NO. OF D'BLE PER SESSION	SPOT ID. BY LETTER ABOVE	ID. OF SPOT PER DOUBLE	SCALE WAGES	PENSION CONTRIBUTION	H & W WHERE APPLICABLE
18 Violin #6 (LEADER)				1		all		78.00	7.80	7.78
19 Violin #7				1		"		78.00	7.80	7.78
20 Violin #8				1		"		78.00	7.80	7.78
21 Violin #9				1		"		78.00	7.80	7.78
22 Viola #1				1		"		78.00	7.80	7.78
23 Viola #2				1		"		78.00	7.80	7.78
24 Viola #3				1		"		78.00	7.80	7.78
25 Cello #1	6			1		"		78.00	7.80	7.78
26 Cello #2	6			1		"		78.00	7.80	7.78
27 Cello #3	6			1		"		78.00	7.80	7.78
28										
29										
30										
31 (½ of $250) Arranger								125.00	12.50	8.25
32 Orchestrator			NOT USED IN THIS EXAMPLE					-	-	-
33 (½ of $250) Copyist								125.00	12.50	8.25
34										

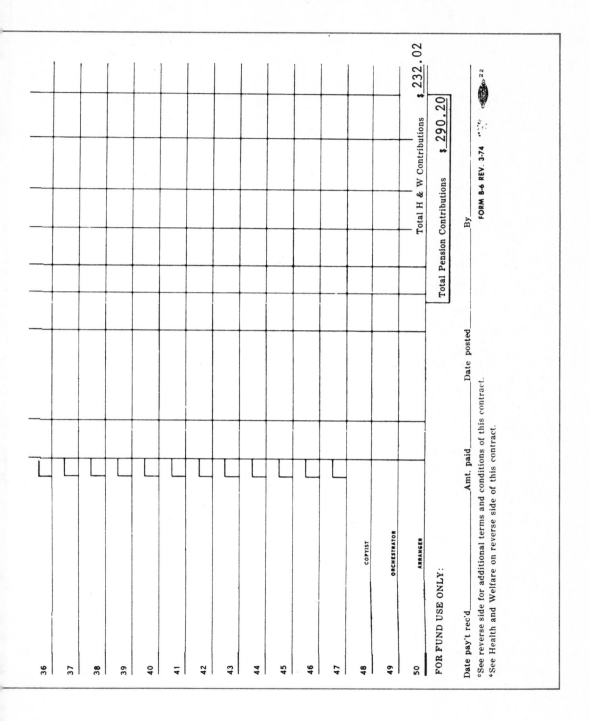

Total H & W Contributions $ 232.02

Total Pension Contributions $ 290.20

By _____

FORM B-6 REV. 3-74

36

37

38

39

40

41

42

43

44

45

46

47

48 COPYIST

49 ORCHESTRATOR

50 ARRANGER

FOR FUND USE ONLY:

Date pay't rec'd _____ Amt. paid _____ Date posted _____

°See reverse side for additional terms and conditions of this contract.
*See Health and Welfare on reverse side of this contract.

Television and or Radio Commercial Announcements and
Electrical Transcriptions Contract Blank

AMERICAN FEDERATION OF MUSICIANS
of the United States and Canada

This page to Pension Fund

S 655039

Broadcast Medium (Check one)
___ TV
_X_ Radio
Foreign Use

Rates (Check one)
___ National
___ Regional
___ Local

Name of Local or Region

Kind of Payment (Check one)
_X_ Original Session
___ Reuse
___ New Use (different medium)
___ Dubbing (same medium)

ADVERTISER _____

PRODUCT _____

ADVERTISING AGENCY World Wide Adv, Inc.

ADDRESS _____

NO. OF ANNOUNCEMENTS 3

IDENTIFICATION (Use Titles, Code Nos. or both)

When identification changes, give prior and new

Original (or Prior) Identification / New Identification

A. GENERIC :60 full vocal
B. GENERIC :60 donut
C. GENERIC :60 instrumental with vocal tag
D. _____
E. _____
F. _____
G. _____

First Air Date _____
Cycle Dates Being Paid _____
Pension Contribution Rate:
Commercials produced on and after 2/7/79 .... 9%
Commercials produced on and after 2/7/82 .... TV–10%
Commercials produced on and after 2/7/82 ...... Radio–9½%

THIS CONTRACT for the personal services of musicians is made this date _____ between the undersigned producer (hereinafter referred to as "the producer"), acting on behalf of the Advertising Agency and its advertiser client specified herein, and 27 musicians (hereinafter called "employees"), all being members of AFM Local _____ unless otherwise noted below.

WITNESSETH: The producer hires the employees as musicians severally on the terms and conditions of this agreement and including the terms and conditions as set forth in Paragraph One on the reverse side hereof. The employees severally agree to tender collectively to the producer services as musicians in the orchestra as follows:

EITHER (If new "live" session, fill in next four lines)

Name and _____

Address of engagement _____

Date(s) and _____

Hours of employment _____

OR (If "ReUse," "Dubbing" or "New Use," fill in next line)

Original Form B Contract No. _____ dated _____

Wages agreed upon scale _____

Producer's Name and Greatest Jingles Inc. on behalf

Authorized Signature of World Wide Advertising, Inc.

Street Address _____

City _____ State _____ Zip _____ Phone _____

Leader's Signature _____

Street Address _____

City _____ State _____ Zip _____ Phone _____

EMPLOYEE'S NAME	LOCAL UNION NO.	SOCIAL SECURITY NUMBER	H'RS W'KED	NO. OF D'BLE PER SESSION	SPOT NO. BY LETTER ABOVE	NO. OF SPOT PER DOUBLE	SCALE WAGES	PENSION CONTRIBUTION	H & W WHERE APPLICABLE
1 Leader (LEADER)			2		all		312.00	29.64	10.12
2 Contractor			2		"		312.00	29.64	10.12
3 Synthesist(double scale)			1		"		156.00	14.82	8.56
4 Drums			1		"		78.00	7.41	7.78
5 Bass			1		"		78.00	7.41	7.78
6 Guitar #1			1		"		78.00	7.41	7.78
7 Guitar #2			1		"		78.00	7.41	7.78
8 Piano			1		"		78.00	7.41	7.78
9 French Horn #1			1		"		78.00	7.41	7.78
10 French Horn #2			1		"		78.00	7.41	7.78
11 Woodwind #1			1		"		78.00	7.41	7.78
12 Woodwind #2			1		"		78.00	7.41	7.78
13 Violin #1			1		"		78.00	7.41	7.78
14 Violin #2			1		"		78.00	7.41	7.78
15 Violin #3 COPYIST			1		"		78.00	7.41	7.78
16 Violin #4 ORCHESTRATOR			1		"		78.00	7.41	7.78
17 Violin #5 ARRANGER			1		"		78.00	7.41	7.78

Total Pension Contributions $ _____   Total H & W Contributions $

FOR FUND USE ONLY:

Date pay't rec'd _____   Amt. paid _____   Date posted _____   By _____

FORM B-6 REV. 8-81

*See reverse side for additional terms and conditions of this contract.
*See Health and Welfare on reverse side of this contract.

CONTINUATION SHEET

EMPLOYEE'S NAME (AS ON SOCIAL SECURITY CARD) LAST FIRST INITIAL	CARTAGE	LOCAL UNION NO.	SOCIAL SECURITY NUMBER	H'RS W'KED	NO. OF D'BLE PER SESSION	SPOT ID. BY LETTER ABOVE	ID. OF SPOT PER DOUBLE	SCALE WAGES	PENSION CONTRIBUTION	H & W WHERE APPLICABLE
18 Violin #6 (LEADER)				1		all		78.00	7.41	7.78
19 Violin #7				1		"		78.00	7.41	7.78
20 Violin #8				1		"		78.00	7.41	7.78
21 Violin #9				1		"		78.00	7.41	7.78
22 Viola #1				1		"		78.00	7.41	7.78
23 Viola #2				1		"		78.00	7.41	7.78
24 Viola #3				1		"		78.00	7.41	7.78
25 Cello #1				1		"		78.00	7.41	7.78
26 Cello #2				1		"		78.00	7.41	7.78
27 Cello #3				1		"		78.00	7.41	7.78
28										
29										
30 (½ of $250)										
31 Arranger								125.00	11.88	8.25
32 Orchestrator		NOT USED IN THIS EXAMPLE						-	-	-
33 (½ of $250) Copyist								125.00	11.88	8.25
34										

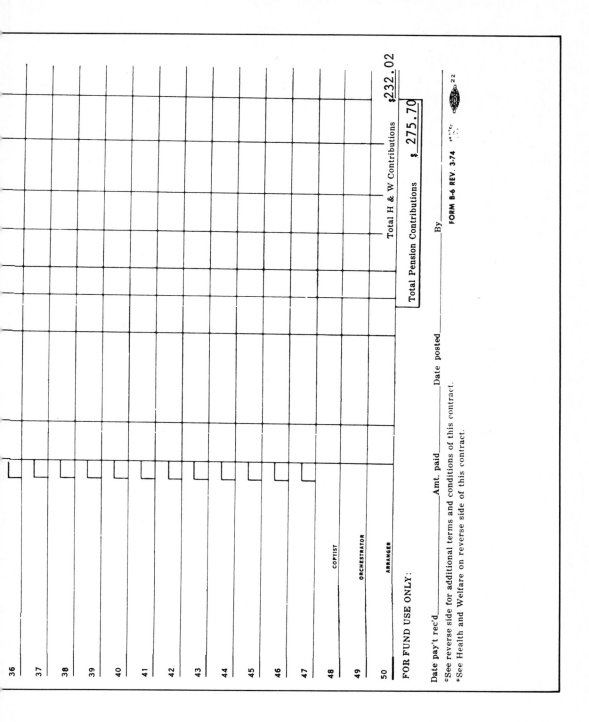

The Cost of Singers

After listening to some vocal tapes, you have agreed with the music director that a girl will sing the solo part, to be backed up by a male vocal group of four.

Unlike payments to musicians, payments to singers are determined first by the number of spots recorded, and then by the number of hours worked.

Current Union Wage Scales. The minimum call for television singers is one spot to be recorded in two hours. Overtime is an additional spot payment for each additional two-hour segment. This means that for a one-spot payment, two hours are available; for a two-spot payment, four hours are available; for a three-spot payment, six hours are available, and so on.

But if one spot takes three hours to complete, the performer would receive payment for the time it would take to do two spots. If one spot takes five hours, the performer gets paid for three spots. (Sometimes I think the code books were written by Abbott and Costello.)

The time minimums for radio are one-and-a-half hours, and two hours for TV.

Your singers estimate will be based on 1989 jingle scales:

FOR TELEVISION (ONE SPOT)	
Soloist session fee (off-camera)	$ 275.65
Group of four ($155.45 plus 50% "doubling" fee per singer = $233.18 × four singers)	932.72
Vocal contractor	58.75
Subtotal	1,267.12
SAG pension (11½%)	145.72
Total singers cost	**$1,412.84**

FOR RADIO (ONE SPOT)	
Soloist session fee	$ 142.00
Group of four ($104.70 plus 50% "doubling" fee per singer = $157.05 × four singers)	628.20
Vocal contractor	48.80
Subtotal	819.00
AFTRA pension (11½%)	94.19
Total singers cost	**$ 913.19**

A sample SAG TV contract and a sample AFTRA radio contract are shown on pages 150 and 151.

Payment for Doubling. To achieve that "fat" vocal sound that became popular in the early '70s, it was the practice to "double" the group (also called "tracking"). Producers found that a different sound was created when four people sang along with themselves, as compared to the sound of eight different voices (which required hiring eight separate singers).

But the singers' unions took the position that if four singers doubled themselves, the producer was denying an employment opportunity to four other singers, and in accordance with the codes, each singer should be paid for each vocal layer they sang. When groups tripled themselves, each layer had to be paid for with an additional full session fee. And all this doubling and tripling and quadrupling (and, believe it or not, even *more*), carried over to residuals as well. With the advent of overdubbing, the cost of singers jumped to one of the highest items on the production budget.

The agencies argued that since there were only four people in the room, only four payments should be made. They protested that they should not be penalized when the modern technology of multitrack recording equipment made it possible for unlimited layers of voices to be created by small numbers of singers. (The same question is raised about the synthesizer when it replaces ten or twenty musicians: should the synthesizer player receive ten or twenty additional scale payments? Or just one? We'll see later.)

TV COMMERCIALS

PENSION AND WELFARE CONTRIBUTION REPORT
SCREEN ACTORS GUILD PRODUCTION AND USE REPORT
ACTORS AND N. Y. EXTRA PLAYERS

IMPORTANT INSTRUCTIONS

1. Use this form for Production, Use and Reuse, or Editing reporting.
2. Mail original of P & W Report with contributions payment check to the SAG-Producers Pension & Welfare Plans, 7755 Sunset Blvd., Hollywood, Calif. 90046.
3. Mail copy of P & W Report to SAG office NEAREST THE CITY IN WHICH THE COMMERCIAL WAS MADE. Addresses of the various SAG offices are listed on the reverse side of the original copy hereof.
4. The filing by Producer of this Report shall be deemed an acceptance by Producer of the Pension & Welfare Fund provisions of the applicable collective bargaining contract of Screen Actors Guild, Inc., and an agreement by Producer to be bound thereby and by the Pension & Welfare Plans established thereunder.

PENSION AND WELFARE

Reporting Company Greatest Jingles, Inc.
on behalf of World Wide Advertising

Address _____

Account No. _____ Date _____

Signature _____

This sheet is page _____ of _____ pages
(a) Total Gross Payment (sum of Col. (1) all pages) . . . $ 1267.12
(b) CONTRIBUTIONS:
Commercials produced after 11/15/74 . . 11½% $ 145.72
Commercials produced prior to 11/16/74 . . 7¾% $ _____

(c) Make checks payable to
SAG-PRODUCERS PENSION & WELFARE PLANS

Product _____
Advertiser _____
Studio _____
Production Company Greatest Jingles, Inc.
Advertising Agency World Wide Advertising, Inc.
Filming/Recording Dates _____
First Air Date(s) _____
Commercial Identification GENERIC :30 FULL VOCAL
_____

Type of Use	Dates of Cycle	Guarantees						CHECK APPLICABLE BOX(ES)*									Fill in Number* No. of Add'l Cities
		Class	8-Use	13-Use	N.Y.	Chi.	L.A.										
Program																	
Wild Spot								Atl.	Balt.	Bost.	Clev.	Dal.- Ft. W.	Det.	Hous.	Ind.	Mpls.- St. P.	
								Phil.	Pitt.	St. L.	S. F.	Sea-Tac	Wash.	Mex. C.	Mont.	Tor.	
Dealer		Type A	Type B														
Holding Fee																	
Foreign																	
Theat.—Indust.																	

Special Comments:
(For Class A program,
Note use numbers)

SYMBOLS FOR COL. C

P - Principal   ST - Stunt Man   G-3 - Group   G-6 - Group   G-9 - Group   NE - N Y Extra
C - Contractor   S - Soloist-Duo   Pup. - Puppeteer   Pil. - Pilot   SA - Specialty Act   HM - N Y Hand Model

(A) Social Security Account Number	(B) PERFORMER'S NAME Last	First	Initial	(C) Category	(D) Cam On Off	(E) No. of Comm'ls	To be filled in when reporting Session Fee (F) Date(s) Worked	(G) Date(s) of Re-Takes	(H) If an Upgrade, insert amt. already paid for cycle	(I) Gross Payment
	Soloist			S	X	1				275.65
	(CONTRACTOR)			C		-				
	Group Singer #1			G4	X	1				291.93
	Group Singer #2			G4	X	1				233.18
	Group Singer #3			G4	X	1				233.18
	Group Singer #4			G4	X	1				233.18

*All boxes which apply in cycle should be checked and total additional cities filled in, even when payment is for an upgraded use.
Form No. SAG—UPW—202. These forms may be obtained from Parker & Son, Inc., Los Angeles, and Dispatch Letter Service, Inc., 25 West 45 St., New York, N. Y. 10036.
1-70

123

THE PRODUCTION BUDGET

RADIO RECORDED COMMERCIALS — AFTRA — P&W REMITTANCE REPORT/PRODUCTION REPORT

IMPORTANT INSTRUCTIONS

1. Use this for for Production, Use and Reuse, or Editing reporting.
2. Make checks payable to AFTRA Pension and Welfare Funds and mail with the white, pink and blue copies of this report to the Fund office nearest the city in which the commercial was recorded.
3. The filing by Producer of this Report shall be deemed an acceptance by Producer of the Pension & Welfare Funds provisions of the applicable collective bargaining contract of AFTRA and an agreement by Producer to be bound thereby and by the Pension & Welfare Funds established thereunder.

1350 AVENUE OF THE AMERICAS, NEW YORK 10019   1717 N. HIGHLAND AVE., HOLLYWOOD 90028   307 N. MICHIGAN AVE., CHICAGO 60601

PENSION AND WELFARE	
Reporting Co. Greatest Jingles, Inc.	
on behalf of World Wide Advertising	
Address	
Account No. _____ Date _____	
This sheet is page ____ of ____ pages.	
a) Total Gross payment (sum of column H all pages) $ 819.00	
b) Contribution: _____ 11½% $ 94.19	
_____ % $ _____	
c) Total Contribution $ _____	
Make checks payable to:	
AFTRA PENSION AND WELFARE FUNDS	

Product _____
Advertiser _____
Recording Studio _____ City _____
Recording Date(s) _____
Advertising Agency World WideAdv. City _____
Producer Greatest Jingles, Inc.
First Air Date(s) _____
Commercial Identification GENERIC :60 FULL VOCAL

	Enter Symbol in Col. (C) — Category		
A	Actor, Actress	S6	Singer Gp. 6-8
ANN	Announcer	S9	Singer Gp. 9 or more
S	Singer Solo or Duo	C	Contractor
S3	Singer Gp., 3-5	SE	Sound Effects Perf.

TYPE OF USE	DATES OF CYCLE	CYCLE WEEKS				NY	CHI	LA	# Units Weighted Cities	# Units Non weighted Cities	NO. OF USES	
		1	4	8	13						26	39
Wild Spot												
Net Prog.												
Reg. Net. Prog.												
Dealer (26 wks.)												
Foreign (18 mon.)												

Special Comments:

(A) Social Security Account Number	(B) PERFORMER'S NAME			(C) Category	(D) # Comm'ls	(E) Dates(s) Worked	(F) Hours From	To	(G) If an Upgrade, insert amount already paid for cycle	(H) Gross Payment
	Last	First	Initial							
	Soloist			S	1					142.00
	Group Singer #1 (CONTRACTOR)		C	S4	1					205.85
	Group Singer #2			S4	1					157.05
	Group Singer #3			S4	1					157.05
	Group Singer #4			S4	1					157.05

Finally, a compromise created a 50 percent overdub wage scale, which permitted unlimited tracking for the single additional 50 percent fee. Residuals were also calculated to include an additional 50 percent.

The net result is that today hardly anyone ever records without doubling the vocal group. The 50 percent overdubbing fee has become a standard, accepted as part of the singer's payment. "Scale" for group jingle singers has, in reality, become scale-and-a-half.

Jingle companies, whose only avenue for continuing income is to sing on their tracks, justify the overdub as a necessary part of the sound (that coincidentally happens to pay a 50 percent higher premium). Overdubbing has an enormous impact on the creative process; you'd be amazed at how often clients have been told that their product name will sound better when reinforced by multi-layering a vocal group. The more layers the better, right? Well, at least one more, to qualify for the extra payment.

The person who said "group is where it's at" certainly knew where it was at.

Recording-Studio Costs

You have estimated four hours of instrument recording, (two hours for the rhythm section, one each for horns and strings), two hours for the vocals, and three hours for all the mixing. In addition you have estimated one hour for dubbing time to make tape and mag copies.

The rate card for a top-quality recording studio will list all the costs that you'll be concerned with. (See page 154.)

Based upon the rate card you calculate the following figures, which include a house engineer:

STUDIO ESTIMATE	
Recording time (six hours Studio B @ $300/hr.)	$1,800
Mixing time (three hours @ $300/hr.)	900
Dubbing time (one hour @ $100/hr.)	100
32-track digital recorder (nine hours @ $50/hr.)	450
Necam automated mix (nine hours @ $40/hr.)	360
One-inch digital tape ($300/reel)	300
Half-inch tape (@ $60/reel)	60

Quarter-inch tape (two reels @ $50/reel)	100
Cassettes (six @ $10 each)	60
Instrument rentals (approx.)	100
Delivery charges (approx.)	100
Miscellaneous costs (your contingency)	1,000
Total studio estimate	**$5,330**

(A good rule of thumb for quickie estimating is $500 to $550 per hour, which includes everything.)

Allowing for Set-up Time. In planning your session schedule (and budget), it is important to allow for set-up time. After the rhythm recording, for example, it may take a few minutes to clear the room and set up the microphones for the horn/woodwind overdub. And simply moving your fifteen-person string section in and out of a relatively small area will take several minutes. (But you'd be amazed at how quickly the old string players move when they are called—it's all that symphony training.) Schedule musicians to allow for breathing room. If you are starting at 10:00 A.M. you might book the horns at 12:15 to begin their hour, and the strings at 1:30 for their hour, leaving enough time in between sections so that you can set up without having the musician meter running simultaneously.

The day before the session, you (or your music contractor) should advise the studio manager about the number of instruments you will be using, and the order in which you will be recording them.

Recording to Film. If you are going to record the music with playback in sync with the picture, the cost of the studio will increase accordingly. You should inform the studio manager prior to the session if you intend to work "to film," and they will provide and prepare any necessary video-tape equipment.

Total Production Estimate

You are now ready to calculate the entire cost of recording a radio :60 and a TV :30 using an independent recording studio with union musicians and singers.

RECORDING STUDIO
RATE SCHEDULE

STUDIO TIME	with house engineer	without engineer
Studio A (music record/mix)	$300 per hour	$260 per hour
Studio B (music record/mix)	$300 per hour	$260 per hour
Studio C (overdub/mix)	$240 per hour	$200 per hour
Production (tape copy room)	$100 per hour	
Film Room (mag transfers)	$100 per hour	

DIGITAL RECORDING*		
32 Track (Mitsubishi X-850)	$50 per hour	
2 Track (Mitsubishi X-80 or Sony 701ES)	$25 per hour	

OTHER SERVICES*		
NECAM automated mix	$40 per hour	
Lockup (BTX Softtouch)	$25 per hour for two machines	
Video Playback	$20 per hour	

DUBS		
¼ inch tape, under 600 ft	$15 each plus production time	
¼ inch tape, under 1200 ft	$25 each plus production time	

TAPE		
2″ Ampex 456	$200 per reel	
½″ Ampex 456	$60 per reel	
¼″ Ampex 456	$50 per reel	
1″ Ampex 467 (Digital)	$300 per reel	
¼″ Ampex 467 (Digital)	$125 per reel	
Cassettes (TDK-SAX C-60)	$10 ea.	
Fullcoat Stock (3M 351)	10¢ per foot	
Stripe Stock (3M 338)	9¢ per foot	

*In addition to studio time

RADIO	
AF of M (contract 655039)	$ 3,409.72
Vocal	913.19
Studio (half of total)	2,665.00
TELEVISION	
AF of M (contract 655038)	3,616.22
Vocal	1,412.84
Studio (half of total)	2,665.00
Grand total production estimate **(excluding creative and arranging fees)**	**$14,681.97**

Polishing the Budget

In our budget example, the costs of musicians, singers, and studio time are figured pretty close to the minimum. The optimist always thinks he will finish in less time, and this is wonderful when it happens.

But what if you run into trouble? If something is not working right? If your client wants to hear it a little faster, or slower, or even differently? It might take more time than expected to get the rhythm to sound right, or to perfect the overdubs, or the vocals. The copywriter might be cranky. While each delay is part of the normal production experience, it can be expensive when the minutes—and fees—keep marching on.

Recording a jingle is a game of catch-up and wait. Nothing happens the way you plan it. When the rhythm section goes like a piece of cake and you finish early, the horns will take longer. When the overdubs take too long, the strings are sitting in the hallway waiting, and being paid while they wait. Then the singers are late (never early). And all the while, the studio time clock keeps ticking.

To be safe, it pays to build a cushion into each portion of your estimate. For musicians, you might budget the rhythm section at two hours and twenty minutes, or 2:40. And figure the horns and strings for 1:20 or 1:40, giving yourself the extra padding "just in case." Adding an extra hour or two into the studio estimate is also quite realistic. Time flies when your engineer begins to use his toys to get that great drum sound you want.

As the composer/arranger of your track, you should also allow your-self the financial latitude to add a few extra musician-units in case you think of something special while you are doing the arrangement. You might even put down an extra 10 or 15 percent of the total budget as a contingency for the unforeseen.

It is better to estimate larger amounts than to have to tell the pro-ducer, after the fact, that you went over budget, which unfortunately happens from time to time no matter how you plan. A fat budget is workable and acceptable if you advise your client that you have pur-posely made it so.

If you are working cost-plus and the extra padding isn't used, it will not be billed to the client. If you are on a package deal, the overage is in your pocket—but so is the financial loss if a problem takes you into your padding. These days, however, most agencies handle all the pro-duction cost payments, and will only pay the actual costs that occur.

Here's one way you can attempt to save money: if you anticipate needing musicians for two hours, book them for only 1:20 plus :40. This way, if you luck out and only use them for 1:20 or 1:40, that is all you will pay for.

A budget should be as flexibly realistic as possible to allow the best possible production of the music track.

BUDGETING THE HOME/OFFICE STUDIO SESSION

We have already seen how the home/office studio is the wave of the present, with jingle companies setting up in-house recording facilities as good or better than the independent studios. Depending on the sophistication of equipment, 30 to 50 percent of the music produced in home/office studios become the "final" on-air-quality track. In some cases, where the equipment is top quality, or the jingle house spe-cializes in electronic sounds, *all* of the tracks go on the air.

The home/office studio offers an alternative route for your produc-tion of the jingle, and also opens up some questions about budgeting.

For our example, we will assume the same type of orchestra sound as we did in the independent studio session. (Of course, instruments produced by a synthesizer will never sound exactly like a live band. No one expects the two to be identical. But what the electronics expert can do is play the parts written by the arranger and create a convincing recording completely out of electronic components. I do not wish to imply that synthesizers are only used in place of musicians. In fact, the opposite is true. Electronic music is a sound and source all its own: inventive, imaginative, and often creating musical expressions that no live orchestra could possibly produce. But for a budgeting comparison, it simply takes fewer bodies to achieve the final product.)

The Cost of Musicians (You, the Synthesist)

For this estimate, we will assume that you were the only musician needed to program the drum machine and play the synthesizers, and therefore only your name will appear on the AF of M contract. How many times depends on your own sense of business and your clout with the agency.

Let's look at an example.

It took four hours to produce all the parts for the jingle—the drum machine and all the layers necessary to create the rest of the orchestra. Because you were working alone in your own studio (in the agency's viewpoint an essentially timeless atmosphere, with your own hours and the depreciation of equipment as your only expense), you played the equivalent of eight parts: drums, bass, two keyboards, percussion, French horns, woodwinds, and strings. In this case you might put yourself down as the leader (double scale), and then eight more times at scale for the amount of hours it took to complete the recording (four), plus once more as arranger (double scale), and once as copyist (scale—obligating you to provide a lead sheet).

In theory, if one synthesist replaced twenty-seven people, his name could be listed twenty-seven times on the contract. Synthesist/composers support this position by pointing out that the advertiser would otherwise have had to pay session fees and residuals to two horn players, two woodwinds, fifteen strings, and a rhythm section.

But the agencies have countered that they should only have to pay you as leader and arranger (double scale), copyist (scale), and then only once more as synthesist (double scale) for however long you worked, no matter how many layers you performed. Why should they be prevented from enjoying the savings offered by the new technology (the same argument raised against paying singers full wages each time they overdub a layer)? An added justification for their position is that if you had hired an independent synthesist, he would only have received double scale for the time he worked.

Other agencies claim that even this is an exorbitant production cost because they are paying a creative and arranging fee on top of everything else. They would prefer that you, the synthesist, appear on the contract only as leader (double scale) and as synthesist (double scale) for only one hour, the minimum time period (and as arranger and copyist—if you can get away with it).

How the situation is handled depends on the agency.

No one ever lists his name twenty-seven times unless he is gouging a client who doesn't know any better. But if a synthesist actually worked for four hours and played eight sections, some agencies will allow a contract that reflects this creative input.

Others are quite rigid about their payment policy—one man, one fee, comrade.

All these factors have an impact on residuals. The leader receives residuals (double scale); the synthesist receives residuals (double scale—and an additional single scale residual for every time he is able to list his name on the contract); the arranger receives residuals (double scale); the orchestrator receives residuals (double scale); and the copyist receives residuals (single scale).

Compare the AF of M contracts showing different payment approaches for the composer/synthesist/arranger. AF of M contracts 655026 and 655027 (pages 160–163) have one name listed eleven times, split into two hours for TV and two hours for radio. AF of M contracts 655028 and 655029 (pages 164–167) have one name listed four times for a one-hour session. Contracts 655023 and 655024 (pages 168–171) show one name listed twice. It is obvious which method provides the most income for the synthesist.

Adding Other Musicians. When additional musicians are needed to sweeten a machine-made track, or to record a "live" track in the home/office studio, they are budgeted at union scale and paid along with the synthesist on the AF of M contract. (The form of payment is discussed in Chapter Eight.)

Home/Office Studio Costs and Billing

The studio budget line item for a session should never be deleted because the work was done in-house. Agencies may suggest that since you are receiving other fees (creative, arranging), and that since you are also the studio, you should charge less for its use. But the investment in equipment necessary for one person (or a few—a staff engineer, maintenance person, or programmer) to do the job must always be considered when making a production budget.

Once you have created the music track, you might bring the tape to an independent studio, perhaps to overdub the vocals and do the final mix with their more sophisticated outboard equipment. Or perhaps your equipment is of high enough quality to complete the entire session in your own studio.

Regardless of where the music is ultimately recorded, there should always be a studio bill.

When a session is produced as a final at a home/office studio, the jingle house charges the agency for studio time the same way it would if an outside studio had to be rented, but at a sometimes lower rate (but not much lower). Where the independent recording studio might charge $300 per hour, a home/office studio might bill $225 to $250. Some with state-of-the-art equipment might charge more.

Assuming the same number of hours as the independent studio, the costs might be as follows:

HOME/OFFICE STUDIO ESTIMATE	
Recording time (four hours @ $225/hr.)	$ 900
Mixing time (three hours @ $225/hr.)	675
Dubbing time (one hour @ $100/hr.)	100
Two-inch tape (@ $175/reel)	175
Half-inch tape (@ $50/reel)	50
Quarter-inch tape @ $40/reel)	80
Delivery charges	100
Cassettes (six @ $10 each)	60
Miscellaneous costs	500
Total studio estimate	**$2,640**

Television and or Radio Commercial Announcements and
Electrical Transcriptions Contract Blank

AMERICAN FEDERATION OF MUSICIANS
of the United States and Canada

This page to Pension Fund

S 655026

THIS CONTRACT for the personal services of musicians is made this
date _____ between the undersigned
producer (hereinafter referred to as "the producer"), acting on behalf of
the Advertising Agency and its advertiser client specified herein, and
9 musicians (hereinafter called "employees"), all being
members of AFM Local _____ unless otherwise noted below.

WITNESSETH: The producer hires the employees as musicians
severally on the terms and conditions of this agreement and including
the terms and conditions as set forth in Paragraph One on the reverse
side hereof. The employees severally agree to tender collectively to the
producer services as musicians in the orchestra as follows:

EITHER (if new "live" session, fill in next four lines)

Name and _____

Address of engagement _____

Date(s) and _____

Hours of employment _____

OR (if "ReUse," "Dubbing" or "New Use," fill in next line)

Original Form B Contract No. _____ dated ___/___/___

Wages agreed upon scale

Producer's Name and Greatest Jingles Inc. on behalf

Authorized Signature of World Wide Advertising, Inc.

Street Address _____

City _____ State _____ Zip _____ Phone _____

Leader's Signature _____

Street Address _____

City _____ State _____ Zip _____ Phone _____

Kind of Payment
(Check one)
X Original Session
__ Reuse
__ New Use
   (different medium)
__ Dubbing (same medium)

Broadcast Medium
(Check one)
X TV
__ Radio
__ Foreign Use

Rates
(Check one)
__ National
__ Regional
__ Local

Name of Local or Region

ADVERTISER _____

PRODUCT _____

ADVERTISING AGENCY World Wide Adv. Inc.

ADDRESS _____

NO. OF ANNOUNCEMENTS 3

IDENTIFICATION (Use Titles, Code Nos. or both)

When Identification changes, give prior and new

Original (or Prior)   New Identification
Identification

A. GENERIC :30 full vocal

B. GENERIC :30 donut

C. GENERIC :30 instrumental with
                        vocal tag

D. _____

E. _____

F. _____

G. _____

First Air Date _____
Cycle Dates Being Paid _____
Pension Contribution Rate:
Commercials produced on and after 2/7/79 . . . . 9%
Commercials produced on and after 2/7/82 . . . . TV–10%
Commercials produced on and after 2/7/82 . . . . Radio–9½%

EMPLOYEE'S NAME (LAST, FIRST, INITIAL)	LOCAL UNION NO.	SOCIAL SECURITY NUMBER	H'RS W'KED	NO. OF D'BLE PER SESSION	SPOT ID. BY LETTER ABOVE	IB. OF SPOT PER DOUBLE	SCALE WAGES	PENSION CONTRIBUTION	H & W WHERE APPLICABLE
1 (double scale) (your name) Leader (LEADER)			2		all		312.00	31.20	10.12
2 Synth Layer #1 (your name) (scale)			2		"		156.00	15.60	8.56
3 Synth Layer #2 (your name) (scale)			2		"		156.00	15.60	8.56
4 Synth Layer #3 (your name) (scale)			2		"		156.00	15.60	8.56
5 Synth Layer #4 (your name) (scale)			2		"		156.00	15.60	8.56
6 Synth Layer #5 (your name) (scale)			2		"		156.00	15.60	8.56
7 Synth Layer #6 (your name) (scale)			2		"		156.00	15.60	8.56
8 Synth Layer #7 (your name) (scale)			2		"		156.00	15.60	8.56
9 Synth Layer #8 (your name) (scale)			2		"		156.00	15.60	8.56
10									
11		NOT USED IN THIS EXAMPLE							
12 (½ of $250) Arranger (your name)							125.00	12.50	8.25
13 Orchestrator (½ of $250)							–	–	–
14 Copyist (your name)							125.00	12.50	8.25
15 COPYIST									
16 ORCHESTRATOR									
17 ARRANGER									

Total Pension Contributions $ 181.00 Total H & W Contributions $ 95.10

FOR FUND USE ONLY:

Date pay't rec'd _____ Amt. paid _____ Date posted _____

By _____

*See reverse side for additional terms and conditions of this contract.

*See Health and Welfare on reverse side of this contract.

FORM B-6 REV. 8-81 PRINTED IN U.S.A. 22

Television and or Radio Commercial Announcements and
Electrical Transcriptions Contract Blank

AMERICAN FEDERATION OF MUSICIANS
of the United States and Canada

This page to Pension Fund

S 655027

Kind of Payment (Check one)
X Original Session
___ Reuse
___ New Use (different medium)
___ Dubbing (same medium)

Broadcast Medium (Check one)
___ TV
X Radio
___ Foreign Use

Rates (Check one)
___ National
___ Regional
___ Local
_____ Name of Local or Region

THIS CONTRACT for the personal services of musicians is made this _____ date _____ between the undersigned producer (hereinafter referred to as "the producer"), acting on behalf of the Advertising Agency and its advertiser client specified herein, and 9 musicians (hereinafter called "employees"), all being members of AFM Local _____ unless otherwise noted below.

WITNESSETH: The producer hires the employees as musicians severally on the terms and conditions of this agreement and including the terms and conditions as set forth in Paragraph One on the reverse side hereof. The employees severally agree to tender collectively to the producer services as musicians in the orchestra as follows:

EITHER (If new "live" session, fill in next four lines)

Name and _____

Address of engagement _____

Date(s) and _____

Hours of employment _____

OR (If "ReUse," "Dubbing" or "New Use," fill in next line)

Original Form B Contract No. _____ dated ___/___/___

Wages agreed upon scale

Producer's Name and Greatest Jingles, Inc. on behalf

Authorized Signature of World Wide Advertising, Inc.

Street Address _____

City _____ State _____ Zip _____ Phone _____

Leader's Signature _____

Street Address _____

City _____ State _____ Zip _____ Phone _____

ADVERTISER _____

PRODUCT _____

ADVERTISING AGENCY World Wide Adv. Inc.

ADDRESS _____

NO. OF ANNOUNCEMENTS 3

IDENTIFICATION (Use Titles, Code Nos. or both)

When Identification changes, give prior and new

Original (or Prior)
Identification   *New Identification*

A. GENERIC :60 full vocal

B. GENERIC :60 donut

C. GENERIC :60 instrumental with vocal tag

D. _____

E. _____

F. _____

G. _____

First Air Date _____

Cycle Dates Being Paid _____

Pension Contribution Rate:
Commercials produced on and after 2/7/79 .... 9%
Commercials produced on and after 2/7/82 .... TV-10%
Commercials produced on and after 2/7/82 .... Radio-9½%

EMPLOYEES (AS ON SOCIAL SECURITY CARD) LAST FIRST INITIAL	T A G E	LOCAL UNION NO.	SOCIAL SECURITY NUMBER	W'KS W'KED	NO. OF D'BLS PER SESSION	SPOT ID. BY LETTER ABOVE	NO. OF SPOT ID. DOUBLE	SCALE WAGES	PENSION CONTRIBUTION	H & W WHERE APPLICABLE
1 Leader (double scale)(your name) (LEADER)				2		all		312.00	29.64	10.12
2 Synth Layer #1(your name) (scale)				2		"		156.00	14.82	8.56
3 Synth Layer #2(your name) (scale)				2		"		156.00	14.82	8.56
4 Synth Layer #3(your name) (scale)				2		"		156.00	14.82	8.56
5 Synth Layer #4(your name) (scale)				2		"		156.00	14.82	8.56
6 Synth Layer #5(your name) (scale)				2		"		156.00	14.82	8.56
7 Synth Layer #6(your name) (scale)				2		"		156.00	14.82	8.56
8 Synth Layer #7(your name) (scale)				2		"		156.00	14.82	8.56
9 Synth Layer #8(your name)				2		"		156.00	14.82	8.56
10										
11										
12 Arranger (your name) (½ of $250)								125.00	11.88	8.25
13 Orchestrator			NOT USED IN THIS EXAMPLE					=	-	-
14 Copyist (your name) (½ of $250)								125.00	11.88	8.25
15 COPYIST										
16 ORCHESTRATOR										
17 ARRANGER										

Total Pension Contributions $171.96   Total H & W Contributions $95.10

FOR FUND USE ONLY:

Date pay't rec'd _____ Amt. paid _____ Date posted _____   By _____

•See reverse side for additional terms and conditions of this contract.
•See Health and Welfare on reverse side of this contract.

FORM B-6 REV. 8-81   PRINTED U.S.A. 22

Television and or Radio Commercial Announcements and
Electrical Transcriptions Contract Blank

AMERICAN FEDERATION OF MUSICIANS
of the United States and Canada

This page to Pension Fund

S 655028

THIS CONTRACT for the personal services of musicians is made this
date _____ between the undersigned
producer (hereinafter referred to as "the producer"), acting on behalf of
the Advertising Agency and its advertiser client specified herein, and
2 musicians (hereinafter called "employees"), all being
_____ unless otherwise noted below.

members of AFM Local _____

WITNESSETH: The producer hires the employees as musicians
severally on the terms and conditions of this agreement and including
the terms and conditions as set forth in Paragraph One on the reverse
side hereof. The employees severally agree to tender collectively to the
producer services as musicians in the orchestra as follows:

EITHER (if new "live" session, fill in next four lines)

Name and _____

Address of engagement _____

Date(s) and _____

Hours of employment _____

OR (if "ReUse," "Dubbing" or "New Use," fill in next line)
Original Form B Contract No. _____ dated ___/___/___

Wages agreed upon   scale

Producer's Name and Greatest Jingles Inc. on behalf

Authorised Signature of World Wide Advertising, Inc.

Street Address _____

_____
City   State   Zip   Phone

Leader's Signature _____

Street Address _____

_____
City   State   Zip   Phone

Kind of Payment
(Check one)
X Original Session
__ Reuse
__ New Use
   (different medium)
__ Dubbing (same medium)

Broadcast Medium
(Check one)
X TV
__ Radio
__ Foreign Use

Rates
(Check one)
__ National
__ Regional
__ Local

Name of Local or Region

ADVERTISER _____

PRODUCT _____

ADVERTISING AGENCY World Wide Adv. Inc.

ADDRESS _____

NO. OF ANNOUNCEMENTS 3

IDENTIFICATION (Use Titles, Code Nos. or both)
When Identification changes, give prior and new

Original (or Prior)   *New Identification*
Identification
A. GENERIC :30 full vocal
B. GENERIC :30 donut
C. GENERIC :30 instrumental with
                          vocal tag
D. _____
E. _____
F. _____
G. _____

First Air Date _____
Cycle Dates Being Paid _____
Pension Contribution Rate:
Commercials produced on and after 2/7/79 ....9%
Commercials produced on and after 2/7/82 ....TV-10%
Commercials produced on and after 2/7/82 ....Radio-9½%

EMPLOYEE'S NAME (AS ON SOCIAL SECURITY CARD) LAST FIRST INITIAL	A B O V E	LOCAL UNION NO.	SOCIAL SECURITY NUMBER	NO'S W'KED	NO. OF D'BLE PER SESSION	SPOT ID. BY LETTER ABOVE	ID. OF SPOT PER DOUBLE	SCALE WAGES	PENSION CONTRIBUTION	H & W WHERE APPLICABLE
(double scale)(your name) 1 Leader (LEADER)				2		all		337.20	33.72	10.37
2 Synthesist (your name)				2		"		337.20	33.72	10.37
3										
4			NOT USED IN THIS EXAMPLE							
5										
(½ of $250) 6 Arranger (your name)								125.00	12.50	8.25
7 Orchestrator								-	-	-
(½ of $250) 8 Copyist (your name)								125.00	12.50	8.25
9										
10										
11										
12										
13										
14										
15 COPYIST										
16 ORCHESTRATOR										
17 ARRANGER										

Total Pension Contributions $92.44   Total H & W Contributions $37.24

By

FORM B-6 REV. 8-81   22

FOR FUND USE ONLY:

Date pay't rec'd _____ Amt. paid _____ Date posted _____

*See reverse side for additional terms and conditions of this contract.

*See Health and Welfare on reverse side of this contract.

Television and or Radio Commercial Announcements and
Electrical Transcriptions Contract Blank

AMERICAN FEDERATION OF MUSICIANS
of the United States and Canada

This page to
Pension Fund

S 655029

THIS CONTRACT for the personal services of musicians is made this
date _____ between the undersigned
producer (hereinafter referred to as "the producer"), acting on behalf of
the Advertising Agency and its advertiser client specified herein, and
_2_ musicians (hereinafter called "employees"), all being
unless otherwise noted below.

WITNESSETH: The producer hires the employees as musicians
severally on the terms and conditions of this agreement and including
the terms and conditions as set forth in Paragraph One on the reverse
side hereof. The employees severally agree to tender collectively to the
producer services as musicians in the orchestra as follows:

members of AFM Local _____

EITHER (if new "live" session, fill in next four lines)

Name and _____

Address of engagement _____

Date(s) and _____

Hours of employment _____

OR (If "ReUse," "Dubbing" or "New Use," fill in next line)

Original Form B Contract No. _____ dated ___/___/___

Wages agreed upon _scale_

Producer's Name and _Greatest Jingles Inc. on behalf_
Authorized Signature _of World Wide Advertising,Inc._

Street Address _____

City _____ State _____ Zip _____ Phone _____

Leader's Signature _____

Street Address _____

City _____ State _____ Zip _____ Phone _____

Kind of Payment
(Check one)
X Original Session
___ Reuse
___ New Use
    (different medium)
___ Dubbing (same medium)

Broadcast Medium
(Check one)
___ TV
X Radio
___ Foreign Use

Rates
(Check one)
___ National
___ Regional
___ Local

Name of Local or Region

ADVERTISER _____

PRODUCT _____

ADVERTISING AGENCY _World Wide Adv,Inc._

ADDRESS _____

NO. OF ANNOUNCEMENTS _3_

IDENTIFICATION (Use Titles, Code Nos. or both)

When Identification changes, give prior and new

Original (or Prior)   New Identification
Identification
A. GENERIC :60 full vocal
B. GENERIC :60 donut
C. GENERIC :60 instrumental with
                            vocal tag
D. _____
E. _____
F. _____
G. _____

First Air Date _____
Cycle Dates Being Paid _____
Pension Contribution Rate:
Commercials produced on and after 2/7/79 . . . . 9%
Commercials produced on and after 2/7/82 . . . . TV-10%
Commercials produced on and after 2/7/82 . . . . Radio-9½%

EMPLOYEE'S NAME (AS ON SOCIAL SECURITY CARD) LAST FIRST INITIAL	RATE	LOCAL UNION NO.	SOCIAL SECURITY NUMBER	H'RS WK'ED	NO. OF D'BLE PER SESSION	SPOT ID. BY LETTER ABOVE	ID. OF SPOT PER DOUBLE	SCALE WAGES	PENSION CONTRIBUTION	H & W WHERE APPLICABLE
1 (double scale)(ycur name) Leader (LEADER)				2		all		337.20	32.03	10.37
2 (double scale) Synthesist (your name)				2		"		337.20	32.03	10.37
3										
4										
5			NOT USED IN THIS EXAMPLE							
6 (½ of $250) Arranger (your name)								125.00	11.88	8.25
7 Orchestrator								–	–	–
8 (½ of $250) Copyist (your name)								125.00	11.88	8.25
9										
10										
11										
12										
13										
14										
15 COPYIST										
16 ORCHESTRATOR										
17 ARRANGER										

Total H & W Contributions $ 87.82

Total Pension Contributions $ 87.82   Total H & W Contributions $ 37.24

FOR FUND USE ONLY:

Date pay't rec'd _____ Amt. paid _____ Date posted _____ By _____

See reverse side for additional terms and conditions of this contract.

See Health and Welfare on reverse side of this contract.

FORM B-6 REV. 8-81   PRINTED IN U.S.A.   22

Television and or Radio Commercial Announcements and
Electrical Transcriptions Contract Blank

AMERICAN FEDERATION OF MUSICIANS
of the United States and Canada

This page to Pension Fund

S 655023

Kind of Payment (Check one)

X Original Session

___ Reuse

___ New Use (different medium)

___ Dubbing (same medium)

Broadcast Medium (Check one)

X TV

___ Radio

___ Foreign Use

Rates (Check one)

___ National

___ Regional

___ Local

___ Name of Local or Region

ADVERTISER _____

PRODUCT _____

ADVERTISING AGENCY _World Wide Adv. Inc._

ADDRESS _____

NO. OF ANNOUNCEMENTS _3_

IDENTIFICATION (Use Titles, Code Nos. or both)

When identification changes, give prior and new

Original (or Prior) Identification / *New Identification*

A. GENERIC :30 full vocal

B. GENERIC :30 donut

C. GENERIC :30 instrumental with vocal tag

D. _____

E. _____

F. _____

G. _____

First Air Date _____
Cycle Dates Being Paid _____
Pension Contribution Rate:
Commercials produced on and after 2/7/79 .... 9%
Commercials produced on and after 2/7/82 ....TV-10%
Commercials produced on and after 2/7/82 ......Radio-9½%

THIS CONTRACT for the personal services of musicians is made this date _____ between the undersigned producer (hereinafter referred to as "the producer"), acting on behalf of the Advertising Agency and its advertiser client specified herein, and _2_ musicians (hereinafter called "employees"), all being members of AFM Local _____ unless otherwise noted below.

WITNESSETH: The producer hires the employees as musicians severally on the terms and conditions of this agreement and including the terms and conditions as set forth in Paragraph One on the reverse side hereof. The employees severally agree to tender collectively to the producer services as musicians in the orchestra as follows:

EITHER (if new "live" session, fill in next four lines)

Name and _____

Address of engagement _____

Date(s) and _____

Hours of employment _____

OR (If "ReUse," "Dubbing" or "New Use," fill in next line)

Original Form B Contract No. _____ dated ___/___/___

Wages agreed upon _scale_

Producer's Name and _Greatest Jingles Inc. on behalf_

Authorized Signature _of World Wide Advertising, Inc._

Street Address _____

City _____ State _____ Zip _____ Phone _____

Leader's Signature _____

Street Address _____

City _____ State _____ Zip _____ Phone _____

168

EMPLOYEE'S NAME (AS ON SOCIAL SECURITY CARD) LAST FIRST INITIAL	LOCAL UNION NO.	SOCIAL SECURITY NUMBER	H'RS W'KED	NO. OF D'BLE PER SESSION	SPOT ID. BY LETTER ABOVE	IN. OF SPOT PER DOUBLE	SCALE WAGES *	PENSION CONTRIBUTION	H & W WHERE APPLICABLE *
1 Leader (your name) (LEADER)			1		all		168.60	16.86	8.69
2 Synthesist (your name) (double scale)			1		"		168.60	16.86	8.69
3									
4									
5									
6									
7									
8									
9									
10									
11									
12									
13									
14									
15 COPYIST									
16 ORCHESTRATOR									
17 ARRANGER									

Total Pension Contributions $33.72

Total H & W Contributions $17.38

FOR FUND USE ONLY:

Date pay't rec'd _____ Amt. paid _____ Date posted _____ By _____

*See reverse side for additional terms and conditions of this contract.

*See Health and Welfare on reverse side of this contract.

FORM B-6 REV. 8-81

Television and or Radio Commercial Announcements and
Electrical Transcriptions Contract Blank

AMERICAN FEDERATION OF MUSICIANS
of the United States and Canada

THIS CONTRACT for the personal services of musicians is made this
date _____ between the undersigned
producer (hereinafter referred to as "the producer"), acting on behalf of
the Advertising Agency and its advertiser client specified herein, and
2 _____ musicians (hereinafter called "employees"), all being
members of AFM Local _____ unless otherwise noted below.

WITNESSETH: The producer hires the employees as musicians
severally on the terms and conditions of this agreement and including
the terms and conditions as set forth in Paragraph One on the reverse
side hereof. The employees severally agree to tender collectively to the
producer services as musicians in the orchestra as follows:

EITHER (If new "live" session, fill in next four lines)

Name and _____

Address of engagement _____

Date(s) and _____

Hours of employment _____

OR (If "ReUse," "Dubbing" or "New Use," fill in next line)
Original Form B Contract No. _____ dated ___/___/___

Wages agreed upon scale

Producer's Name and Greatest Jingles Inc. on behalf
Authorized Signature of World Wide Advertising, Inc.

Street Address _____

_____
City   State   Zip   Phone

Leader's Signature _____

Street Address _____

_____
City   State   Zip   Phone

Kind of Payment
(Check one)
X Original Session
___ Reuse
___ New Use
   (different medium)
___ Dubbing (same medium)

Broadcast Medium   *Rates*
(Check one)   (Check one)
___ TV   ___ National
X Radio   ___ Regional
___ Foreign Use   ___ Local

_____
Name of Local or Region

**This page to
Pension Fund**

S 655024

ADVERTISER _____

PRODUCT _____

ADVERTISING AGENCY World Wide Adv, Inc.

ADDRESS _____

NO. OF ANNOUNCEMENTS 3

IDENTIFICATION (Use Titles, Code Nos. or both)
When identification changes, give prior and new

Original (or Prior)   *New Identification*
Identification

A. GENERIC :60 full vocal

B. GENERIC :60 donut

C. GENERIC :60 instrumental with
                            vocal tag

D. _____

E. _____

F. _____

G. _____

First Air Date _____
Cycle Dates Being Paid _____
Pension Contribution Rate: _____
Commercials produced on and after 2/7/79 ....9%
Commercials produced on and after 2/7/82 ....TV–10%
Commercials produced on and after 2/7/82 ....Radio–9½%

EMPLOYEE'S NAME (AS ON SOCIAL SECURITY CARD) LAST FIRST INITIAL	C B T A C E	LOCAL UNION NO.	SOCIAL SECURITY NUMBER	HRS W'KED	NO. OF D'BLE PER SES-SION	SPOT ID. BY LETTER ABOVE	ID. OF SPOT PER DOUBLE	SCALE WAGES •	PENSION CONTRI-BUTION	H & W WHERE APPLI-CABLE •
1 Leader (your name) (LEADER)				1		all		168.60	16.02	8.69
2 Synthesist (your name) (double scale)				1		"		168.60	16.02	8.69
3										
4										
5										
6										
7										
8										
9										
10										
11										
12										
13										
14										
15 COPYIST										
16 ORCHESTRATOR										
17 ARRANGER										

Total Pension Contributions $ 32.04   Total H & W Contributions $ 17.38

FOR FUND USE ONLY:

Date pay't rec'd _____ Amt. paid _____ Date posted _____

By _____

*See reverse side for additional terms and conditions of this contract.

*See Health and Welfare on reverse side of this contract.

FORM B-6 REV. 8-81   PRINTED U.S.A. 22

Total Home/Office Studio Production Estimate

At this point you can calculate the entire cost of recording a radio :60 and a TV :30 using the home/office studio. There are three possibilities, depending on how you charged for your synthesizer tracks. Using one named listed eleven times:

RADIO	
AF of M (contract 655027)	$2,077.06
Vocal	913.19
Studio (half of total)	1,320.00
Subtotal	4,310.25
TELEVISION	
AF of M (contract 655026)	2,086.10
Vocal	1,412.84
Studio (half of total)	1,320.00
Subtotal	4,818.94
Grand total	**$9,129.19**

Using one name listed four times:

RADIO	
AF of M (contract 655029)	$1,049.46
Vocal	913.19
Studio (half of total)	1,320.00
Subtotal	3,282.65
TELEVISION	
AF of M (contract 655028)	1,054.08
Vocal	1,412.84
Studio (half of total)	1,320.00
Subtotal	3,786.92
Grand total	**$7,069.57**

Using one name listed twice:

RADIO	
AF of M (contract 655024)	$ 386.62
Vocal	913.19
Studio (half of total)	1,320.00
Subtotal	2,619.81
TELEVISION	
AF of M (contract 655023)	388.30
Vocal	1,412.84
Studio (half of total)	1,320.00
Subtotal	3,121.14
Grand total	**$5,740.95**

Recall that the total production estimate for the independent recording studio was $14,681.97, and compare it with the home/office studio estimate.

These are only examples, but they clearly illustrate the variance in cost between using real people and machines (where a string section is just a button away). These significant dollar differences have changed the way business is done. It is obvious which way saves more money.

Musician's Yearly Income. Table 4 (page 174) shows the amount of income a musician can earn from a single commercial that runs for a year. (The session fee is one hour for this example; the payment to arranger and orchestrator is computed at double scale; and the copyist payment is computed at scale. Even if the session fee were higher it would have no effect on the residuals—residuals are paid by the spot. Each payment provides the advertiser with unlimited use of one commercial on one media during each thirteen week cycle, whether local, regional, national, network, or all four).

TABLE 4. MUSICIAN ONE-YEAR INCOME FOR ONE COMMERCIAL

	Session Fee	2nd Cycle Residual	3rd Cycle Residual	4th Cycle Residual	Year Total
Leader (double scale)	$156.00	$117.00	$117.00	$117.00	$507.00
Contractor (double scale)	156.00	117.00	117.00	117.00	507.00
Synthesist (double scale)	156.00	117.00	117.00	117.00	507.00
Sideman (scale)	78.00	58.50	58.50	58.50	253.50
Arranger (double scale)	156.00	117.00	117.00	117.00	507.00
Orchestrator (double scale)	156.00	117.00	117.00	117.00	507.00
Copyist (scale)	78.00	58.50	58.50	58.50	253.50

THEY WANT THE DEMO

With technology traveling at light speed, it is entirely possible that the agency might decide to put your demo on the air. When determining what to charge, the same rules should apply: there should be a creative fee, an arranging fee, a studio bill, and union contracts filed.

RULES AND REMINDERS

1. Don't cramp your creativity because of an underestimated budget. It's better to figure a higher budget (assuming you can get it approved) than to try to scrape by and then have to rush. Effective and competitive advertising is a battle of production value. Your client wants originality and should be prepared to spend the money to achieve it. If it costs an extra fifty dollars an hour to record with a certain type of new equipment, and it makes the track sound better, the cost is minor compared to the overall budget. The difference between good and great could be as simple as that extra "one more time." You should seek the creative dollar freedom to "go for it."

2. Sometimes ballpark figures aren't in the ballpark.

8
TALENT
PAYMENT

ALTHOUGH THE SESSION
has not yet taken place, you have made a commitment to the studio,
the musicians, and the singers. On everyone's calendar, the date is
"firm." You have obligated the agency to the minimum time/cost of
the call. Before the session, it is important to understand the subject of
talent payment. Afterward will come the mad scramble to complete
the paperwork and get everything processed in time to meet union
deadlines and avoid late penalties. (The studio bill should be paid
within thirty days. Musicians and singers must be paid within twelve
to fifteen working days of the date of the session. The AF of M permits
fifteen days, while AFTRA and SAG allow twelve. Singers and announcers obviously have to pay their rent sooner than trumpet players
do.)

WHO WRITES THE CHECK?

In the vast majority of cases, the jingle house serves only as a mid-
dleman, passing along talent paperwork to the agency. Studio bills are
sent directly to the agency producer. When agencies allowed their
creative suppliers to actually write the talent checks, the jingle house
would then bill them for all the production costs, plus a markup fee,
saving the agency the paperwork and hassle.

But today, in order to save money (where have we heard *that* one before?), it's practically an industry standard for agencies to pay all talent through independent payroll service companies such as Talent Partners (formerly Talent and Residuals and Donovan Data Services) or Broadcast Traffic and Residuals, Inc. Where a jingle house might charge 12 to 15 percent of gross as a handling fee (in addition to the mandatory costs), a big payroll company will charge only 3 to 4 percent and make a profit due to the greater volume they process. For the jingle house, the loss of payroll handling has cut back a former source of operating income.

But as an independent contractor, if you stay in business long enough there will be instances when you will be requested to advance monies for production costs. What can you do? Can you afford to be on the hook for large amounts while you await payment of your invoice? The fact of life is that unless special arrangements have been made beforehand, your company will not be paid by the agency for thirty to sixty days or *more* (would you believe ninety to one hundred twenty days?), far beyond the limit allowed by the unions. This is one of the risks of doing business for yourself, and the main reason that, early in your dealings with an agency, you should inform them that you would appreciate prompt payment of your invoice. Delays are usually explained when the agency says they are waiting to be paid by their client. This is "check-is-in-the-mail" excuse number seventeen. Most of the time you will accept this, even though it won't satisfy the people *you* hired. If you're late in paying them, try explaining to the union that you are waiting for *your* payment from the agency, and see what happens. You'll learn a lot about the business world, and why it's sometimes easier to be the payee than the payer.

YOUR MARKUP

The total amount you charge for the service of handling payrolls and other production costs is called your markup. Again, it should come to 25 to 30 percent of gross, with a portion covering employer mandatory costs and the remainder covering handling.

Employer Mandatory Costs

These include (a) the employer social security payment, currently 7.51 percent of gross salary up to $45,000 per year; (b) the cost of carrying a workmen's compensation insurance policy and liability insurance; (c) the cost of a disability insurance policy; (d) the cost of state and federal unemployment insurance policies. The above costs must be paid by an employer according to state and federal law and by union agreement. In addition, the employer (you) must withhold taxes from the employee and pay the money over to the state and federal governments. (Your accountant can help you set up procedures for withholding taxes and advise you on how to get the appropriate insurance policies.) The unions will not accept talent payment of a gross amount without the appropriate deductions, except if the talent is independent (i.e., incorporated or an individual proprietorship doing business with a trade name). Most singers and some musicians have their own corporations, and deductions are not required. If you have achieved your full markup, your savings on not paying mandatory costs for incorporated talent becomes profit. These mandatory costs average at about 12 to 15 percent of gross wages.

Employer Handling Costs

These include (a) the salary of the person who writes the checks; (b) the cost of printing the checks; (c) the expense of appropriate book-keeping, accounting, processing bank requisitions, filing quarterly tax returns, and at year end providing each employee with a withholding statement. (If, for example, you handled payrolls for three sessions, each with a thirty-piece orchestra and a five-singer group, your office will have to write one hundred and five checks and process all the paperwork for one hundred and five people, a service that costs work hours and money). Typical handling fees are figured at 10 to 15 percent of gross.

Therefore, small suppliers who handle payrolls charge 25 to 30 percent of gross wages as a markup (not including any P&W—union pension and welfare). Running an office with modest volume makes the 12 to 15 percent handling fee just about a breakeven situation.

But for the most part, the effort to keep production costs down (even to the point of spawning agency in-house production companies) has made jingle house payroll handling a service of the past.

TAXES

But if you are indeed handling the payroll for a jingle session, the following nuts-and-bolts guidelines apply. According to current law, if at the end of any month your total undeposited social security and withholding deductions are $500 or more, but less than $3,000, you must deposit the taxes within fifteen days after the end of the month. If amounts withheld exceed $3,000 at any time during the month, then federal deposits must be made within three business days after the date of the deduction (the date of the check).

Woe shall befall the company that doesn't pay its withholding or social security deductions on time! While *you* may have to accept that "the check is in the mail," Uncle Sam is not interested, and will charge penalties and interest for every day that payments are received after the legal deadline!

In the event that you are working nonunion, be sure to obtain a written confirmation of the disbursements your company makes, either by paying everything by check, made out to the name of each talent, or by insisting on a receipt if you're doling out the green stuff in the studio. Talent may grumble that since they are working for cash, or underscale, they are doing it as a favor, and that there should be no records. (As President Nixon said, "Cash is cash.")

While talent may not want their off-the-books income declared, the agency will definitely deduct as a business expense on their tax returns any amounts they have paid *your* company as a fee; at the end of the year you will receive a 1099 form from the agency. So it is your responsibility to verify your write-offs, including payments to talent and studio. Obtaining written evidence—paid bills, cancelled checks, or signed cash receipts—is the only acceptable practice.

ESTABLISHING A RELATIONSHIP WITH A BANK

Unless you are well-heeled enough to advance money without borrowing any, it is advisable to establish a working relationship with a bank. Being in debt is the American way.

Early in my career, I composed a background track for a Score Haircream television commercial and was asked to handle the payroll. It was strictly a union spot using a large orchestra, and the payments were more than my fledgling company had on hand. Knowing that my obligation was secured by the confirming purchase order and rights contract given to me by Score's agency, Grey Advertising, I debated whether to borrow the money from family or friends or go to a stranger, a bank. I recognized that if I ever hoped to have my company taken seriously in the business world, borrowing operating capital from friends would never do. So, right off the street, with no appointment, wearing my best suit and tie, I marched into my local bank, and up to a loan officer, produced my purchase order and contract, and requested to borrow $1,500 for thirty days to pay my band and studio (a twenty-piece orchestra was cheap in 1968). It took an hour of describing every facet I knew about the advertising music industry to convince him to make the loan, and to cross another hurdle: he wanted to make it a personal loan, and I wanted it lent to my company, as a proof of its viability. Today, whenever I see a commercial for a bank that indicates a banker "who understands," I am warmly reminded of the kindness of the man who made my first loan and officially put my company in business.

SIGNING THE PAPERWORK

All paperwork, regardless of who writes the check, should indicate your services on behalf of your client: "Greatest Jingles, Inc., on behalf of Worldwide Advertising, Inc." This clearly states that you are producing "on behalf of . . . ," and though it will not legally release you from any employer obligations (you are a signatory company, remember?), it provides someone to share the load if problems arise.

UNION BOND

If the unions don't know you, they may insist that you put up a bond that will guarantee any payment. If they do know you, or if they know the agency for which you are handling the payment, they won't require a bond. But in any case, timely payment will be expected.

CHECK-WRITING SYSTEMS

There are many check-writing forms available that permit payment, bookkeeping, and posting in one operation. If you can work with a home computer, there are also simple accounting programs that will do it all for you. Well, almost all—everything except provide the person to type in the information.

PAYING MUSICIANS AND SINGERS

The AF of M requires that payment for jingle dates be sent directly to the union. A musician goes to his local to receive his checks, and he is charged an amount equal to 3 percent of gross wages as work dues.

AFTRA also requires that singers' checks be sent directly to the union for distribution, but does not deduct a work tax. AFTRA mails the checks to the performers.

The Screen Actors Guild, unlike AFTRA, requires that the employer mail checks directly to the performers, and at the same time supply the union with the appropriate pension fund payment and correct backup paperwork.

For years there have been ongoing discussions about a merger of AFTRA and SAG. If and when this happens, it will probably resolve the differences in payment procedures.

YOUR OBLIGATIONS

Your word is your bond, and if you have hired talent and booked a studio, you have made a personal commitment to them, and you should be certain that everyone gets paid promptly, regardless of who is making the payment. *You* hired everyone, and if there are any questions, they will come to you first. If the agency has made timely payments, you will know it by the receipt of your union checks (as leader/arranger or singer). If you don't receive them, call the agency producer.

RESIDUALS

Union residuals (always processed by the agency) are the most sought-after form of talent payment, representing continuing income for the continuing uses of a performer's work.

For singers, actors, and announcers, the concept of repayment began in the early days of radio, when commercials were all done live. When a radio network broadcast a program like Jack Benny or Fred Allen, it was actually performed twice, in front of two different studio audiences: first for Eastern and Central time-zone listeners, then again three hours later for Mountain and Pacific. Everything was reperformed, including the commercials.

Then came the recording machine, providing the ability to save that first performance and use it again later by simply pressing a button and playing the recording. (Doesn't pushing a button sound familiar?)

Management loved it: they didn't have to pay the actors or the studio a second time. Labor hated it: performers who formerly were paid for *two* shows were only doing *one*, and potentially suffering a 50 percent loss of income.

The unions, due in large part to the support of many big stars, fought for and achieved residual payments for the reuses of performers' work, and a system has since evolved in which every two years both sides negotiate contracts covering wage scales, residuals, and working conditions.

Residuals for Composers

While the sponsor pays continuing financial homage to singers, announcers, and actors—all union talent who perform words written by others—there are no residuals of any kind for composers of advertising music. The music that represents the biggest corporations in America, with very rare exceptions, is sold to the advertiser for a one-time fee, and the composer earns nothing more for the life of the work.

Through the years, advertising composers have tried to achieve residual status or continuance fees for the uses of their music. Some composers seek a renewable creative fee payment every thirteen weeks, or yearly for as long as their work is broadcast. Some try to negotiate payments equivalent to what actors, announcers, or singers earn. But the overwhelming majority of jingle composers sign away their rights without a whimper, allowing the vocal residual to provide the ongoing payment they seek.

If you intend to be a serious composer of advertising music, you will have to decide whether to fight for a fair residual for the uses of your music, or give in to the current industry practice, which provides no ongoing income.

Residuals for Others

The argument brought up when jingle writers seek residuals is: "If we give it to composers, then we'll have to give it to film directors, cameramen, and the agency employees who thought up the work. They'll want residuals, too." So far it hasn't helped to point out that other creators in the process *do* earn continuing income from their creative efforts; agencies pay salaries to successful creative people, with all the benefits. These are residuals—ongoing payment for ongoing uses of their ideas. And film directors and cameramen, unlike composers, have the opportunity to earn continuing money by filming new spots for the product (using the old song—*your* song). It is only the person who has provided the instantly recognizable audio platform for the sponsor's message who is shut out—even if his song runs for twenty years. (I hear someone saying that when an agency copywriter changes agencies—or gets fired—he no longer receives his "salary residual" for the work he created at his former agency. This sad fact is true of the corporate system, and is one of the strongest arguments for self-employment, where you can attempt to achieve your own terms and run your own show.)

The following chart shows the variation in payments allotted to different participants in the jingle-making process.

THE MAGICAL MADISON AVENUE RESIDUAL CHART			
Title	*First Spot*	*Other Spots First Year*	*Other Spots Later Years*
Composer	full fee	nothing	nothing
Arranger	full fee	arranging fees plus residuals (if hired)	arranging fees plus residuals (if hired)
Jingle House	full fee	arranging fees (if hired)	arranging fees (if hired)
Agency Employee	salary	salary	salary
Film House	full fee	full fee	full fee
Singer/Actor/ Announcer	full fee plus residuals	full fee plus residuals	full fee plus residuals

Someday things may be different.

RULES AND REMINDERS

1. Always ask for a purchase order, or even a contract, from the agency producer. You should have something in hand or at least in the mail before production begins. Having a purchase order provides you with the security that if anything goes wrong during the process, such as a last minute client cancellation of talent and studio, that the agency has given its word to pay the costs of your commitments.

2. Seek a relationship at the bank where you do your checking. You'll know right away if they can help you. If they cannot, try another bank; someone will listen if you have the proper paperwork. A bank will need to see the evidence that you have really been hired (the P.O. and contract), and will want assurance that you won't use the money to buy medical books.

3. If the money is lent in your company name, the bank may expect you to personally guarantee the loan. While they might take a chance on your honest face and lend money to your company, they probably will never have heard of the agency that hired you. And they need their security, too.

4. Be frugal. Don't borrow much more than you need for your payroll. Avoid borrowing amounts that include your creative and arranging fees (unless you're starving), or there will be nothing left when your invoice is finally paid.

5. If you are requested to handle the payroll and you are unable to do so, for any reason, it is your duty to advise the agency before you begin. *No surprises* is a good rule for any business.

6. Make sure to get each performer's social security number for correct reporting. Don't hire anyone who won't give it to you. You may feel magnanimous at the time of the session, and say "to-hell-with-it," but three years later when your corporate tax return is being audited by the IRS, you'll have to scramble to prove that you actually paid out the money.

7. Always get a receipt. The man with a receipt rules the world (almost).

9
MAKING
THE DEAL

UP UNTIL NOW, everything has been a piece of cake. They love your work at the agency; they've approved an unlimited production budget (something they've never given to anyone else before and which you have promised not to exceed); and they are whispering about your potential in all the bar cars to Greenwich, predicting that your breathtaking talent will win recognition in Harry Wayne McMahon's Top 100.

"Oh, just a moment, there. That's right—*you*. The fair-haired composer with songs in your heart. It's time to take care of business."

"Business? What's that? Go away. Don't bother me. I just want to write songs about fried chicken."

" 'Business,' my friend, means signing the agency contract."

Stop.

Before you, the innocent composer, put pen to paper, you'll have to travel through the darkest part of the jingle jungle and arm yourself with knowledge about the forces that will determine the future of your participation in the successes of your artistry.

Eat lightly before we leave. It's not good to travel down these roads on a full stomach.

People become composers so they can work with their brains—there's no heavy lifting. And there is the real potential to earn substantial amounts of money. It is in part this financial potential that keeps a creator's juices flowing and his imagination sharp. Inspired by dreams, spurred on by the successes of others, he lays out his notes like a mariner's chart and sails through the stormy waters of the music industry in search of recognition for his talent and lasting income from his songs.

Marvin Hamlisch is a part of the dream. *A Chorus Line* has been on Broadway for years, and sets new records daily. With touring companies performing it throughout the world, Marvin's musical score has become a theatrical standard. Every day, Marvin earns income from the ongoing uses of his work. Bravo, Marvin.

Paul Simon is a part of the dream. His songs and unique poetic commentary—the work of a serious genius—have touched generations. Every day Paul earns income from the ongoing uses of his songs. Not money for *yesterday's* work (like writing the song) or *yesterday's* uses (like on the radio last night), but money for the uses of his songs that are going on *right now*, as you read this. Bravo, Paul, *bravo*!

Everyone marvels at Michael Jackson's purchase of the Northern Songs music catalog, which contains most of the Beatles' songs, for almost $50 million. Can you imagine owning the Beatles' song library? The income it provides for ongoing uses will probably continue forever. The next sale price will certainly be higher. Mr. Jackson outbid Paul McCartney, another businessman who recognizes that the ongoing uses of music—in this case his own—should, and *do* provide continuing income for their composers and publishers.

The list goes on and on: Broadway composers, popular songwriters, composers of songs and scores for movies and television, all earn continuing income from the continuing uses of their music.

The single exception is the composer of advertising music. The jingle writer is hired by the agent of a sponsor who wants to own, unconditionally, everything that has been created for his advertising and who, when dealing with the custom-made-jingle community, always gets it. Unfortunately, the jingle writer has not been affected by the traditions and values that have been established for other composers. In the advertising world it is the tradition for the jingle writer to continue to dream. And also to agree to any conditions that are put before him, without question or reservation, regardless of how one-sided or disadvantageous they might be.

The terms under which the jingle writer creates, delivers, and earns money from his jingle are embodied in the "work-for-hire" contract, which provides only for the payment of a one-time fee.

Of course, other composers, especially those who work in television, sign work-for-hire contracts for a one-time fee, and someone else also ends up owning "everything." But these composers are able to retain their all-important performance rights because it is the tradition in their musical world to do so.

Performance income provides the greatest portion of the economic pie for composers of TV music, and when forces appear, ready to threaten the well-being of the system, these TV composers and their publishers rally together to fight for their performing rights.

In jingles, the only rally is around the vocal residual.

The Hollywood image of a songwriter is of a dedicated artist who locks himself away in some dark corner to create beautiful melodies, but who rarely gets involved in the business aspect of selling his work. He writes the hit, the world applauds, he wins the girl, reaps the golden rewards, and lives happily ever after. In jingles, something goes wrong after the "winning the girl" part.

Tin Pan Alley lore tells the story of John (Joe) Black, a destitute composer who sold all the rights to his most popular song for $50. "I Want to Buy a Paper Doll That I Can Call My Own," went on to become a standard, but the composer received nothing after that first and only $50. Today, it's hard to believe that any composer in his right mind would do something like that. Yet, in advertising, it happens all the time.

The rules of the business part of the jingle business are so one-sided as to make impossible an impartial account of what goes on when a composer sells his music for use in commercials. In the following description, however, every attempt has been made to present both sides in as unbiased a way as possible, leaving any judgments to the discretion of the individual participant, based on the demands of his specific work situation.

WHAT THE ADVERTISER WANTS

What an advertiser wants, and pays for, is the secure right to use a composer's music in his commercials. Whether he licenses a popular song from an independent music publisher or commissions a custom-made jingle from a composer-for-hire, he strives to achieve one main objective: unrestricted and unlimited determination of the uses that are made of his music.

The simplest way this happens is for an agency to buy a custom-made jingle under a work-for-hire contract. They then submit the jingle for copyright protection as an unpublished work in the name of the client, and forget about it. This is currently the policy at many agencies. There is no music publisher, no registration with ASCAP or BMI for performing rights, no nothing. The music remains safe and sound, forever protected, drifting in limbo. On the occasions when someone requests a nonadvertising use of the jingle, such as sheet music to be played by a high-school band at halftime, the client has it printed up, supplies it free, and writes off any costs to promotion. It's the ultimate control. There is no ongoing expense since the composer is owed nothing beyond the original fee.

However, agencies with a broader outlook toward creative people know that a composer can supplement his small one-time creative fee with performance income from jingles, without any cost to their clients. (Performance money is paid to composers by ASCAP and BMI, which are in turn paid by broadcasting stations, not by advertisers.) Sometimes they will grant to the composer the right to *attempt* to register his jingle with ASCAP or BMI (this will be explained later), and even permit him to own the copyright in the name of his own publishing company. They know that their contract gives them complete control over their music, and that whichever entity acts as publisher or is called publisher is relatively unimportant, as long as it doesn't cost the client anything.

The Agency Music Publishing Company

As the world of musical uses gets more complex and more lucrative, advertising agencies are recognizing that income can be generated from non-advertising uses of their jingles. And from broadcast performance fees for commercials. Some agencies have formed their own music publishing companies, or have assigned their publishing rights to companies that represent their interests. They know that shows like ''Saturday Night Live'' and ''Greatest TV Commercials and Bloopers'' require licenses to rerun their commercial parodies in syndication. This means income for the agency music publisher and for the client, who traditionally shares in the publisher's income from the jingle. Suddenly, there are $1,000 syndication license fees for jingle parodies. And $2,500 fees for motion picture synchronization rights for a jingle use. And income from the sale of sheet music and band arrangements, as well as big bucks from the occasional jingle hit record. Some agency publishers, especially those who provide schedules to ASCAP/BMI confirming broadcast performances (schedules usually not available to composers), are beginning to see six-figure incomes.

For jingle composers, the advent of the agency music publisher was a good sign. It meant that income from jingles could be more than just a one-shot deal. When a publisher earns money, he traditionally shares it equally with the composer.

And best of all, agency publishers could register their jingles with ASCAP and BMI, who otherwise would not pay the composer his share.

For the jingle writer there is now the possibility, for the very first time, of earning ongoing income from the continuing uses of his work without him having to qualify as a singer.

Sounds wonderful doesn't it?

Wait.

To better understand the current situation, let's take a look at the way music is licensed for broadcasting.

═══ PERFORMING RIGHTS—HOW BROADCASTING WORKS ═══

Years ago, long before there was advertising music, or even broadcasting, composers and publishers of popular music wanted to be paid when their songs were used in public places, bars, nightclubs, theaters, and concert halls. They claimed that these establishments benefited from the public demand to hear their music, and as writers and publishers they were entitled to remuneration for providing this benefit. They formed an organization called ASCAP (The American Society of Composers, Authors, and Publishers), the purpose of which was to act as a central licensing organization for the uses of their songs, so that individual establishments wouldn't have to go directly to an individual music publisher each time they wanted to use a specific song.

The concept was that ASCAP would issue a single license, called a "blanket license," which, in return for a percentage of the establishment's income, allowed the unlimited use of any song in the ASCAP catalog. The theater or nightclub made a payment, agreed to report the music that was used (or ASCAP would do its own survey), and then ASCAP would distribute the income among the composers and publishers whose songs were performed.

Later, when that new infant, radio, was born, and still later, when television came into our lives, ASCAP was successful in applying the same blanket license concept to the broadcasting stations: they could pick and choose from any song in the ASCAP catalog, pay a percentage of their income, and the money would be distributed among those whose music was broadcast.

If there were instances when a station wanted to bypass ASCAP and deal directly with a certain music publisher, the publishers were free to do so in accordance with their ASCAP agreements, and they could then issue what is called a "direct" or "source" license.

For many years the blanket license system worked, even spawning another performance rights society called BMI (Broadcast Music Inc.). It was convenient: a songwriter and his publisher registered their works with ASCAP or BMI, who took care of all the paperwork, and when the songs were broadcast, they earned income.

The Impact of Syndicated Television

But then the rules changed. As broadcasting technology became more sophisticated, with videotape as one of its by-products, the stations began to question the practicality of the blanket music license concept. A major catalyst in this unrest was the advent of "syndicated television."

The real profits for a TV producer, after the high production costs of the initial taping of his shows like "Dallas," "All in the Family," and "M*A*S*H," come from his ability to license reruns to local TV stations. This process, which takes place after the original network broadcast, is called "syndication," and it provides the producer with ongoing income from continuing uses of his programs. (See? *Everyone* wants to profit from the future uses of their work!)

An example of the power of syndication is "I Love Lucy." When Desi

Arnaz negotiated the deal to produce the show for CBS television, he held out for the right to own the films of the programs, which he later sold over and over, continuing to earn ongoing income from the ongoing uses of his work.

Before syndication, local TV stations broadcast local programming, local sporting events, local news, and then mainly old movies. From the stations' point of view syndication was wonderful. Not only could they now broadcast top programs in place of the limited supply of old movies, but the fees they paid to the shows' producers included everything connected with the program: residual payments to creators, actors, writers, singers, musicians, all of which were handled by the producer—with one glaring exception. This was the money that still had to be paid by the stations to ASCAP and BMI under the blanket license for the music in these programs.

"Unfair!" cried the stations. "We paid a fee to the producers to include *everything*. Why should we pay for the music separately? We don't need the blanket license. We don't choose the music from the ASCAP/BMI repertoires. Why shouldn't the producers of the shows also provide us with a music license—a direct license—included in the overall fee? The music in the show is *their* choice, not ours."

Recognizing that this would cause a tremendous loss of income to ASCAP/BMI writers and publishers, the two performing rights societies resisted. And finally, the local television stations, through their representatives, the All-Industry Committee, sued ASCAP and BMI in what has come to be known as the Buffalo Broadcasting Case, arguing that they should not have to pay separately for what they believed should be included in the one-time payment.

And they won, in the lower court, only to have the decision reversed on appeal. The reversal was based partly on an earlier court decision in another case called the CBS Case, in which the CBS Television Network tried to do essentially the same thing: eliminate the blanket license and pay only for music that it actually used. ASCAP/BMI won the CBS Case partly because they were able to convince the courts that the blanket system was necessary: it would be impossible for the stations to contact each individual publisher every time they wanted to use a song.

Imagine a station that wanted to broadcast an old movie like *Casa-*

blanca: it would have to contact the music publisher and secure a license that covered each airing. And movies most often contain music from several publishers. Without the blanket license each station would have to negotiate a fee with each publisher. And considering the number of movies that a station broadcasts, the amount of time and paperwork spent securing licenses would be overwhelming.

But the local stations are persisting, and have taken their case to Congress, asking for a law that would free them from having to pay separately for the music in local and syndicated TV shows when their deals with producers include everything else.

Unfortunately, they have lumped advertising music into the same category with basically the same argument: the sponsors pay residuals for everyone else, the actors, the singers, the announcers, the musicians; why should they, the stations, have to pay separate performance fees under the blanket license for the uses of music in commercials? And now, legislation has been proposed that would place the responsibility for obtaining source music licenses directly in the laps of the Hollywood producers for TV shows and the sponsors for the music in commercials.

The legislation is on hold at some stage in the Congressional process, but it is obvious that the stations intend to pursue this issue because they believe it is a fair position and in their best financial interests.

The Cost of Source Licenses

Nonjingle composers, especially those who provide music for TV shows, make the bulk of their income from performances. If Hollywood producers were required to provide a source music license with each syndicated sale, the expense of compensating the composer for what he would have earned under the blanket license would be prohibitive. So in order to make supplying a source license to the station feasible, the producers would have to insist on including the purchase of the composer's performance rights in the initial one-time fee.

Music publishers and film and TV composers, of course, are resistive of this, recognizing that if it happens they would probably lose most of their income. (Contractual negotiations would certainly be ruled by the person who signs the check—the producer. Remember the dock boss? "You give up your performance rights, you work. You don't give up your rights . . . " You know the rest.)

The Advertiser Responds

When the possibility of having to provide a source music license for commercials arose, the advertisers were among the loudest to complain, arguing that the added cost would increase their production budgets dramatically. Of course they were talking about the instances when they licensed popular songs, whose publishers would not give up their performance rights for use of their music in the commercials without a substantial additional fee.

But they did cover themselves with regard to the custom-made portion of their music. In order to insure that it would not cost them anything more if they ever had to issue a source license for a custom-made jingle, the agencies updated the language in their contracts. Now when they pay a creative fee, the composer's performing rights are included in that fee, exactly what the Hollywood TV producers would have to accomplish to satisfy the broadcaster's demand for a source license. At agencies that are currently permitting composers to attempt to collect from ASCAP/BMI, these rights can be withdrawn at any time, meaning if advertisers ever had to provide a direct or source music license, at their own option they could do so at no cost.

The Effect on the Jingle Writer

What all this means to the jingle composer is that if the stations succeed and eliminate the blanket license in local and syndicated television (with network television stations certain to follow close behind), it will effectively deny the advertising composer his only chance for continuing income from the ongoing uses of his work. (The dock boss who works on Hollywood and Vine has a franchise on Madison Avenue.)

ASCAP/BMI PAYMENTS FOR JINGLES

Through the years I have been a participant in the industry struggle to achieve fair performance income. Twice in the earlier text I used the word *attempt* when referring to the jingle composer's quest to collect income from the performance licensing societies. While performance royalties seem the perfect way for a jingle composer to earn ongoing fees for the continuing uses of his music without having to sing, an attempt to register work with ASCAP or BMI brings the jingle writer up against resistance of another kind.

Since so much of the music on radio and television is advertising music, one would expect that there would be a big pot of gold waiting for the composer who had the tenacity to retain his performance rights. After all, wasn't the blanket license system devised to distribute income proportionally among those whose music was played?

Unfortunately, under the present ASCAP/BMI system, jingle composers are treated differently than composers of other kinds of music. Each society requires specific language in the agency contracts that gives them control of the music so they can license the jingles to the stations. As we know, the agencies don't wish to give up control—work-for-hire contracts give the ownership of performance rights to the client.

At ASCAP, when the composer is able to work out language satisfactory to both the society and the agency legal department, he discovers that even though his jingle was broadcast several times during an hour, he only got credit for one performance, and then at a greatly reduced rate. He also learns that his category of music is only valued at 3 percent of what a popular song earns: a popular song is given 100 percent of a credit and a jingle is given 3 percent.

BMI uses another approach to calculate payments for jingles: the jingle writer is given credit if fifteen seconds of his work are broadcast "in the clear," without an announcer. In the disappearing world of the sixty second spot, and in the real world of the :30, and in the new world of the :15, it is almost impossible to find commercials with enough music in the clear to satisfy the BMI fifteen-second rule.

Advertising composers claim that since there is so much advertising music broadcast, the rate for jingles should be higher. But raising the jingle payment rate would mean a new distribution of the income pie, shifting money from composers and publishers whose music is played less. The performance societies are, of course, resistant to this.

ASCAP and BMI argue that the air time for a commercial is purchased by the sponsor, and that the music is played not to satisfy some listener demand (as they claim there is for the music they license) but because the air time was bought. The jingle industry counters that there is as much *demand* for advertising music as there is for the background scores in "Dallas" and "M*A*S*H," the air time for which was also purchased by advertisers, but whose music is paid at much higher performance rates than the just-as-recognizable and more-often-heard music in jingles.

But composers don't like to fight; they like to write. When the amount of energy that they have to expend to get proper contract language results only in minor payment amounts, the vocal residual remains the easiest way to achieve ongoing payment for ongoing uses. All the composer has to do is keep his mouth shut and sing.

Like the legislation before Congress, the industry effort to achieve fair performance income remains in the channels waiting for Godot.

FINALIZING THE DEAL

Samuel Goldwyn said that "an oral agreement isn't worth the paper it's written on." To have an accurate record of the deal, there must be something in writing. Whether it only takes the form of terms annexed to a purchase order or bid sheet, or clauses spelled out in a letter of agreement, you should insist on a written document. It is the only responsible way of confirming the understanding between the parties.

Now, having digested the intricacies of achieving continuing income and performing rights, you must negotiate a contract with the agency that will provide their client with the legal right to use your jingle. Knowing that the only sure road to progress and fairness lies in your ability to say no when presented with less than acceptable terms, let's take a good look at the contract forms that agencies use.

THE WORK-FOR-HIRE (EMPLOYEE-FOR-HIRE) CONTRACT

The standard contract negotiated between a composer and an advertising agency is called a work-for-hire or employee-for-hire contract. Within it, the work-for-hire composer agrees to work for a single one-time fee. (As we have seen, advertising composers who are lucky enough are allowed their performing rights on a short string.)

The work-for-hire contract can take many forms, including an initial "bid sheet," covering work done by the jingle writer before his work is selected, and a final, all-encompassing contract that lays down the terms and conditions of the agency/composer business relationship *after* the jingle has been picked for production.

Agency Bid Sheets

The way one agency begins the paperwork process is to have their music production bid sheet signed before any creative work begins. A bid sheet is essentially a pre-contract, and is just as binding as the final.

WORLDWIDE ADVERTISING, INC.
MUSIC PRODUCTION BID SHEET

Supplier _____   Client _____

Composition _____   Product _____

Agency Producer _____   Job Number _____

1. For a Demo Recording of the Composition (if requested by Agency) for the purposes of evaluating the acceptability of the Composition as provided for in paragraph 5a below. No grant of rights. $ _____

2. For the Composition and Rights including Original Arrangement as specified in Paragraph 5b below. $ _____

3. For Additional Arrangements (if requested by the Agency) of the Composition. No Exclusivity or Right of First Refusal. $ _____

4. Supplier's estimated cost of Artists to be paid by Agency as specified in Paragraph 5(c) below. All Artists to be booked at the minimum union scale rates.

    (a) Number of Musicians: _____

    (b) Number of Singers: Solo/Duo ____ Group ____ $ _____

5. Supplier's estimated cost for Recording Facilities to be paid by Agency as specified in Paragraph (c) below, including recording, edit, mix, elements—15 ips ¼" trk; 35mm mag stripe and 35mm full coat tracks.

    Name of Studio _____ Hours _____ $ _____

(a) *Demo:* If requested by Agency, Supplier will make available on a timely basis to Agency a demo recording for the purpose of enabling Agency to evaluate Composition. Supplier will furnish and pay for the studio as well as costs and salaries of all personnel used in the making of each demo.

(b) *Grant of Rights:* Supplier hereby agrees to sell, transfer and assign to Client in perpetuity all right, title and interest in and to the Composition, including but not limited to the right to secure copyright therein throughout the world, without any restrictions whatsoever as to use. Supplier will execute, without charge or expense, any additional documents Client or Agency deems necessary to further evidence such transfer of ownership in the Composition.

(c) Supplier will book Artist and Facilities. Agency will employ Artists and pay Facilities.

BY: _____   DATE: _____

This bid sheet spells out everything that the agency wants to know about your deal. In paragraph 5b, "Grant of Rights," the composer/jingle house agrees to transfer all rights, and indicates he will sign a contract to that effect at some time in the future.

If you have any additional terms or any differences in the way you want to work, you should put them on this bid sheet, or not sign it.

Another agency negotiates test- or limited-market use on their demo bid sheet (in paragraph 3a on the facing page) and is specific about the kind of demo they want. This sheet also obligates the composer to sign a later confirming agreement.

UNIVERSAL ADVERTISING, INC.

Supplier: _____   Client: _____

Composition: _____   Job Number: _____

Supplier Invoice Number: _____   Date: _____

1. Supplier shall provide a demo of the Composition in the following form:

    _____ (a) a piano or guitar presentation;
    _____ (b) a demo quality tape;
    _____ (c) an on-air quality tape; or
    _____ (d) other (specify) _____

2. In consideration for the above demo submission and for the right to conduct off-air testing of the Composition for 6 months from the date hereof ("Demo Term"), Supplier shall receive the sum of $_____.

3. During the Demo Term Client shall have the following options, exercisable by written notice of such election:

    (a) to utilize the Composition in broadcast advertising in not more than _____ markets and for not more than _____ months, commencing with date of initial broadcast use, in consideration for the payment to Supplier of $_____; and/or

    (b) to purchase all rights to the Composition in consideration for the payment to Supplier of $_____.

4. If Client exercises its option under Paragraph 3(b), Supplier shall transfer and assign to Client all right, title and interest, in and to the Composition, including the copyright thereto, and shall enter into Standard Music Purchase Agreement, a copy of which is attached hereto.

Very truly yours,

ACCEPTED AND AGREED: On Behalf of _____

_____   By: _____

Agency Standard Form Contracts

The standard form contract backs up the bid sheet once the music is accepted and spells out in detail the agreement regarding the agency's use of your composition.

The following contract does it all, from a complete "Grant of Rights" (paragraph 2) to specific language about ownership of the recorded materials (paragraph 3).

Note the line on the bottom of the contract about not getting paid unless you sign. It was prepared by the lawyer-son of the dock boss.

WORLDWIDE ADVERTISING, INC.
MUSIC CONTRACT

Supplier _____   Date _____

Composition _____   Job # _____

Client/Product _____

This contract is entered into between Worldwide Advertising, Inc. as agent for Client, and Supplier, on the above date under the following terms and conditions.

1. WARRANTY:
Supplier warrants and represents that
(a) It is the sole author as an "employee for hire" of the Composition, a copy of which is annexed;
(b) The Composition has never been published;
(c) No application has been made to register the Composition for copyright as either a published or unpublished work;
(d) Supplier has full right, power and authority to make and enter into this agreement, and the rights granted to Client hereunder will not violate the legal or equitable rights of any person, firm or corporation;
(e) No assignment has been made of any of the rights in the Composition.

2. GRANT OF RIGHTS:
Supplier hereby sells, transfers and assigns to Client, its suc-

cessors, assigns and licensees, in perpetuity, all rights of whatsoever kind, nature and description, that are presently known or hereafter ascertained, in and to the Composition, including, but not limited to the right to secure copyright therein and all renewals thereof throughout the entire world, without any restriction whatsoever as to use. Supplier further sells, transfers and assigns to Client all recordings made of the Composition. Supplier will execute, without charge or expense, any additional documents Client or WAI deem necessary to further evidence such transfer of ownership, establishment of copyright or renewal of copyright in the Composition.

3. OWNERSHIP:

The commercials or other productions hereunder, shall be and remain the absolute property of Client forever. Without limiting the preceding sentence, it is understood that Client shall have the right during the term hereof, to use any production produced hereunder for broadcasting and telecasting over any network or networks, station or stations, in any country or countries, at any time and from time to time and for programs, spots, or on any other basis whatsoever, as well as the right to revise the picture and/or sound therefor.

4. INDEMNITY:

Supplier hereby agrees to defend, indemnify and hold harmless Client, WAI and their respective associated or affiliated companies, successors, assigns and licensees (hereinafter called "Indemnitees") from and against any and all damages, costs, charges, legal fees and disbursements, recoveries, judgments, penalties, expenses or losses of whatsoever kind or nature which may be obtained against, imposed upon or suffered by the Indemnitees by reason of any breach by Supplier of any of its warranties or representations hereunder or any infringement or claim of infringement of copyright, or violation or claim of violation of any other rights resulting from any use made by the Indemnitees, of the Composition. WAI will similarly indemnify Supplier and hold harmless with respect to any laterations of or additions WAI makes to the Composition.

5. CONSIDERATION:

In full consideration of Supplier's performance hereunder, and for all rights granted by Supplier herein, Client agrees to pay Supplier and Supplier agrees to accept the sum of $_____.

6. INJUNCTIVE RELIEF:

It is agreed that the services of Supplier are special, unique, unusual, extraordinary and of an artistic character giving them a peculiar value, and are impossible of replacement and that any breach of this agreement by Supplier will cause Client and WAI irreparable damage. Therefore, Client and WAI shall be entitled as a matter of right, and without notice, to equitable relief by way of injunction or otherwise, in the event of any violation of the provisions of this agreement.

7. ENTIRE AGREEMENT:

This agreement constitutes the entire understanding between the parties with respect to the subject matter of this agreement and supersedes all prior agreements. No waiver, modifications or addition to this agreement shall be valid unless in writing and signed by the parties hereto. This agreement shall be construed pursuant to the laws of the State of New York.

Your signature, together with ours, shall constitute this a binding agreement between us.

AGREED: WORLDWIDE ADVERTISING, INC.
                           AS AGENT FOR:

BY: _____   _____

TITLE: _____   BY: _____

SUPPLIER INVOICES WILL NOT BE APPROVED FOR PAYMENT WITHOUT A SIGNED CONTRACT AND LEAD SHEET RETURNED TO BROADCAST BUSINESS MANAGER.

Here are some additional points of interest:

1. Note that in paragraph 2, "Grant of Rights," the composer transfers all rights to the composition "without any restriction whatsoever as to use." This includes the right of determination about performance rights. ASCAP/BMI will not accept this contract.

2. Note that there is no provision for the composer to participate in any ancillary income from his jingle, whether it be through sales of phonograph recordings, or of sheet music, band arrangements, or any other format.

In the following paragraph, an agency has you state that you are an "independent contractor" and that you are responsible for payments and all other employer obligations.

> You agree that you are an independent contractor and that any and all contracts entered into by you in the performance of this agreement, whether contracts of employment or otherwise, shall be entered into by you as principal. You shall make or cause to be made full payment of all compensation payable by you to persons rendering services or furnishing materials in connection with this agreement. You agree to discharge all obligations imposed by any applicable union code or by any federal, state, or local law, regulation, or order now or hereafter in force with respect to employees, including, without limitation, the payment of required minimum fees and pension and welfare contributions, the withholding of all taxes, the filing of all returns and reports, and the payment of all assessments, taxes, and other sums required to be withheld, filed, and paid by employers.

Rider to Contract

In a separate rider to its music contract, one agency grants back to the composer the right to register with a performing rights society. This language is acceptable to ASCAP/BMI.

WORLDWIDE ADVERTISING, INC.
RIDER TO AGREEMENT

Dated_____

BY AND BETWEEN WORLDWIDE ADVERTISING AS AGENT FOR CLIENT AND _____

Notwithstanding anything to the contrary set forth in the agreement between the parties dated _____ (The Main Agreement), it is specifically agreed that Supplier retains the non-dramatic public performance rights to the composition conveyed pursuant to the Main Agreement which rights shall be licensed through the American Society of Composers, Authors and Publishers (ASCAP) in accordance with its rules and regulations. However, Supplier warrants and represents as a condition to this Rider, that under its membership agreement with AS-CAP Supplier has a right to direct licensing free of charge to any user and that under and pursuant to such right, Supplier is authorized to and hereby agrees to issue a direct license without charge upon written request of Agency or Client in any of the following events:

a) ASCAP shall no longer be in existence.

b) Publisher shall no longer be a member of ASCAP.

c) ASCAP shall no longer offer general blanket licenses that are in actual use by most United States radio and television local stations and networks.

d) Agency or Client specifically request a direct license for uses on a radio or television local station network which is then currently unlicensed by ASCAP.

Supplier further agrees that within ten days following receipt of a written request by either Agency or Client for the assignment to Client of the non-dramatic performing rights in the Composition, Supplier will execute and deliver to Agency or Client all documents necessary to effect such assignment.

_____

(Publisher)

_____

(Agency)

APPROVED AND ACCEPTED BY:

_____

(Composer)

Points of interest in this rider include the following:

1. It allows the composer to also act as music publisher.

2. All conditions are based on the survival of the blanket license system.

3. In the event that pending legislation changes the picture of performing rights, the advertiser clearly has the right to issue a free direct or source license at any time, thereby eliminating the composer's ability to collect performance income.

Warranty and Indemnification Explained

In his contract, the composer must state to the agency that his work is original and that he will stand behind that statement financially if it is proven false. In legalese, you "warrant" (claim) that you are the sole author and that the work is original; then you "indemnify" the agency and client against a breach of your warranty. The warranty is the claim; indemnification is the protection against breaches of the claim.

In advertising, it is easy to *say* that your work is original, but proving originality in a court of law is much more difficult. And expensive.

As the composer, therefore, you should never forget that you are only one participant in the collaborative process. It's not like writing a song, where you are influenced only by your imagination. In advertising, the direction of a musical approach or lyric or sound might be firmly dictated by the agency creative team.

You will almost always be given a preset campaign theme and provided with sample lyrics or fact sheets that contain phrases written and approved by many people. Sometimes the agency lyric is unchangeable. Melody patterns and sounds might be agency-suggested especially to please a client who has been watching a rough cut accompanied by a top 40 record and been promised "something like it." Or the audio direction might even come from the client himself, who wants to sound as good, or better, than his competitor.

"Make it sound like _____, but stay far enough away so we won't get sued," is a direction not unknown to the jingle supplier.

Yet the composer is the only member of the creative team who is required to provide indemnification against plagiarism.

Indemnification Clauses. In the paragraph below, you are agreeing to indemnify against any possible claim against your music. This indemnification is unlimited, and potentially terrible for the composer.

Supplier hereby agrees to defend, indemnify and hold harmless Client, WAI and their respective associated or affiliated companies, succesors, assigns and licensees (hereinafter called "Indemnitees") from and against any and all damages, costs, charges, legal fees and disbursements, recoveries, judgments, penalties, expenses or losses of whatsoever kind or nature which may be obtained against, imposed upon or suffered by the Indemnitees by reason of any breach by Supplier of any of its warranties or representations hereunder or any infringement or claim of infringement of copyright, or violation or claim of violation of any other rights resulting from any use made by the Indemnitees, of the Composition. WAI will similarly indemnify Supplier and hold harmless with respect to any alterations of or additions WAI makes to the Composition.

Note the last sentence, where the agency correctly acknowledges their own influence on the creative process and resulting potential liability. The dock boss has a heart after all (although a small one). It is only recently that agency contracts have begun to contain this kind of language, but it is an important consideration worth fighting for when you negotiate.

Types of Breach. If someone attacks your originality, your indemnification should not become effective until the claim against you has been *proven*.

Quacks and cranks will always attempt to jump on the bandwagon of a successful advertising campaign. Accusatory letters and phone calls should be handled by your attorney. The serious claimant will institute a legal action against the agency and whichever entity owns the copyright. (When someone sues, they sue *everyone*). You will probably have to defend against this action. The number of cases that actually reach trial are minimal, and the rest are usually only expensive, time-consuming paperwork makers, ultimately resolved in an out-of-court settlement. Therefore, you should not indemnify against *alleged* breaches, or you will be paying fees to attorneys for something that might not have been your responsibility. You should only indemnify against proven breaches.

In the following clause, you are indemnifying against an alleged breach. Another no-no.

> You agree to indemnify and forever hold us and our Client harmless from any and all liability, damages and expenses (including reasonable attorney's fees and expenses) resulting from or by reason of a breach or alleged breach of any representation or warranty herein made by you or of the failure to satisfy an obligation assumed by you under that agreement.

The Need for Insurance. Although agencies and clients carry their own plagiarism insurance ("errors and omissions" insurance), the jingle composer has usually been unable to obtain such a policy, having somehow been lumped together in the same high risk category as doctors (even though they hardly ever perform brain surgery). Premiums are financially prohibitive even when the insurance is available.

Modern law is expensive, and what is known in legal parlance as "reasonable attorney fees" are usually measured in staggeringly large amounts, especially when compared with creative fees for advertising music. If the originality of your work is challenged, the claim might never reach a trial on its merits, but will still end up costing lots of money. The agency's legal fees will be paid by the insurance company (or the insurer will defend on behalf of the agency), while you, who cannot get insurance, will have to finance your defense out of your own pocket.

Most agencies will want the right to make an out-of-court settlement and then, since you have indemnified them, have you pay for any uninsured loss. You should never permit an out-of-court-settlement without your written consent. Your approval should be required before someone gives away your money. The sensibility of this policy speaks for itself.

The following clause requires you to carry insurance, even though it may be financially prohibitive for you to do so.

> You will indemnify and hold harmless the Client and us, and any other person, firm or corporation making use of the Composition, from and against any and all loss, damage, costs or expense, including reasonable attorneys' fees resulting from any use of the Composition or any claim based upon a breach or alleged breach of any representation, warranty or agreement made by you herein and you agree to carry sufficient insurance to protect yourself, Worldwide Advertising, Inc. and its client against any such claim based upon a breach or alleged breach.

If you can't obtain or afford insurance, how can you protect yourself?

Limiting Your Idemnity. When it comes to dragging bucks out of your pocket to back your claim of originality, you should accept responsibility for what you did, not what you didn't do.

Acknowledging the collaborative nature of the business, a fair dollar value of personal liability should not exceed the amount you have been paid during the creative process (not including residuals, as these are use fees).

An arranger warranting the originality of his arrangement should limit his indemnification to no more than the amount of the arranging fee paid. You don't want to be the arranger who gets sued because the agency told you to find a jingle singer to imitate a star's voice. Arrangers who rearrange popular songs for advertising should be especially careful about the indemnification clauses that they sign.

A point to remember is that all advertising agencies and their clients carry their own insurance policies, duplicating each other, which completely protect them from any loss suffered because of an action against your work. Also bear in mind that none of the agency employees have anything to lose when they ask you to risk financial exposure from unlimited indemnification. The cruel rules are made by people who don't have to back them up themselves. The agency business manager who insists upon a certain condition in a contract risks nothing; the lawyer who drew up the clause risks nothing; the agency and client who decide what kind of settlement to make, or what caliber of attorney to hire to defend the case, all have absolutely nothing to lose. If there is a dollar loss, their plagiarism insurance will cover all except the deductible. Their one risk, beyond the loss of this small amount, is that the insurance premium will go up, just as if you had several accidents with your car and they raised your rates. (The agency's liability may at times include any production costs to fix the commercials that might have been pulled off the air until they could be retracked with different music—but while lawyers would like composers to believe that this can really happen, most will acknowledge that it never does. It's just on the list of things to protect against.)

It seems unfair that a jingle composer who basically works at someone else's direction must assume unlimited risk and provide unlimited indemnification upon the insistence of people and corporations who risk absolutely nothing.

Since the agency's financial exposure is limited to the deductible on their insurance policy, this is ideally the amount that you should be liable for. But it is beyond the scope of your job to inquire about the agency's insurance deductible.

The solution is to limit the amount of your indemnification to the creative fee paid, and then have it be effective only for a proven breach. By doing this, you will have in effect insured yourself.

Copyrighting Your Work

All agency music contracts require that someone (either the agency or the composer) apply for a copyright as an unpublished work. Doing this will officially record the earliest claimed date of creation, and will establish a written record of the artistic content of the work.

In advertising, a copyright comes into play only after a client has accepted a work for broadcast. If you have written a jingle that has been rejected it doesn't pay to copyright it. Wait until you use it for something. But if you feel it's special, you might consider spending the ten dollars per song necessary for registration.

Forms can be obtained by writing to the Register of Copyrights, Library of Congress, Washington, D.C. 20559.

The Need for Lawyers

Do you need a lawyer? Can you afford a lawyer? Can you afford not to use a lawyer? You will certainly need a lawyer if your originality is challenged. Therefore, it is advisable to seek counsel at least once in the formative stages of your advertising music career. It's worth the expense just to establish a relationship with someone who can help you if you get into trouble.

One thing you can do without the help of an attorney is reach an understanding of the issues contained in the agency contract. Knowing which rights you can retain and which you must give away will help protect you against a costly mistake that probably wasn't your fault anyway.

THERE IS ANOTHER WAY

When an agency licenses a popular song (or some other form of nonadvertising music), it is the music publisher who usually provides the contract of agreement. You could approach your business in much the same way, by forming a music publishing company and then trying to license (not *sell*) your jingles. Popular songs are not *sold* to agencies, they are *leased* under very specific terms. For the agency the only difference would be that instead of licensing an existing pop song from a nonadvertising publisher, they will be licensing one that is custommade for them by you.

The agencies will not like this. They will immediately begin thinking of you in a different way, because each of your attempts to avoid Big Brother's standard form will require that you deal with a lawyer on the other side (or at least a business affairs person). And this will happen for each job you do.

Using your own contract will take courage. Seeking terms other than "the agency standard" will undoubtedly cost you work at the agencies that are adamant in their zeal to own everything.

If you believe in your bargaining power—if you believe that you are a fair person whose creative efforts deserve fair treatment—then you might consider the licensing route using your own contract form.

It can be done.

When making your deal you might be warmed by the words of Bertrand Russell, who in his *Liberal Decalogue* said: "Do not fear to be eccentric in opinion, for every opinion now accepted was once eccentric."

The Composer/Publisher Advertising License

In reading the following contract (which is meant to be prepared on agency letterhead and addressed to "you," the composer/publisher) note the following:

Paragraph 1 gives you, the jingle publisher, the right to apply for and own the copyright.

Paragraph 2 states that the agency agrees to display your copyright notice wherever required by law. This protects everyone.

Paragraph 3 gives the agency the exclusive right to use the work, and the sole right to determine how it is used. It also limits the use to advertising only, and specifically for one product.

Paragraph 4 names the one-time creative fee.

Paragraph 5 allows the agency complete freedom to hire whomever they wish to do rearrangements of the song, as long as they pay your continuance fee.

Paragraph 6 lists the continuance fee, in this case the equivalent of a double-scale on-camera actor or announcer for all broadcast uses of the jingle. (This particular amount is approximately 30 percent higher than the payments that the agencies now make to the singing composer and singing arranger at scale plus 50 percent for overdubbing.) You may wish to begin your process of licensing at "scale." In return for receiving this residual you might agree not to sing on your tracks. You would benefit greatly from the trade-off.

This paragraph also says that your residuals are the essence of the agreement, and if they are not paid, you shall have the right to cancel the contract.

Paragraph 7b acknowledges that the agency is responsible for talent payment, regardless of who writes the check. (In this contract, you are the person who will pay the talent. If the agency wants to process payments, eliminate the second and third sentences.)

Paragraph 8 provides your warranty of originality.

Paragraph 9a provides your indemnification against a proven breach up to the amount of your creative fee.

Paragraph 9b provides that the agency indemnify you in the event that you suffer any loss resulting from their failure to display a proper copyright notice.

Paragraph 10 retains, without condition, your performing rights. This language is acceptable to ASCAP.

Paragraph 11 names the potential battlefield in the event of a dispute.

Paragraph 12 lists the participants.

Paragraph 13 states that everything must be in writing.

WORLDWIDE ADVERTISING, INC.
MADISON AVENUE
NEW YORK, NEW YORK

Greatest Jingles, Inc.

Gentlemen:

The following constitutes our agreement:

1. You have created and written a certain musical "work" entitled _____ consisting of music and lyrics to be used in radio and television advertising of the products of our client, _____. You warrant and represent that you have applied for U.S. copyright registration to said work or will do so promptly following the execution hereof.

2. (a) You hereby license to us and our successors and assigns the exclusive rights in the United States and its territories and possessions and Canada in such work in all areas of advertising, promotion and merchandising (excluding, however, the use thereof in any mechanical device for sale and the right to perform, as explained in paragraph 10 herein), for the full term of the statutory copyright to such work.

(b) It is our mutual desire to control the uses of the composition under all applicable laws. You have advised us that it is necessary on all newspaper, magazine, television, and other graphic advertising that uses the music or lyrics or both, in whole or in part, to display the copyright notice "© 19___ Greatest Jingles, Inc." We may determine that for any reason whatsoever we will not do so and such determination will not cause us to be in breach of this agreement except to the extent of the indemnity contained in paragraph 9(b). You agree to reserve and hold in trust for us the phrase/slogan "_____ _____" for the full term of the copyright and will authorize no uses of such phrase/slogan other than in the work.

3. It is specifically understood and agreed that we shall have the right to alter, expand, adapt, shorten, change lyrics or slogans, and make any arrangements of said work, hereinafter collectively referred to as "uses" of all or part of said work, and we shall have sole right to decide whether and in what manner said work shall be advertised, publicized or exploited by us, our successors or assigns, provided that any such use shall be limited to the advertising and promotion of our client's product.

4. We agree to pay you and you agree to accept in full consideration for all services rendered by you to us and for all rights granted by you to us, except only as specifically otherwise provided below, the sum of _____ receipt whereof is hereby acknowledged by you. We acknowledge that this contract does not require you to provide the services of any specific individual unless such individual is named herein.

5. It is specifically understood that we shall have the right to authorize others to furnish arrangements, or other uses of the work, in part or in whole, for the purpose of making recordings of it for the purpose of commercial advertising, and in such an event, no compensation will be payable to you with respect to any such arrangements, except as provided in paragraph 6.

6. We agree that you will be entitled to compensation as provided below, for all uses of the work, in whole or in part, in radio, and television, whether or not the arrangements or other uses were furnished by you.

(a) With respect to uses in television, the compensation shall be equivalent to the fees (including session fees and residuals and Pension and Welfare payments) payable to a double-scale on-camera actor (or 220% of scale) pursuant to the Screen Actors Guild Commercials Contract in effect at the time the use is made.

(b) With respect to uses in radio, the compensation shall be equivalent to the fees (including session fees and residuals and Pension and Welfare payments) payable to a double-scale actor (or 220% of scale) pursuant to the AFTRA National Code of Fair Practice for Transcriptions for Broadcast Purposes in effect at the time the use is made.

(c) Amounts due to you as computed under such collective bargaining agreements shall be paid to you or your designees at the same time as we pay talent reuse payments and we agree to supply you with a schedule of the uses of each commercial.

(d) Notwithstanding any provision to the contrary contained herein, we hereby acknowledge that these residual payments are the essence of this agreement, and our failure to render same when due shall be a material breach of this agreement, giving you the right to terminate this agreement and revoke this license by written notice to us. Provided, however, it is hereby agreed that if within thirty (30) days after our receipt of such notice, we render to you the payments originally due pursuant to this sub-paragraph 6(c), the breach shall be deemed cured upon such payment.

(e) We agree to supply you with an audio tape of all radio commercials and a ¾-inch videotape print of all television commercials using the work.

7. (a) We shall not be responsible for any agents or booking commissions in connection with the services or materials to be supplied to you hereunder.

(b) We accept responsibility for all AF of M, AFTRA, and SAG reuse and residual payments. We will notify you at least fifteen (15) days prior to use and you agree to compute and process these payments on our behalf. We shall pay you the amounts shown due promptly upon our receipt of your invoice and supporting information.

8. You represent and warrant to us that except to the extent it is based on the phrase/slogan described above or other copy submitted by us:

(a) the work by you is original;

(b) it does not and will not infringe upon or violate the copyrights or any other rights whatsoever of any person or entity;

(c) no adverse claim exists with respect to it;

(d) it has not heretofore been published or exploited in any form anywhere in the world; and

(e) you have the full and exclusive right and authority to enter into this agreement and to make the grant herein contained.

9. (a) You will indemnify and save harmless to us, our client, and any other person, firm, or corporation making use of such work from and against any and all loss, damage, or expense, including reasonable attorneys' fees, resulting from or by reason of any proven breach of any representation or warranty herein made by you. This indemnification shall not cover losses of any nature whatsoever caused by our failure to display a proper copyright notice on print, television or other material or media. The amount of your total indemnification of us shall not exceed the total compensation paid to you pursuant to paragraph 4 above.

(b) Should we fail to include the copyright notice as provided in paragraph 2(b), we shall indemnify you and any other person, firm, or corporation making use of such work fram and against any and all loss, damage, or expense, including reasonable attorneys' fees, resulting from our failure to display a proper copyright notice on print, television, or other material or media. We shall similarly indemnify you with respect to the phrase/slogan or copy submitted by us and incorporated by you in the work.

(c) We agree to refer all claims regarding the work to you for disposition.

10. All rights in the work not specifically granted to us are deemed retained by you. Specifically, no right to perform the composition publicly for profit is granted herein. Notwithstanding anything to the contrary contained elsewhere in this agreement, it is expressly agreed that the term "use" shall not mean or be deemed to mean "perform" and that no performing right license is granted hereunder by Greatest Jingles to Agency or its client.

Greatest Jingles is a member of ASCAP and the "composition" is part of the ASCAP repertory. The parties acknowledge that the right to perform the composition publicly has been reserved exclusively to Greatest Jingles for licensing only through ASCAP. ASCAP's agreement with Greatest Jingles permits Greatest Jingles, hereafter, to grant a nonexclusive license to perform the "composition" and, if Greatest Jingles shall later do so, Greatest Jingles must promptly notify ASCAP. In the event any such license is granted, the "composition" would remain part of the ASCAP repertory, and ASCAP's licensees would have the right to perform the "composition," but Greatest Jingles would not then be entitled to be paid by ASCAP for surveyed performances.

11. This agreement shall be interpreted by and construed under the laws of New York State applicable to contracts executed and wholly to be performed therein.

12. All notice or other documents to be delivered pursuant to this agreement shall be given by registered or certified mail to the parties at their respective addresses set forth hereunder.

Greatest Jingles, Inc. _____

Worldwide Advertising _____

13. No waiver, modification, or addition to this contract shall be valid unless in writing signed by the parties hereto. The waiver by either party of any breach of any provision of this agreement shall in no event constitute a waiver of any subsequent breach.

If the above accords with your understanding and agreement, kindly indicate your consent hereto by signing in the place provided below.

Very truly yours,

ACCEPTED AND AGREED:
GREATEST JINGLES, INC.

ACCEPTED AND AGREED;
WORLDWIDE ADVERTISING

_____   _____

Final Warnings

Seeking to own the copyright of your own music will make big waves, and may exclude you from job consideration.

Seeking a fair residual for your composition will make bigger waves. But it is fair, especially if you can't sing or don't want to for moral or ethical reasons. And it is obtainable.

Dabbling with indemnification language will make tidal waves with the lawyers. Having a contract to nitpick is a juicy job for an attorney. Lawyers love to change other lawyers' work.

Don't give in on indemnification; it's not necessary. The client is completely protected already.

And if you want your financial position to grow, you will have to say no to the job when the terms are less than your minimum standards. Now that you understand the business part, you should begin to have a sense of what your work is worth.

DOWN TO EARTH

Before we leave business affairs issues to the seeding ground of your practical experiences, let's eavesdrop on a conversation between a young jingle composer and an agency business manager. (Charlton Heston, the voice of God, should play the business manager. The jingle writer's face is left to the reader's imagination.)

"If I understand the terms of this contract, it means that I'm giving up all rights to my work. Is that right?"

"That's correct."

"My performance rights, too?"

"Yes."

"But I'll be losing potential income. Will you pay me for my performing rights?"

"No. Our music budgets are high enough. Look at all the money we pay out in residuals to singers and musicians. It has to stop somewhere. Sorry."

"Are composers of popular songs used in advertising giving up their performing rights, too?"

"No. They can still charge for them because they never had to give them up in the first place. In jingles everyone gives them up. Old habits die hard, you know. Of course, you can try to change things—it's a free country and all that—but you probably won't succeed."

"I don't get it. How can writers of popular songs keep control of their performance rights, while jingle writers can't?"

"I guess that somewhere down the line they were willing to stand together and fight. I've never seen a jingle house stand up for anything, except for singing on their own sessions. Strictly between the two of us, we see all the composers come through here, the big companies and the small ones. Contrary to what they say in public, they'll sign anything as long as they can sing on their commercials. So we let them sing. But pretty soon most everything will be nonunion anyway, and eventually that will end, too."

"May I ask your advice? I don't want to sing on my work, but I also don't want to sell it without a continuance fee. Do you think that if I stand up for my rights that anyone will join me?"

"Are you kidding?"

"How could such a thing happen?"

"People in your business never say no—not as long as they can sing. If we want to compete twenty houses against each other, no one ever refuses. If we want free demos, no one ever refuses. If we want unlimited indemnification, no one ever refuses, even if it means potentially risking everything they have. And I don't want to make you feel bad, but if you try to be different, chances are you will never be called to work at this agency again."

"Well, I certainly don't want to make trouble. Maybe I'll sing on my work, too, to make up for my lost performance income."

"You'd better clear that with the agency producer. Again, just between the two of us, at the next SAG/AFTRA negotiation the agencies are going to insist that employees of jingle houses be prohibited from listing themselves as performers. After all, agency employees and employees of film and editing houses aren't allowed to sing. The same rule should apply to jingle companies."

"I see your point."

"So if you want to do this job, you'd better sign the contract."

"Oh."

"You can't eat principle, you know."

"I guess not. Where do I sign?"

RULES AND REMINDERS

1. Learn about biting on bullets.

2. Indemnify only against a proven breach, and only up to the fee you were paid.

3. Remember the 4 P's: "Proper Payment for your Powerful Product."

4. Good luck in the real world.

10
THE DAY OF
THE RECORDING
SESSION

YOU HAVE CLEARED your mind of all the heavy stuff, those nasty words like contract, indemnification, alleged and proven, performance rights, license, and work-for-hire. You may not have won everything you wanted in the contract negotiation, but there's always next time.

Now there is only one thought that sends energy coursing through your body: today you are going to produce the best possible music track of your magnificent composition.

BEFORE THE SESSION

Although the union permits you to begin recording at 8:00 A.M., you have decided to start at 10:00, acknowledging a request from the account exec who has to travel an hour to get to the studio. Leaving the boonies at the crack of dawn to make an 8:00 A.M. start will raise havoc in his household, and you don't wish to bear the guilt for his divorce on your very first session.

You arrive at the studio at 9:00, an hour early, to check things out, to get the feel of the room. With pride, you announce to the receptionist that you are the composer/producer of the 10:00 A.M. session in Studio B. She smiles and points the way. A "closed session—no admittance" streamer is plastered across the schedule board for Studio A. You wonder if Diana Ross is in there working on her next album; you had heard that she often works here. Or maybe Ennio Morricone is scoring the next Brian de Palma film. (His last music score won an Academy Award nomination; maybe this one's a film about medical school . . . but you quickly squelch the thought.)

The control room of Studio B is cold and stark. You are alone. The only sound is the almost inaudible hum of the collective recording machine motors, a soft, whirring drone on the flight deck of the Starship Enterprise. In the dim light, five recording machines stand waiting—a Mitsubishi thirty-two-track digital recorder, a Studer twenty-four-track analog recorder, a Studer four-track recorder, and two Studer two-track machines, one for stereo, the other for two-track mono—their meters glowing in anticipation of receiving your beautiful notes.

The chair near the very center of the control console is worn from the rubbing and twisting of many sessions. This is the location from which the pilot, your sound engineer, will guide your ship. The Neve control board is enormous and you count a possible forty inputs and two jillion buttons and knobs. Directly behind where the engineer will sit is an island loaded with outboard gear: equalizers, digital delays, compressors, noise gates, space-age electronics whose operation will be in his masterful hands.

Connected to the far end of the console is a small desk. You assume that this is the spot for the music producer, the captain's perch. You claim the territory by spreading out your "immediate" file containing the approved lyrics and the storyboard. You put your stopwatch on the table as a further sign that it is *your* spot, and then slide your briefcase, which contains every other scrap of paper that has anything to do with this job, under the desk.

Your plan is to supervise the orchestra rehearsal in the studio, refining the band parts to perfection, then to continue supervising from the control booth. You have heard that these responsibilities are sometimes split between members of a jingle house team: the composer/arranger remains in the studio with the band for the entire session while the jingle house producer supervises from the control room, schmoozing the client at the same time. Today, you'll wear both hats.

Yesterday, when your contractor called the studio with the setup, he followed your instructions and ordered coffee and bagels for the rhythm section and the handful of expected clients, as a gesture of friendship and welcome. But the order hasn't yet arrived, and you're not sure who to ask about this detail.

After about ten minutes of apprehensive silence, a technician appears, nods a fast hello, and begins aligning each tape machine using a tone generated through the console. You watch as he sets every meter to zero, pleased to be with another living person in this operating-room atmosphere. You are tempted to ask what he is doing but decide not to reveal your inexperience. He obviously knows his job, and you certainly can't contribute anything at this stage.

MEETING THE ENGINEER

"Hi," says a tall, lanky, youngish, unshaven man wearing a Hawaiian shirt and carrying a feedbag over his shoulder. "I'm Sam, the engineer. You are . . . ?"

You quickly tell him that you're the composer/producer of the session, and you shake hands. Sam motions to someone you had not noticed before, who is out in the studio, moving chairs and setting up microphones. "That's Brenda, my assistant."

Then, ignoring you, he proceeds to enter into a rather detailed discussion with the technician about a buss that was frying. You don't recall hearing about any bus fires on the radio this morning, but then you realize that he's describing one of the gadgets on the console. Or something like that. This is not your department.

You listen for a moment, trying to appear interested in these technical matters, and when you find an opening you tell Sam that you'd like to discuss the project with him before everyone else arrives. Then you give him the speech you rehearsed, referring to the list that you've prepared of all the things you want your pilot to know about your song.

"It's a :60 and a :30, big band, rhythm first, horns and flutes at 11:40—assuming I'm on schedule—strings at 1:00, vocals at 2:00, and hopefully we'll be mixing by 4:00 or 5:00. It's radio, probably TV later on, so we should record sync."

Sam tells the technician to check the sync (synchronization) signal that must be recorded on all the versions of the tape so that any audio changes that happen later will all remain in sync with any visual.

"This is my first job with this agency, so I don't know who's going to show up . . ."

"Oh, I know them all real well," Sam interrupts. "They do lots of work here. Their music producer's a good guy . . . "

". . . so if there are any comments or questions, please direct them to me. Just so you understand the way I work, this is not music-by-committee. Any questions you have, direct them to me. All changes will be authorized by me, and me only."

"No problem," he says, starting to open up microphone lines.

Even though there is a half hour to go, Sam is working, getting as much of the technical stuff out of the way before the musicians arrive. Suddenly, the control room is filled with the sound of drums, one at a time, absolutely huge. You've never heard drums this loud in your life. It's like sitting under them, or worse . . . and better. You are immediately impressed with the sound system. Brenda is out in the studio, sitting in the drum cage, pounding on each drum, one at a time, and listening to instructions from Sam on headphones. You watch as he opens microphones and sets equalization levels.

"Can we talk about tracks?"

He keeps on working. "Go."

You run down the list of how you envision the track split, saving enough empty channels to overdub the vocals last. Sam agrees, improving your split here and there. His comments give you a sense of confidence that he knows what he's doing.

BEFRIENDING THE BAND

Your contractor, also one of your woodwind players, has booked the band on your behalf, and when the musicians begin to arrive, you go out to meet them. You plan to do everything possible to win them over, recognizing that they will be indispensable tools in the construction of your jingle (and your career). You shake hands with everyone, offering the just-arrived coffee and bagels (without the milk, or a knife to cut the cream cheese; Brenda goes off to correct this while the guitar players spread the cheese with their fingers). The conversations cover everything from yesterday's baseball scores (usually the older guys) to computer-equipment talk (usually the synthesizer players) to the latest foul, bigoted, raunchy joke (usually the fret players—bass and guitar—but attended by everyone), and you try to blend in with them, to establish a good working rapport.

Your copyist comes in. It had taken ten hours for you to complete the arrangement, and he looks as worn now as you felt yesterday when you delivered the score to him. He has worked most of the night, but has arrived on time. He asks about a section where you had left out the cello part. He has duplicated the bass line at that point, but will correct it at your instruction. Looking through the pages you confirm that he did the right thing.

Your contractor passes through the room putting the parts out on the individual players' music stands.

You stiffen a little. Over your shoulder you see three agency types arriving in the control booth: the agency producer and two suits (one male, one female), both of whom you have never seen before. You wave hello, but continue to check the score.

At exactly 10:00 the contractor claps his hands, and you call everyone to attention. The point about the importance of starting on time reverberates in your head: time is money, as the business manager had reminded you in your last phone call.

"Please put your headphones on," you ask, and everyone follows. The click track is pumping in the cans.

You explain the feel that you are looking for, pointing out little sections in the score that need special attention, singing parts of the lyric for example.

"Okay, let's try it," you direct, kicking off the tempo.

REHEARSING THE RHYTHM

Sixty seconds speed by, that never-to-be-repeated first birthing of your song. In your headphones you begin to hear the individual instruments as Sam opens microphones and adjusts levels, trying to get you a working "cue" mix as quickly as possible. You concentrate as the song takes shape. First the drums, then the booming bass, then the piano (you've never heard a piano like that before) and the guitars. You marvel as Sam positions each instrument in its own audio space. At times like this, you learn later, it's best not to be in the control booth, where all that might be heard are drums (and where the client might be *worrying* that there's too much drums).

Magically, after several rundowns in which both you, as composer/arranger, and Sam, as audio designer, each get a chance to make adjustments, the piece is beginning to sound like music.

During one of the rehearsals you check your stopwatch to confirm that the track is exactly the proper length. Finally, you tell the band that they sound wonderful, and that if there are no questions, you'll be going inside to supervise the recording.

You glance over your shoulder, and through the control booth window you see that the music director has arrived and seems to be in intense conversation with everyone. But you can't quite make out expressions through the glass. You later learn that the talk had nothing to do with music; they were discussing the stock market. (Sound engineers have the indispensable ability to concentrate on their duties while competing for attention with the Dow Jones average.)

You wonder if it sounds as good in there on the big speakers as it does to you in the headphones, and you suppress the sudden bolt of fear that they might not be liking what they are hearing.

The guitar player brings you back by asking if he can loosen up a little at letter C on the music score.

You are reminded of the words of Moss Hart, the great playwright who directed the Broadway shows *My Fair Lady* and *Camelot*: "To gain control of a cast, to get control early and to keep this control in an iron grip, is essential to a director facing a new company for the first time. There will be times—even whole days, perhaps—when a director, if he is a good one, will not always know what he is doing or if what he is doing is actually right for the actors or the play. He must proceed to do it, nevertheless, with certainty and surety and never relax his control for a moment—the more uncertain he feels, the more sure-footed he must appear. He can always change everything he has done at the next rehearsal, but on the day that he is floundering and insecure himself, he must never allow the actors to know it. All is lost if he does."

"Show me," you permit, wanting to take advantage of his talent and experience. He demonstrates a few fills.

"That's a little too busy, but how about something here?" You suggest an idea inspired by his riffs. Everyone plays it again and you acknowledge that the addition helped.

The time has come to leave the sanctuary of the studio and go to the control booth, which looks like anything *but* a sanctuary. You grab your almost-empty coffee cup and push through the heavy door. This is the moment of truth. You have taken twenty-five minutes to teach the band all the nuances of your chart. Now it's "Author Meets the Critics."

RECORDING THE :60

Up until this point no tape has been rolling: you and Sam have each been doing your individual jobs. Now you will come together to begin the recording.

Occasionally, you might consider asking that the last rehearsal be recorded. That way you'll have something on tape for immediate reference. This is helpful when you want to quickly check the track against picture. Note: if the engineer is up to Take 8 on the tape when you arrive in the booth, it would not be unreasonable to suspect that he has been rolling to beat up the tape cost.

"Sounds great," the account exec says as you enter.

"It's beginning," you reply graciously, fumbling with your score.

"I love it," adds the smiling producer.

This provides an immediate lift. "It'll really grow when the horns and strings come in," you add.

Someone introduces the lady suit as a representative of the client. They're all here.

The music director is sitting in your chair.

You ask politely if you can have your seat back. "So far we're right on time," you say, glancing at your watch, trying to be casual as you displace the person who is in the position of hiring you for other jobs. But after he has moved, you diplomatically demonstrate, for his benefit, what the horn and strings will be playing later.

He nods silently.

You move into the captain's chair (warm from the music director's body), press the talkback, and ask for another rundown.

This time the drummer is ad-libbing where he wasn't ad-libbing before, and you stop in the middle to tone him down.

You listen to each individual track, making sure you are hearing what you heard and approved in the headphones.

Sound engineers usually have a favorite instrument, whether drums, bass, keyboard, or guitar, and they subconsciously (sometimes not so subconsciously) tend to make that particular instrument more prominent than the rest of the band. And like all super-skilled, highly trained technicians, they have strong opinions. A sound engineer with an overactive ego may try to impose his tastes on your song. Engineers like to play producer. At those times, you must be firm and insist that the balance be as you direct, or you will not achieve the sound you have planned and sold to the client. Never let a sound engineer take control of your session. The good ones will recognize that the job comes first and will do everything to make you come off as the star. They will look to you for guidance and ultimate approval.

You make minor fine tunings, asking Sam to make the acoustic guitar louder and the piano softer and to fatten the sound on the bass drum, and after ten minutes of this and that, recording everything as you go, you arrive at what you believe is the best take.

You turn to everyone for approval.

Everyone says it's great with the exception of the music director, who thinks that the track should have more punch.

But before you can can respond and defend your work, the agency producer and account exec each jump in to remind him that the client has specifically said that they wanted an anthem, and *not* a heavy-metal cruncher. This position is confirmed by the client rep. After a brief discussion, through which you have remained neutral (except for nodding when someone praised the track), everyone agrees that this approach is correct.

You play it back again as some of the musicians drift in to comment. A studio musician's opinion is a deeply valued item, especially if you keep in mind that he is usually listening to his own part. Since you have hired only the best available players, you should have an interest in whether they thought they did their best. No one wants to discover a clam in the mix after the session is over.

RECORDING THE :30

"Okay, let's do the :30," you announce to everyone, relieved that this first step of many is completed. You dictate the cuts in the score that will shave the music down to thirty seconds. "We'll start with the same intro, play four bars of letter A, delete letter B, play all of C (at this point the pianist plays the music for "All of Me," and everyone laughs), then cut to the tag for the ending."

On the first run-through, someone fails to make the correct cut. This brings forth a caustic comment from the music director, who points out that it was the guitarist, "the one with the glazed look." (You are reminded that you insisted on calling your own musicians, and did not use any of his suggested players.) But on the next run-through, the musicians all play together and your clients agree that the track and message work exceptionally well in the thirty second format.

There is only one problem: the track is thirty-one seconds long.

THE FIRST BREAK

It is now five minutes to eleven, past the due time for the union-mandated break.

"Let's take ten now," you say to the contractor. "We'll finish the :30 after the break."

While the musicians rush out of the studio, the music director notes that you could have rushed to complete the :30 and not gone into the first overtime segment. But you are playing by the rules, and the break proceeds. You can use this time to figure out an appropriate way to shorten the music.

When the band returns, you direct them to make a 2/4 bar out of the phrase one bar before the tag, and now the track is a perfect :29.5, the correct length for television.

"The best music for advertising is modular, isn't it," jokes the music director, after you've made your first musical concession to reality.

OVERDUBBING

When the rhythm is completed, you hold the synthesizer player for an additional twenty minutes while he overdubs a bell part, a low bass synth line (for the intro only), and a melody line that will be used to replace the vocals wherever it is decided that the announcer donut will occur.

It is wise to record a melody line throughout even if there is no present intention of using a version with an announcer. If the campaign is a success, they may want to make donuts. Also, this Utopian version, with a melody line, can serve as a presentation piece for the agency to show off their music to the client. Instrumental versions are wonderful at sales meetings, played while everyone walks in, or as background music, or just to get everyone up and into the advertising.

Now you're ready to start the rest of the overdubs, to add the other instruments layer by layer until the full orchestra is on tape.

Since the advent of overdub recording, a constant challenge for the sound engineer is the elimination of leakage. In order to record only pure music, he must control the level of the prerecorded track—the track that the musician listens to as he records the overdub. (The mikes can sometimes pick up the sound of the playback coming through the headphones, and also the level of the ever-pulsing click track, cranked up to keep everyone together.) Some players wear both ears of the head set, some only one. It is the "single ear" Van Gogh players who cause the most havoc.

Overdubbing the Horns

You have returned to the studio to rehearse the horns and woodwinds. You give the players an opportunity to correct any copying errors and to listen once or twice on the big speakers before putting on headphones, just to help tune to the track. For a musician, learning to play in pitch with headphones is an art unto itself.

When the parts are learned, you return to the flight deck and supervise the overdub.

After a few run-throughs, they play along perfectly. But someone flubs near the end, and you have decided that the rest was so good that you will just "punch in" the ending (listening to playback up to a specific point and then switching into record for as long as necessary to correct the error). It is important that someone in the booth other than the engineer directs the spot of the punch (your engineer may not appreciate this). This is one of those times when it is essential that you be your own producer. Nothing is more embarrassing than wiping out something it was your intention to save simply because someone didn't know where the punch was. The someone is you, and this is your responsibility.

Overdubbing the Strings

String sections are usually recorded as one of the last musical overdubs, the icing on the cake. Strings tend to pull the pitch up, and it is again important that the players hear a playback on a big speaker, in order to tune properly, before going to headphones.

String players will tell the same jokes you heard three hours ago, and you will laugh again, while the older players pine for the good old days.

As you proceed through each section of overdubs, you ask Sam to solo the individual channels so you can confirm that all the notes are correct. Take the time now, so you won't be disappointed later. The string track sounds quite dramatic on its own, and you marvel at the way this building-block process of musical creation comes together into one whole.

Sometime during the day you will have ordered lunch, either the most exotic Japanese or fabulous deli available, and in copious portions. For agency and client types, sustenance is important. But while others munch on the goodies, you will continue to work, pausing momentarily to take bites as you charge ahead, cognizant of the never-stopping clock.

(The studio will usually include the food cost on their bill, either as food or as a tape charge.)

Overdubbing the Vocals

When it comes time for the vocals everyone perks up. Here is a language that everyone understands: the lyrics. This is the part of the session where those with limited musical expertise can have their say.

You have hired five singers on the basis of their reputations for consistency and interpretation, and you go back into the studio to teach them their parts. Again, you begin on the big speakers so they can be bathed in the fullness of the track.

This time, achieving a clean vocal track, one that contains the minimum amount of leakage, is critical. Orchestra leakage, which sounds squashed like a 1920 radio, will interfere with the overall sound of the track when the real background music is added.

As you record, punching in and out to correct errors and save the good stuff, you ask approval from your clients after every vocal layer.

Even though your sense of ethics prohibits you from singing in the group (they hired you as a composer, not as a singer), you have decided to "double" the group, to thicken the sound. Groups expect this as standard procedure. As they sing along with their prerecorded selves, the sound changes—instead of five voices, now there are ten on the melody, plus two layers of harmony—a grand total of twenty singers, creating a rich, full vocal sound. You pay particular attention to their articulation and cajole them to heights of enthusiasm as they sing the name of the product. Last of all, you give each potential soloist a chance, and after a quick discussion with the agency and client, you choose one to record.

Finally, six hours after you began, all the materials are on tape.

THE MIX

Much like a construction crew assembling materials, you and your engineer have recorded all the elements. Now it is time to mix everything into an acceptable form.

An advertising sound engineer is like a dentist: he has lots of clients, and he works with a lot of different mouths, but if he's a pro, he'll know that *each* client is expecting him to be a genius, or that client won't be back. Your Sam is no exception. You have decided to give him creative leeway during the mix. This is the chance for the engineer to display his craft—if you hear anything you don't like, you'll say so.

The account exec and the client left after the vocals were completed, and the music director has been on the phone talking to another jingle composer at a different studio. Before the mix begins you remind everyone that Sam is doing his thing, and it is best if they are quiet.

You sit back and watch a true marvel of technology. Sam literally performs the session again, opening each track one at a time, panning each instrument to an appropriate place (assigning it to either the left or right stereo channels or anywhere in between), adding special effects and equalization as he goes along. First the drums, then the bass, then the keyboards, until slowly, carefully, with beauty and precision, all the instruments have been brought back to life, one by one, section by section, with the tender love and care that only you and your mother would devote to your music. Finally, your song is an entire orchestra, fine-tuned and sounding better than you had ever hoped.

Sam has spent more than an hour nuancing the band. Now, as he adds the singers, all efforts are directed to making each word audible. Each little adjustment in instrument level helps the clarity.

You listen on small speakers, at a level so soft that everyone has to stop breathing to hear it. You confirm that there is enough bass, enough bass drum, enough strings, and most important for the client, enough vocal.

Finally, everyone agrees that this is *the* mix.

Going to Tape

The final mix to tape occurs in one of two ways: (1) the engineer rehearses the physical fader movements he must execute each time during the dubdown, or (2) the mix is made with the aid of an automated console, where a computer remembers all the moves for each individual channel and plays them back automatically. Today you are working on an automated Neve console, and you watch as the faders move up and down by themselves in response to their computerized instructions.

The Four-Track Tape

You will mix to four-track, which can serve as the master for a full-coat mag (magnetic film stock containing multitrack audio material) that can be put in sync with the film. The four-track will also be the master for the creation of versions that will alternate lyric and announcer copy. These are typical four-track splits for TV:

    A. 1. Orchestra (stereo) left channel
          2. Orchestra (stereo) right channel
          3. Vocal group and soloist
          4. Sync tone

This version is used to control vocal levels against the band.

    B. 1. Orchestra (monaural)
          2. Vocal group and soloist
          3. Instrumental melody
          4. Sync tone

This version is the most common and most flexible and is used for mixing donuts for the voice-over, with the melody and the voices used interchangeably.

C. 1. Orchestra (monaural)
2. Vocal group
3. Solo voice
4. Sync tone

This version allows control of the solo voice against the vocal group and the band and provides the easiest way to change a solo lyric.

D. 1. Orchestra (monaural)
2. Vocal group and soloist
3. Special effects of any kind
4. Sync tone

Special effects can also be recorded on a two-track tape—one channel for effects, one for sync—to be matched with the film by the editor.

These are typical four-track splits for radio:

A. 1. Orchestra (stereo) left channel
2. Orchestra (stereo) right channel
3. Vocal group and soloist
4. Instrumental melody

B. 1. Orchestra (stereo) left channel
2. Orchestra (stereo) right channel
3. Vocal group
4. Solo voice

C. 1. Orchestra (monaural)
2. Vocal group
3. Solo voice
4. Instrumental melody

D. 1. Orchestra (monaural)
2. Vocal group and soloist
3. Special effects of any kind
4. Instrumental melody

You will most often make only one four-track split, the one that is the most appropriate for the specific job.

Protecting Your Mix

Maintaining the artistic integrity of your music can be difficult when you create a four-track tape which can be remixed by someone else later. Providing separate, individually adjustable tracks always permits another person to fiddle with your creation.

At the film mix or at the announcer session, the sound mixer might decide, after listening over his studio's equipment, that your track needs adjustment: more bottom, less bottom, more melody, less melody, or some alteration of the vocals. Providing a four-track tape allows someone the freedom to act on his perceptions.

This person may decide to rework your tracks into a "chicken mix"—a version that has mostly all vocal, and very little orchestra. This kind of mix is popular with clients who don't like loud music.

"Let's do a real mix, and a chicken mix for the client."

The best way to avoid the loss of control is to take the extra effort and time to produce any donut versions or chicken mixes on your session, rather than risk having another engineer dabble with your painted picture.

Mixing to Two-Track in Stereo or Mono

Your final mix element will be a quarter-inch tape.

When a recording is made for phonograph records, the producer knows that, with the exception of AM radio, it will always be heard in stereo, in cars and on home systems, on FM radio, and on MTV-type stations.

But the vast majority of homes do not have stereo television, and unless you are careful, there can be a significant difference when you listen to a stereo track on a mono system.

Ideally there should be a separate mix for each type of use: stereo for radio, and monaural for television. But these days stations that broadcast in stereo also make their own monaural signal by combining both channels of the stereo mix.

For this reason you should not be fooled by the spread of the stereo, which will sound fabulous. Always check the mono mix. Since the stations will combine your stereo channels, you should do the same, and listen to the results. It is wise not to position many audio elements too far left or too far right as these will tend to be heard less in mono.

Center stereo information will be more predominant; a mono playback of a stereo mix will have more vocal.

Make the necessary pan adjustments, and take the time to approve both the stereo and the mono versions.

Although most TV commercials will be released with stereo sound-tracks to accommodate state-of-the-art broadcasting technology, mon-aural listening on the old set is still the most important advertising version.

ON YOUR WAY HOME

Sometime, hours later, it is all done. You are bone weary, eye weary, ear weary—*especially* ear weary. You have listened to your song over and over and over again, checking and double checking it in every length. Even your mother would have left two hours ago, as did the music director, who won the argument over whether he or the agency producer would stay for the dregs of the mix. Your last task is to order appropriate tape copies to be sent to the agency in the morning and an extra set for yourself (all of which will be made tonight by the Brenda long after everyone else is tucked in bed).

You are sushi'd out, pizza'd out, coffee'd out, and you feel grungy after spending the last twelve hours of your life in the confines of this tiny capsule. Bravo, John Glenn! How'd you ever do it? How many times today did the image of Jackie Gleason in *The Hustler* pass through your head—how he stopped the game to clean up, dress up, freshen up, and get ready for the next round? Next time, you decide, you'll bring a shaving kit and a towel. It's tough to feel clean and washed after wiping your face with Bounty.

But, taking a deep breath, confident that you have done the best possible job that you could have done, you pack your bag, pick up the music parts left in the studio by your contractor, and head out the door towards home.

RULES AND REMINDERS

1. The recording studio is where you bring to life everything you have imagined in your head. Never be satisfied with anything less. "Set-tling" is a nonexistent word in the production of advertising music. Recognize that while everyone—the musicians, singers, and engineer—will move along to other jobs, your reputation is on the line to the end of this one. When you are responsible, it behooves you to get it the way you want it.

2. Be nice to the assistant engineer. She may some day end up running a music department at a major agency.

3. When something goes wrong, learn to make do without getting crazy. Your ability to show confidence will be matched by your client's confidence in you.

4. It's not smart to order a Coke when your client is Pepsi-Cola.

5. Always get to the studio before your client.

6. Take the time to check out the studio setup yourself. Guitar microphones might have been mistakenly set for acoustic when you wanted electric; classical guitars may be next to the drum cage and not in soundproof isolation as they should be.

7. Dress comfortably and enjoy the session. The studio is the fun part.

11
POSTPRODUCTION

THERE IS NOTHING quite like the satisfaction of knowing that you have done the job well. For the creator, there is a delicious inner glow of accomplishment that supercedes all the effort and emotion and exhaustion experienced during the creative process.

The glow lasts for about eight minutes.

The morning after the session you are awakened by a nervous phone call from the agency producer wondering where the tape copies are ("Everyone's waiting!"). You immediately call the studio only to learn that the package left a half hour ago. As soon as you hang up, the producer calls back and tells you not to panic; they've just arrived.

You struggle out of bed and throw on the cassette that you took home last night. From out of the past come the thundering bass notes of your great new jingle! You relive the excitement, the highs, and the complexities of yesterday's studio adventure.

Later in the day, you check in with the agency producer, who knows that you are concerned about everyone's reaction. The approval process is going very well, the account people all like the music very much, and the creative team is also impressed with your arranging ability. One member even suggested that he might give you a shot at another job.

During the next week, approvals come in from the client, who thinks that this is the most inventive stuff since Saran Wrap.

But there is also bad news: the legal department has criticized one of the *bon mots* and insists that it be changed before the spot can go on the air.

THE REMIX AND RE-SING

Since it is easiest to pass judgment on a finished product, at this point everyone has become an expert.

In addition to the lyric change, there have been comments like: "Too much bass" (from the account exec who listens on a system with no tweeters), "Can the strings be louder? They cost so much!" (the business manager, of course, putting his two cents in), or "It needs more drums" (this from the ex-drummer/producer who hired you).

For the agency, this process—fixing the recording to everyone's satisfaction—is called a remix. For the composer, it is often the un-mix.

Fortunately, the computer will remember the fader moves, and all Sam will have to do is punch in the new lyrics and then make them match the rest of the track.

If the change is simple enough he might even bump your four-track mix up to thirty-two-track digital (with no loss of generation), and use some of the empty channels for the new lyrics. This way you can simply bring in the singers and punch in the tiny change without having to remix everything.

Paying Talent to Fix Lyrics and Music

In accordance with union rules, singers and musicians are supposed to be paid full session fees when they rerecord tracks. Most times, however, the "fix" session is thrown in free (at least by the singers), who know when not to rock a very profitable boat. They'll make up any minimal session-fee loss when the grand residuals of broadcast start rolling in.

Musicians may also help out on the budget by not charging, but the professional producer knows that for players, business stinks, and because their residuals are so low he should pay his band for their time.

THE FILM MIX

If your music is to be used on television, it will be subject to a "film mix."

After all final editing to the picture is completed, a session is held in which the announcer track, the sound effects, and the music are all married together on one track. In Hollywood they call it dubbing. In New York, it's mixing. This introduces yet another professional entity with the power to make musical changes: the film mixer.

You may doubt that a lot of damage can be done when you have only four music tracks to work with, one of which is sync tone. But too much vocal means very little musical impact. If the spot has a lot of announcer or sound effects, the mixer might keep the background music down and the lyric up.

As a safeguard against major changes to the mix that you and the agency both love—the one you spent all those hours perfecting—you should prepare your four-track mix (from which the full-coat mag is made) with tones at the head. Sam should do this automatically, but it never hurts to remind him. That way, if another engineer uses the tape and correctly lines up the tones, what he will hear is the exact mix that you approved. But if the film mixer doesn't use the tones, his mix will replace your mix. Just hope he is a good mixer.

The film mix can be unsatisfying for the composer. The music is no longer the star, and will be downplayed to accommodate the announcer and any sound effects. Some advertising film mixers believe that people always remember dog barks, bird chirps, and engine sounds, and there goes that beautiful string run that you took extra time to perfect.

But, as the agency for a large brewer once said to a composer who complained that his music was buried in the film mix: "There's beer in the spot, too, you know."

WHEN THE CHECK IS NOT IN THE MAIL

The last part of postproduction is the paperwork. As soon as possible, usually along with all the AF of M and vocal contracts and schedules, you should provide your invoice with whatever breakdown is appropriate for this job. Everything should be mailed (or delivered) to the business affairs manager—not to the agency producer. The producer will certainly have to approve your invoice, but by sending it to the business affairs department you can avoid the delay of your package getting stalled on the producer's desk while he is off for three weeks shooting in Mexico. Union penalties are embarrassing and can be easily avoided by sending contracts and paperwork to the right people.

When it comes to not receiving payment for creative and arranging fees, people have different levels of tolerance before they start to get crazy. That's why it's best to find out about the agency's payment policy *before* you begin work.

Many businesses send out statements if they haven't received payment within thirty days. This written form reminds the payer that the payee is waiting. In smaller, less formal operations, a polite phone call to the accounts payable department will do, asking if there is any reason that payment has been delayed. If nothing appears after a week or so, try calling the producer who hired you. He can usually push things along.

What's fair is fair. You have earned the money owed. While the ideal relationship is one in which the agency pays you as promptly as they pay the musicians and singers, reality and business practice dictate that most agencies will not. Being in business for yourself requires more patience than Friday's cry, "Hey, baby. The week's over. Where's my check?"

RULES AND REMINDERS

1. When the job is all finished, say thank you to as many people in the process as you can. With a little luck you'll be meeting them all again.

2. Don't expect the agency to call you after the job and tell you how things went. While yesterday you may have been the star at the session, today you are again a vendor.

3. Celebrate. You've earned it.

12
YOU'RE ON
THE AIR!

THE REAL LEARNING process begins after the job is over. The time to really judge the sound of your commercial is when it's on the air. Only when it is integrated into all the other programming will you be able to find out if your inventions are competitive and your creative decisions justified. What the spot sounds like on the tube in your living room or in your car should be the only confirmation of your direction. Not the sound in the studio on those magnificent speakers.

Every radio and television station has its own audio image. Your spot will sound different on the all-news radio station than it does on the hard rocker. As you spin your dial, you can easily pick out stations because you recognize their "sound." Some broadcast everything with echo, or equalize everything to their own standards—compressing, limiting, innovating for their specific listener. From the production standpoint, there is nothing you can do about this except make the best possible mix. No matter how hard you try to outguess the stations, you cannot. They are the final master, and while they don't have the ability to change the interior mix of your music, *your* sound will be different when heard on *their* sound.

When you hear your jingle on the air, you should ask yourself these questions: Can you understand all the lyrics? Are they too loud? Is the mix too "chicken"? Should you have fought at the remix when the music director insisted that the vocal level be raised, and the bass lowered? (Here's a good lesson to remember about the power vested in the person who pays the bills.)

Are the horn fills audible, the ones you and Sam worked so hard to perfect in the mix?

Do you hear enough band?

Enough string run?

Is the band drowning out the message?

Is the announcer too loud?

At the film mix the producer asked the engineer to load as much level onto the tape as possible. Now that you're hearing it on the air, with everything being compressed and limited by the station, is the final result satisfactory? Would you approach the same project in the same way if you had to do it again? Would you use the same combination of instruments?

THE PRIDE AND FRUSTRATION

Sometimes spots will go through a final recording, filming, editing, mixing, and shipping, only to be pulled before they run (or immediately after) because a higher-up at the client didn't like them. When this happens no amount of mail from your mother can help.

For the 1975 car year, Pontiac's agency came up with a James Bond look for its spots. A Bond swashbuckler type and a Pussy Galore imitation were to be chased all over America by a villain who wanted to capture their Pontiac. (Sounds swell, doesn't it?) The heavy was played by Gert Frobe, the German actor who played Goldfinger, who kept calling the car a Ponjack. The commercials were lavishly produced adventure spots, with bridges blowing up and helicopter chases and speeding cars all over the place.

In those days there was no overdubbing, and we shoehorned a forty-piece orchestra into a small studio and kept them there for nine hours and forty minutes, recording Bondish arrangements of the Pontiac theme. There were fourteen spots of different lengths, and the production costs that day were huge. Yet, when they went on the air at announcement time, they lasted for less than a week. Someone at GM thought they were awful and pulled them.

A job is a success only as long as it runs. When it gets pulled, kiss it goodbye and move on.

YOU'RE OFF THE AIR

The cemeteries are filled with irreplaceable people.

—OLD FRENCH PROVERB

Nothing is as old as yesterday's jingle. With popular music it's a different story. When a pop song slips from vogue, there is always the possibility that it will be reborn again some time in the future, catching the fancy of a new generation, finding new success, and sometimes earning even more income than on the first go around.

But no one is clamoring to hear the music for the 1975 Pontiac. From the first airing, your hit creeps with each successive broadcast toward its predestined demise. You may do everything possible to keep the patient alive and healthy by creating new arrangements, new approaches, new lyrics, and cute little variations that extend the life of the campaign. But the end always comes. Sooner or later someone is bound to say (or think), "Oh, that old tune again?"

On Madison Avenue few things are as threatening as last year's campaign growing stale (and that includes the audio). Agency people are always trying to outguess and out-create their current hits. How to make things better, to serve the hungry future, is the advertiser's never-ending quest. If this means changing the music, the client quickly says, "Let's go get some demos." (When word of a music search hits the street, it strikes terror into the hearts of on-air jingle singers with big mortgages. If the commercial is pulled, there go the residuals . . . and the palace is back on the market.)

When a jingle composer's work is replaced by someone else's, he experiences a unique kind of rejection. Getting through it requires the understanding that the industry you have chosen is always in flux, ever searching for new, fresh ideas and product. The sponsor needs to change with the economic and social climate and with the fluctuations of the marketplace.

It has been said that advertising is a young person's business. Members of every new generation want to make their own mark, to develop their own people and formulate their own new directions. And they often strive to disassociate themselves from the suppliers of their predecessors. You may at some point be among the "former suppliers." This doesn't make you a bad person.

The satisfactions and rewards to be gained in the jingle business should not be confused with an agency's loyalty to you. Don't expect loyalty. You're only as good as your last jingle. The person who seeks loyalty from his advertising client is shortsighted and will spend his life doing someone else's bidding. If you put out your best effort, you will satisfy your most severe critic: yourself. Doing this is the only sure way to survive when the loyalty you mistakenly expect does not appear.

Secretly you may hope that the world will loudly reject any new effort-without-you, halting product sales because everyone hates the new song. But the world never complains. Old man business, he just keeps rollin' along, with new faces to feed the new desires, and new music where once your mother had proudly pointed her finger.

Your real satisfaction should come from the knowledge that you worked hard, were paid fairly (you hope, but probably not), produced your music under the best possible conditions, and that your creation made a difference, touching the public mind and pocketbook even though your name has not become a household word and your songs don't go marching on to continuing glory.

LOOK MA—THE TOP OF THE WORLD!

It's Super Sunday and the game will begin in two minutes. The coin has been tossed. Sides of combat have been chosen. America waits breathlessly for this encounter of encounters, and no one is more excited than you. You have invited your entire family over to watch the spectacle, even including the relatives you don't like, along with several friends who will make the relatives palatable.

The reason for your elation? The matching of two titans? No.

The client who originally told you that your work would only be running in test markets has now spent the enormous funds necessary to buy time on the Super Bowl. Your music is about to be heard by *billions* of people.

"We'll be right back for the kickoff after these messages," says Pat Summerall, sounding overly enthusiastic as if he, too, were waiting only for your commercial. The media department has informed you that the spot will be in the slot before the kickoff. And this is it! Vindication! You didn't have to go to medical school after all to make it in the big time! Behold, world! Behold my artistry!

The room is suddenly hushed . . . your chest is doing the Heartbeat of America . . . all those years . . . all that effort . . .

The spot fades up, but the sound is too soft. You leap to the screen and crank the knob . . . now it distorts . . . you adjust it to a tolerable level . . . in a blink the spot is half over! . . . you shush your mother when she calls out that *it's wonderful!* . . . the pictures are beautiful . . . the bass sounds big and full just as you planned in the mix . . . the singers are singing their hearts out . . . you can understand *all* the words . . . as the logo approaches, the soaring strings fill the room . . . you can sense the rapt attention of your near and dear as they stand in awe of your mighty genius.

The spot fades out and you are replaced by a commercial for Kayopectate. You proudly glance around for approval, the approval you deserve, the approval you have *earned!*

But you are alone.

Alone!

Everyone, your mother included, has rushed to the kitchen for a last-minute snack. The game is about to start—that's what really counts for everyone. Except for you.

At this pivotal, poignant moment you realize that your work will forever be regarded as a distraction, an interruption, a time-out in the public's search for diversion, and at your client's whim you will be heard by millions, or never again.

You have become a professional in the field of musical advertising.

A jingologist.

13
FINDING OUT WHERE THE "HITS" ARE

WHILE MANY PEOPLE set their sights on a profession and then do whatever is necessary to achieve their chosen goal, others fall into a line of work largely by chance, their career directions guided more by enthusiasm than by premeditated plan. Starting out with focused schooling and pretaught skill does not necessarily get you where you want to go.

When I began my career as a composer in the early 1950s I had no formal musical training. My parents, having lived through the fears of the Great Depression, believed that the only way to endure uncertain economic conditions was to have a profession that would provide a steady income through hard times. With that as an underlying guide, they raised their children: my seven-year-older brother, destined to become a physician, and me.

Unfortunately, their concept of professionalism did not include the music business. To them, music was something that you did on the weekend after your regular job. My father, a Russian-born immigrant who had earned his college degree at night school and worked for the City of New York with the title of Civil Engineer, and my mother, also a college graduate with an unswerving commitment to the values of higher education, tried to instill professional values in their children by creating a sterile atmosphere of study in our small West Bronx apartment. Music was rarely played on the radio (television was in its infancy and we could not yet afford one), or on any instrument, although we had an old circa 1920 upright piano in our living room (last tuned during the circa) that stood as a silent repository for the doilies that my mother crocheted during the long quiet evenings while we studied.

But somehow, with an instinctive gift, I was drawn to music as my own form of expression, and I taught myself to play when no one was home. It came quite naturally. There was a recorder, a small wooden flutelike whistle that my brother had brought home during high school, and when I was ten I found that I could produce simple songs by blowing into it and covering the holes with my fingers. And there was my father's mandolin, a relic from the old country that he took out occasionally to play the only melody he knew: a Russian folksong. I learned to play this instrument, too, picking at the double strings until I had mastered a tune or devised a fingering to make a chord. And I played the piano, banging away until I came up with something that pleased me. Later I learned to tune and repair the notes I broke with my over-enthusiastic pounding.

When I was eleven, a miracle happened: an uncle gave me the saxophone that an older cousin refused to play anymore, and for the first time, music became a real part of my life. When the glorious instrument arrived, my father asked one of our neighbors, an ex-musician (now in the umbrella business), to show me how to set it up.

I soon discovered that saxophone fingering was similar to a recorder's, and by the end of that first day I had mastered "Auld Lang Syne" and given my mother a migraine headache. A week later I gave my first unaccompanied saxophone recital to my bored eighth-grade classmates. Yet, in spite of the natural ability I demonstrated, when I graduated from grade school and wanted to go to New York's High School of Music and Art, my parents insisted that I apply to the Bronx High School of Science, to continue on the road to a profession.

But it was the dawn of rock and roll, and in high school I met other nonscientific types who had also discovered music as their personal form of expression. We formed a five-piece band and began playing at school dances, parties, and weddings, jumping at any opportunity to make music, paid or not. Music, by this time, had completely captured my mind and energies.

After graduating—barely—from high school, I reluctantly began college in a last-ditch attempt to appease my parents. But I soon recognized that I was not the academic type. I knew that I would never feel satisfied if I didn't give music a fair chance. So early in my freshman year I quit.

In the mid-'50s, folk songs and calypso music were the rage, and I learned to sing and play the guitar, and put an act together. I began auditioning and working in small nightclubs in New York City—intimate eastside bistros that would hire self-contained acts. By this time I was writing songs and trying to get them recorded by other people. I even made a few records that, to my enormous disappointment, didn't sell. There is nothing quite like the enthusiasm that is squandered on hoping for a hit record.

When the waning folk fad brought fewer and fewer jobs, I decided to set my career sights toward acting and the theater. I enrolled in a small acting school, the Lane Theatre Workshop, one of the many backroom competitors to the Actors Studio.

But because of my limited experience, the only acting job I was able to get was in a low-budget exploitation film about neighborhood kids who prevent a Mom-and-Pop pizzeria from being taken over by the bad guys. I didn't exhibit much in the way of thespian talent, but I was able to convince the producer to include some of my songs along with the records he used for background music.

A few days after the film opened he offered me the job of writing the score for his next movie.

At this point, a word of explanation: while it may seem a bit far-fetched for a beginning songwriter to be offered the chance to write a music score for a motion picture, the motivation in this case was that of a smart businessman recognizing potential talent willing to work cheap. My patron producer specialized in films where the music wasn't of any particular importance in the grand scheme of things. He produced nudies, and I quickly learned that no one pays attention to the music in a skin flick. From the consumer point of view the visual product was far more arresting than the audio, and in the semi-lit theaters where these films played, the sound systems were usually so old and bad that everything distorted anyway.

My producer cared little about the artistic quality of his films; he was a realist, ultimately concerned only that they came in at the minimally correct length, sixty-five minutes each, and that he could produce them cheaply enough and show enough flesh to attract a distributor. During the next four years he allowed me to write the music for all of his movies.

It was in this seamy world of underground show business that I learned the real beginnings of craft. I would spend hours at the moviola trying to invent styles of music that would be appropriate for the on-screen action, which was mostly outdoor travelog shots of photographers on their way to take pictures of naked ladies. Inventing music to keep things interesting became quite a challenge.

Our studio sessions were a mad scramble to record everything in one take—there was no money for retakes—and this made great demands on the talent of my musicians. There was never enough budget for projection to allow us to watch the film as we recorded, but fortunately my producer had taught me tricks with a stopwatch that eliminated the unnecessary distraction of the visual (a fact that never pleased my musicians).

I began by hiring musician friends from high school, later expanding to other young players I met who were willing to work quickly and cheaply.

In one film, a group of traveling salesmen were seen sitting on a funky couch watching some ladies performing a striptease. This particular scene ran for ten minutes—*ten full minutes* of the same three women dancing around and around. The monotony was only occasionally broken up by a new camera angle.

For this epic, my producer wanted to depart from the clichéd, bluesy strip music he always used for this kind of scene. He wanted something different, and Indian belly-dance music was ordered, complete with oboe, finger bells, tabla drums, and sitar-like sounds.

For the session, I prepared a leadsheet that could be played over and over until the required ten minutes had been filled up. This worked out well, except that for my oboe player, ten minutes of nonstop blowing was like playing *forever*. After a few choruses his eyes began pleading with me to tell him that the time had expired. Ten minutes of boom-ditty-boom-ditty-boom-ditty seemed like it would never end. It was like falling asleep on a long plane flight, and waking seven hours later to find out that there are still five more hours to go. This was truly music-by-the-pound.

But for a new writer it was a chance to learn, providing the opportunity to work with film editors who taught me how to cut the mag tracks when my music was over-length, and how to extend and repeat bars when I came in short. And even how to edit the actual picture, adding or removing a few imperceptible frames from each scene to make up for some timing error that I had brought back from the studio.

And on the business side, I learned how to ask for and receive payment, at least for my band, before I entered the studio. I wanted to believe that my producer's intentions were honorable, but sometimes found that his checkbook wasn't.

I have extolled the story of my childhood and career roots to illustrate that it is possible to reach certain levels without training, simply by persevering with raw talent and enthusiasm. Everyone starts somewhere and stumbles along until a crossroad is reached. Mine came with my first chance at a commercial.

There were many young professionals doing their apprenticeship in the nudies, people who today are top film editors, advertising producers, and art directors. (Don't ask; I won't tell who they are.) One who was daylighting on a commercial got me an interview to write the background score. I quickly put together a tape of my best nudie movie music and impressed the agency music director enough for him to give me the job. But when we met at the film editor's to "take counts," I learned how little I actually knew. (Taking counts is the process of measuring the film by individual frames to determine where specific actions occur: the door slams at 14 feet 8 frames; the lips touch at 43 feet 12 frames, and so on).

The commercial was a thirty second spot for Maxwell House Coffee which was currently being packaged in a specially shaped clear glass jar. The object of the commercial was to illustrate the many uses that one could devise for this wondrous jar: first it was a place to putt a golf ball, then a fish tank complete with splashing goldfish, then a flowerpot, then a piggybank. The list went on and on—sixteen different uses, sixteen different "hits," all in thirty seconds.

The music director sat with me and we discussed his concept of what should happen and which instrumentation to use. Naturally I wanted to be agreeable, so his concept immediately became my concept. He suggested that I might use a harpsichord, perhaps going for a classical approach with a little rock flavoring thrown in. Then he gave me the names of some studio musicians, suggesting that I try to book them for the session. Before this, I'd only had my music played by musicians who were my friends.

But as I watched the film counter zip by, and filled my page with the numbers and the lengths of all the quick hits, discussing with the music director what he felt should happen at each point, I realized that I was terribly unprepared to handle this enormous job. Oh, I could write the music without any problem, I thought, but I certainly did not have the technique to guarantee that my music would "catch" the hits each time.

After the music director left, I remained to talk to the film editor.

"Want standard punching?" he asked.

I decided not to fake it. "What's that?"

He had sensed my inexperience. "Four singles and a double—that's where the music starts. A single warning at the end, and then a double at the end of sound."

"How do you determine what the right tempo is to make the hits?"

"Compose at any tempo that has a whole number of frames—no fractions—and watch the holes go by during the leader. I can punch them ten frames apart, eleven, nine, eight, whatever you want. The holes will be your tempo guide. If the studio has the equipment, get them to set up a monitor near the drummer. It helps when two people see the starting punches."

I agreed to call him as soon as I established a tempo for my music.

But now my most serious problem had to be confronted: in the nudies I could fake and re-edit my way around any deficiencies in my studio technique, but in the professional world I had hit my first stone wall: I knew of no way to determine from the numbers where the hits would occur in the music.

I called on one of my high school colleagues who had written music for some industrial films. "How do you determine how many beats of music it takes to get to a certain place in the film?"

"I watch the picture and use my pocket metronome set to the tempo I want, then clock it on my stopwatch until I reach the hit. Try to use full-frame tempos like nine, ten, eleven—it's easier to punch the film. (This confirmed the editor's remarks.) He then described how to convert the frames into metronome settings.

"But how do you know that these spring-wound clocks are accurate, especially on occasions when the cues are really close together?"

"Oh, I adjust it after, by eye, on the session. It's usually only a beat or two here and there."

I could not imagine taking the time on a session to adjust a music track with sixteen cues to catch. It would take forever and cost a fortune while the musicians sat around and I did homework.

Using the name given to me by the film editor, I called the president of a major jingle house. Expecting the same sense of camaraderie that I enjoyed with my own musicians, who always guided me through technical matters when I got in over my head, I introduced myself. Then I asked if he would share what he knew about finding out where the hits are.

He replied brusquely that I represented competition to his company and it would not be appropriate to share anything with me, especially technical information. When I explained that I was just starting out, doing my first job, and was not in his exalted league, and merely wanted to ask some questions and not steal business, I found it was to no avail. Without an apology, he hung up. He must have been having a bad day. (Being unwilling to share information with your colleagues makes you a very bad person.)

In desperation I turned to the one person who I knew would help me puzzle through the problem. I called my father and explained the situation in detail.

"How fast does the film move?" he asked.

"Twenty-four frames per second."

"Your counts are measured in feet and frames? How many frames to a foot?"

"Sixteen frames per foot."

"What tempo do you want to use?"

"One hundred twenty beats per minute would be okay, that's twelve frames per beat, but what if I want to change the tempo?"

"One problem at a time," he said patiently, promising to call back as soon as he had a solution. Twenty minutes later the phone rang.

"At a tempo of one hundred and twenty beats per minute the golf ball hits the jar in nine-and-a-half beats . . . it's eleven beats to where the fish jumps, thirteen-and-a-quarter to the flower pot . . . "

"How did you do that?" I asked, suddenly relieved and mightily impressed.

This is how he described it: Film travels past the projector's film gate at 24 frames per second, or 1,440 frames per minute. Each frame represents a moment of time, and the job is to find out what portion of a beat at your chosen tempo, measured in beats per minute, can be heard during that time span. By dividing the tempo (120 beats per minute in this example) by the film speed (1,440 frames per minute—a standard), you can determine what portion of a beat of music occurs during each frame at that tempo. Then you take the result and multiply it by the number of frames from the start of the picture to the place where the hit takes place. At a tempo of 120 beats per minute:

the golf ball hits the jar at 7 feet 2 frames (114 frames)
$(120 \div 1,440) \times 114 = 9.5$ beats

the fish jumps at 8 feet 4 frames (132 frames)
$(120 \div 1,440) \times 132 = 11$ beats

the flower pot appears at 9 feet 15 frames (159 frames)
$(120 \div 1,440) \times 159 = 13.25$ beats

That's the formula for determining how many beats it takes to get to any spot in your picture. If you want to change the tempo, just change the beats-per-minute calculation and do the rest the same way.

"Give me a few days," my father said, "and I'll develop a chart you can use."

On the day of the session, I arrived at the studio an hour early and asked that the projectionist run the film over and over so I could get accustomed to watching the punches go by.

Needless to say I hit every cue, and thanks to my father's ability to find a way to make it work, the track I wrote was accepted by the Maxwell House client.

To prepare myself for more jobs, I developed my father's charts for every setting on my metronome. It took two years to complete. Then I learned that there were books in existence that had done all the calculating already, and in much greater detail, breaking down counts into eighth-of-frames to conform with the new digital metronome that was becoming the standard of the industry.

But throughout my entire career I have used my own books and my own system. Recently I've begun to use a small RhodesSystem computer, moving into the next phase of figuring out where the hits are.

My first commercial didn't run for a very long time—not even thirteen weeks, which was just enough for the jar promotion. And there is no way to measure the impact that my music had on product sales. But the impact of the commercial on my professional life was indelible and taught me several important lessons:

1. Never be afraid or embarrassed to seek advise. There is always a way to get *anyone* on the phone. If your requests are reasonable and interesting, you'll find out what you need to know. Those who fear you will not respond, but with patience you will always find someone who will take time to help.

2. Make friends with the film editor. His genius can make you one.

3. Love your work. There's nothing else like it out there.

APPENDIX

EXTRACTS FROM THE BRUSKIN REPORT ON
TELEVISION AND RADIO ADVERTISING MUSIC

THE FOLLOWING TABLES are from a 1983 study designed and executed by R.H. Bruskin Associates to measure the proportion of broadcast time that is devoted to music and the proportion of music time that is advertising related. The study was conducted in twenty-five areas of dominant influence (ADI*), selected to achieve a nationally representative sample.

TABLE A1. TELEVISION—
Percentage of Broadcast Time That Involves Music,
and Percentage of Total Music Time That Is Advertising Related

Total TV Broadcast Time	100%
Non-Music	66.6
Music	33.4
Total TV Music Time	100%
Advertising	40.8
Non-Advertising	59.2

TABLE A2. RADIO—
Percentage of Broadcast Time That Is Devoted to Music,
and Percentage of Total Music Time That Is Advertising Related

	AM Radio	FM Radio
Total Radio Broadcast Time	100%	100%
Non-Music	39.5	21.1
Music	60.5	78.9
Total Radio Music Time	100%	100%
Advertising	11.7	8.9
Non-Advertising	88.3	91.1

*An ADI is a geographic area defined by Arbitron, Inc. for the purpose of classifying and measuring television viewing and radio listening behavior.

TABLE A3. AM RADIO—
Variation by Programming Format in the Percentage of Broadcast Time
Devoted to Music (Advertising and Non-Advertising)

Programming Format*	Broadcast Time			Music Time		
	Non-Music	Music	Total	Advertising	Non-Advertising	Total
Middle of the Road	40.7	59.3	100	12.7	87.3	100
Country	38.2	61.8	100	11.0	89.0	100
Standard	45.7	54.3	100	11.9	88.1	100
Contemporary	19.2	80.8	100	9.1	90.9	100
All Other	49.3	50.7	100	12.4	87.6	100

TABLE A4. FM RADIO—
Variation by Programming Format in the Percentage of Broadcast Time
Devoted to Music (Advertising and Non-Advertising)

Programming Format*	Broadcast Time			Music Time		
	Non-Music	Music	Total	Advertising	Non-Advertising	Total
Middle of the Road	23.5	76.5	100	10.5	89.5	100
Country	28.5	71.5	100	8.2	91.8	100
Standard	19.3	80.7	100	6.7	93.3	100
Contemporary	13.0	87.0	100	10.9	89.1	100
All Other	13.2	86.8	100	8.1	91.9	100

*Middle of the Road refers to stations that program soft rock and popular adult music, generally accompanied by news and personalities; Country refers to stations that play country and western music; Standard stations are those that program "beautiful" music or big band and swing music; Contemporary stations program top 40 and contemporary hit radio in a high-energy manner; All Other refers to any formats not included in the above descriptions.

ASSOCIATIONS

ADVERTISING CLUB OF NEW YORK
155 East 55th Street
Suite 202
New York, New York 10022
*Conducts courses, classes, and clinics in
production, marketing, and
management.*

AMERICAN ASSOCIATION OF
ADVERTISING AGENCIES
(THE FOUR As)
666 Third Avenue
13th Floor
New York, New York 10017
*Represents the interests of advertisers
and their agencies, and advances the
cause of advertising as a whole.*

ASSOCIATION OF INDEPENDENT
COMMERCIAL PRODUCERS
Kaufman Astoria Studios
34-12 36th Street
Astoria, New York 11106
*Serves independent television
commercial producers.*

ASSOCIATION OF NATIONAL
ADVERTISERS
155 East 44th Street
New York, New York 10017
*Conducts workshops and seminars on
various aspects of advertising.*

CLIO AWARDS
336 East 59th Street
New York, New York 10022
*Produces the annual CLIO Awards
honoring excellence in advertising.*

INTERNATIONAL ADVERTISING
ASSOCIATION
342 Madison Avenue
Suite 2000
New York, New York 10017
*Serves individuals in advertising and
related fields.*

RADIO ADVERTISING BUREAU
304 Park Avenue South
New York, New York 10010
*Serves radio stations and networks, and
produces the annual Big Apple Awards.*

SOCIETY OF PROFESSIONAL
AUDIO RECORDING SERVICES
4300 Tenth Avenue
Lake Worth, Florida 33461
*Composed of studio owners, engineers,
suppliers, producers, and users.
Promotes all aspects of this industry.*

TELEVISION BUREAU
OF ADVERTISING
477 Madison Avenue
New York, New York 10022
*A trade organization that promotes
television advertising.*

ORGANIZATIONS

AMERICAN SOCIETY
OF COMPOSERS, AUTHORS
AND PUBLISHERS (ASCAP)
One Lincoln Plaza
New York, New York 10023
*A nonprofit music licensing organization
that collects fees from music users on
behalf of the music creators.*

ARTISTS SERVICE
7014 13th Avenue
Brooklyn, NY 11228
212/785-1500
*An answering service primarily for
commercial singers and announcers.*

BROADCAST MUSIC INC. (BMI)
320 West 57th Street
New York, New York 10019
*A nonprofit music licensing organization
that collects fees from music users on
behalf of the music creators.*

BROADCAST TRAFFIC AND
RESIDUALS, INC.
16 West 22nd Street
New York, New York 10010
*Processes talent payments for
performers in commercials.*

COPYRIGHT OFFICE
Library of Congress
First and Independence Avenue,
Southeast
Room 401
Washington, D.C. 20540
*Administrates the statutory protection
due to authors, composers, performers,
and publishers.*

RADIO AND TV REGISTRY
314 West 53rd Street
New York, New York 10019
212/582-8800
*Serves jingle writers, musicians, and
producers. Many, if not most, jingle and
record dates are booked through this
"Work Phone" answering service.*

UNIONS

AMERICAN FEDERATION
OF MUSICIANS OF THE
UNITED STATES AND CANADA
(AF of M)
Paramount Building
1501 Broadway
Suite 600
New York, New York 10036
*The musician's union. Represents all
kinds of musicians. Affiliated with the
AFL-CIO.*

AMERICAN FEDERATION
OF TELEVISION AND
RADIO ARTISTS (AFTRA)
260 Madison Avenue
New York, New York 10016
*Serves the interests of videotape and
radio performers and personalities,
including jingle singers, actors and
announcers.*

AMERICAN SOCIETY
OF MUSIC ARRANGERS
P.O. Box 11
Hollywood, California 90078
*Conducts educational workshops and
"How to Write For" clinics.*

AMERICAN SOCIETY
OF MUSIC COPYISTS
1697 Broadway
Room 805
New York, New York 10019
*Represents copyists of all forms of music
from symphonic to commercial jingles.*

SCREEN ACTORS GUILD (SAG)
7065 Hollywood Boulevard
Hollywood, California 90028
*Represents actors and actresses,
including jingle singers and announcers
in filmed commercials.*

BOOKS

THIS BUSINESS OF MUSIC
By Sidney Shemel and
M. William Krasilovsky, 1985
Billboard Publications, Inc.
1515 Broadway
New York, New York 10036
*An excellent discussion of the business,
economic, and legal aspects of the
music industry.*

LIVINGSTON'S COMPLETE
MUSIC INDUSTRY BUSINESS AND
LAW REFERENCE BOOK
By Robert Allen Livingston

Music Business Consultants
P.O. Box 147
Cardiff by the Sea, California 92007
*A dictionary of legal and business terms
encountered in the music industry.*

MUSIC SCORING FOR TV
AND MOTION PICTURES
By Marlin Skiles, 1976
Tab Books
Blue Ridge Summit, Pennsylvania 17214
*Covers the mechanics of scoring;
includes interviews with leading
arrangers.*

DIRECTORIES

BILLBOARD INTERNATIONAL
RECORDING STUDIO AND
EQUIPMENT DIRECTORY
Billboard Publications, Inc.
1515 Broadway
New York, New York 10036
*A yearly listing of recording studios,
record producers, and equipment
suppliers.*

BUSINESS-OF-MUSIC
SCHOOLS DIRECTORY
By Charles Suber, 1986
Charles Suber & Associates, Inc.
600 South Dearborn Street
Chicago, Illinois 60605
*A directory of colleges, universities, and
other educational institutions that offer
courses and programs in the music
business.*

CALIFORNIA MUSIC DIRECTORY
Augie Blume & Associates
Music Industry Resources
Box 190
San Anselmo, California 94960
*Includes producers, studios, radio and
television stations, suppliers, and
publishers.*

CELEBRITY SERVICE
INTERNATIONAL
CONTACT BOOK
Entertainment Industry
Celebrity Service International
1780 Broadway
New York, New York 10019
*A trade directory of the entertainment,
media, and allied industries. Covers
New York, London, Paris, and Rome.*

HANDBOOK OF ADVERTISING
AND MARKETING SERVICES
Executive Communications, Inc.
919 Third Avenue
New York, New York 10022
*Covers producers, promoters, designers,
and others affiliated with the advertising
industry.*

THE LIVELY ARTS
INFORMATION DIRECTORY
Gale Research Company
Book Tower
Detroit, Michigan 48226
*A guide to the fields of radio, television,
theater, film, music, and dance for the
United States and Canada.*

MADISON AVENUE HANDBOOK
Peter Glenn Publications
17 East 48th Street
New York, New York 10017
*Lists agencies and related services in
New York, Los Angeles, Chicago, San
Francisco, Dallas, Houston, Detroit,
Miami, San Antonio, Toronto, and
Montreal.*

MUSIC BOOKING SOURCE
DIRECTORY
Somerset Communications
6525 Sunset Boulevard, Studio A
Hollywood, California 90028
*A directory of artists, equipment, and
services.*

STANDARD DIRECTORY
OF ADVERTISING AGENCIES
(THE REDBOOK)
National Register Publishing Company,
Inc.
3004 Glenview Road
Wilmette, Illinois 60091
*A directory of agencies with company
name, top management, annual billing,
major accounts, and branch offices.*

THE WORKBOOK
Scott & Daughters Publishing
940 North Highland Avenue
Los Angeles, California 90038
*Includes over 20,000 agencies,
producers, free-lancers, and related
services in California.*

PERIODICALS

ADVERTISING AGE
Crain Communications, Inc.
220 East 42nd Street
New York, New York 10017
Weekly news on advertising, marketing, and promotion in the United States and elsewhere.

ADWEEK'S MARKETER'S GUIDE
TO MEDIA
A/S/M/Communications
49 East 21st Street
New York, New York 10010
Nationwide quarterly guide to the advertising media.

ADWEEK'S MARKETING WEEK
A/S/M/ Communications
820 Second Avenue
New York, New York 10017
Nationwide coverage of the advertising industry. Regional editions serve the East, Midwest, New England, Southeast, Southwest, and West.

BACK STAGE
Back Stage Publications
330 West 42nd Street
New York, New York 10036
A weekly trade paper for the entertainment business; contains information about radio and television commercial production.

BILLBOARD
Billboard Publications Inc.
1515 Broadway
New York, New York 10036
A professional entertainment publication for the recording industry and related fields.

DAILY VARIETY
Daily Variety, Ltd.
1400 North Cahuenga Boulevard
Hollywood, California 90028
Trade news of the entertainment business.

MARKETING AND MEDIA DECISIONS
C.C. Publishing, Inc.
19 West 44th Street
Suite 812
New York, New York 10036
Examines trends affecting national and regional marketing and media.

MEDIA INDUSTRY NEWSLETTER
Media Industry Newsletter
145 East 49th Street
New York, New York 10017
Reports developments in the media and advertising industries.

MUSICIAN
Musician Magazine
Box 701
Gloucester, Massachusetts 01931-0701
A top consumer title in the popular music field.

NEW YORK PUBLICITY OUTLETS
Public Relations Plus, Inc.
Drawer 1197
New Milford, Connecticut 06776
Media listings for radio, television, news services, and syndicates in the New York City area.

WORDS & MUSIC
U.S. Publishing, Inc.
17 Sylvan Street
Rutherford, New Jersey 07070
Contains articles of interest to song writers and lyricists.

INDEX

Account executive, 61
Account supervisor, 61–62
Adaptations of music from other
    sources, 23–24, 95
Advertising
    impact of, 6–8
    information sources on, 48
    local/regional/national, 67–68
    in movie theaters, 7–8
    political, 86
    public service, 6–7
    testing, 67
    See also Automobile advertising; Beer
      advertising
Advertising Age, 48
Advertising agency
    account team of, 60–63
    business affairs manager, 62–63, 236
    change in campaigns, 240–41
    creative meeting with, 71–78
    creative team of, 59–60
    job seeking in, 47–52
    music department of, 56–59
    music publishing by, 187–88
    in new business pitch, 65
    and payment delays, 176, 236–37
    See also Contract; Presentation
Advertising music
    beginnings of, 8–11

forms of, 20–26
quality of, 5
role of, 4, 8, 24
    See also Jingle composer/writer;
      Jingle house; Jingle industry;
      Jingle-making process
Adweek, 48, 100
AF of M, 12, 15, 16, 17, 18, 19, 40
    contract form of, 140–47, 160–71
    wage scale of, 134–47, 158
AFTRA, 12, 15, 16, 17, 126, 128, 149, 151,
    180, 211, 212
Agency Redbook, 48
American Federation of Musicians. *See*
    AF of M
American Society of Composers,
    Authors and Publishers, The. *See*
    ASCAP
Arranger, 109–10, 136, 137
Arranging fee, 13, 17, 18, 69, 136
Art director, 59
ASCAP, 12, 14, 15, 200, 202, 210, 213
    -BMI payment system, 187, 188–89,
      192–94
Automobile advertising
    musical style of, 83–84, 93–94
    Pontiac jingle, 116–17

Back Stage, 48

Bank, relationship with, 178–79, 183
Beer advertising
  lyrics in, 88–92
  musical style of, 94
  tag in, 21
Bid sheet, 195–97
BMI, 12, 14
  -ASCAP payment system, 187,
    189–89, 192–94
Booth/conductor part, 111
Broadcast Music Inc. *See* BMI
Budget. *See* Production budget
Budweiser jingle, 21, 89–92
Buffalo Broadcasting Case, 190
Business affairs manager, 62–63, 236

Cartage costs, in production budget, 137
CBS case, 190
Child jingle singer, 126–27
Chiquita Banana jingle, 9–10
Cigarette advertising, 85–86
Cola advertising, 94
Commercials. *See* Advertising
Contacts, using, 48
Continuance fees, 14, 69–70, 181, 182,
    185–86, 192–94, 216
Contract
  amending terms of, 71
  bid sheet, 195–97
  composer/publisher advertising
    license, 208–14
  copyright requirement in, 207
  indemnification clause in, 95, 203–7
  legal advice in, 207–8
  performance rights and, 192, 215–16
  rider to, 201–3
  standard agency form, 70–71, 194,
    198–201
Contractor
  music, 112, 218, 221
  vocal, 126
Copyist, 110–11, 136, 221
Copyright, 111, 187, 204, 207
Copywriter, 59
Corporation, forming, 35
Creative director, 60
Creative fee, 13, 16, 17, 66–69, 192
Creative meeting, 71–78

Demo
  billing for use of, 174

competitive, 57, 73–74
equipment for, 41–43, 53
fees, 12, 16, 43, 64, 66
  crediting, 66
free, 65–66
length of, 75–76
ownership of, 76–77
presentation of, 104–5
quality of, 43, 57
scheduling time for, 43–44
Donut, 22, 225

Engineer, recording, 130, 219, 223, 224,
    226, 228, 236
Equipment, 41–43, 53

Fees
  arranging, 13, 17, 18, 69, 136
  continuance, 14, 69–70, 181, 182,
    185–86, 192–94, 216
  creative, 13, 16, 17, 66–69, 192
  demo, 12, 16, 43, 64, 66
    crediting, 66
  payroll handling, 176–77
  performance, 14, 186, 187, 192–94,
    215–16
  rearranging, 14, 17, 70
  See also Residuals
Film, recording to, 103
  taking counts in, 247–51
Film mix, 235–36
First refusal, right of, 70
Follow-up call, 49–50
Four-track mix, 229–30, 236

Hook, 20–21
Horns
  overdubbing, 226
  in production budget, 136

"I Love New York" jingle, 113–15
Indemnification clause, 95, 203–7
Instruments
  cartage, 137
  rentals, 138–39
Insurance, plagiarism, 205–7

Jingle, defined, 20
Jingle composer/writer
    and agency. *See* Advertising
    agency

in collaboration, 33
income sources for. *See* Fees
in job search, 47-52
lyricist, 29
musical training for, 28
and performance rights. *See*
Performance rights
pros and cons of business ownership,
34–35
in recording session, 217–32
rep for, 39–41, 53
and residual status, 14–15, 181–82,
185–86
working in jingle house, 29–32, 53, 64
Jingle house
forming, 32–35
hired talent, 109–32
income sources for, 12–15, 16, 19, 64,
186, 187
incorporation of, 35
nonunion, 36–38, 178
pros and cons of working for, 29–32,
53, 64
union signatory, 35–36
See also Payroll handling; Production
budget
Jingle industry
current state of, 5–6
and demise of studio musician, 120–21
pros and cons of working in, 3–4, 6
Jingle-making process
adaptations, 23–24, 95
agency directions in, 57, 88, 203
belief in product, 85–87
creative block in, 97–99
endings in, 96
generating ideas, 79–81
musical style in, 83–84, 92–93
matching with product, 93–94
original musical motifs in, 83–85
plagiarism *vs* imitation in, 94–95
product information in, 72–73, 85
scheduling time in, 81–83
steps in, 11-12
taking counts, 247–51
time limitations in, 45, 50–51, 75–76,
95–97
See also Demo; Lyrics; Recording
session
Jingle parody, 187–88
Jingle singer
affiliated with jingle house, 123–24
children as, 126–27
demo reels of, 124–25
finding work, 125–26
free-lance, 123
income of, 13–14, 15, 20, 121–22
in production budget, 148–52
putting on hold, 128–29
qualifications for, 122–23
star performer as, 129–30
See also Vocals

Lawyers, 207–8
Lead sheet, 111
Liberty Mutual Insurance jingle, 118–19
Library music, 24–26, 56
Logo, musical, 21
Lyrics, 29
from agency script, 88
internal, 88–92
presentation of, 101
product name in, 87–88
slogan in, 87

Madison Avenue Handbook, 126
Management supervisor, 62
Metronome, 42, 248–49, 250–51
MIDI music, 25, 44, 120–21
Mix, 22–23, 228–29
film, 235–36
to four-track tape, 229–30, 236
protecting, 231
remix, 235
stereo/mono, 231–32
Mnemonics, 21
Mono mix, 231–32
Musical style, 83–84, 93–94
Music department, agency, 56–59
Music director, agency, 58
Musician, studio, 112, 220, 224
decline of, 120–21
income of, 10, 173, 174
in production budget, 133–47
putting on hold, 128–29
qualifications for, 112
Music producer, agency, 58–59
Music publishing
by agency, 187–88
by composer, 208

New York Times, 48

Orchestrator, 137

Overdubbing
    elimination of leakage, 226
    horns, 226–27
    melody line, 225–26
    vocals, 227–28

Payroll handling
    through agency, 175
    bank loans for, 178–79, 183
    check-writing systems for, 179
    markup for, 176–77
    purchase order as security in, 183
    through service companies, 176
    signing on behalf of client, 179
    tax guidelines in, 177–78, 183
    unions and, 179, 180
Pension payments, in production
    budget, 137–38
Pepsi-Cola jingle, 8
Performance income, 14, 186, 187,
    192–94, 215–16
Performance rights
    blanket license concept of, 188–89,
    190–91
    impact of television syndication on,
    189–91
    under source music licenses, 190,
    191–92
Plagiarism
    vs imitation, 94–95
    indemnification against, 203–5
    insurance, 205–6
Political advertising, 86
Pontiac jingle, 116–17
Presentation
    dealing with rejection, 105–7
    live, 74, 102–4
    by mail, 105
    on phone, 100–102
    of single idea, 74–75
    tape, 104
Producer, agency, 60
Production. See Recording session
Production budget, 23, 43
    for fix session, 235
    for home/office studio, 43, 157–59,
    172–73
    musician costs in, 133–47, 157–58
    polishing, 155–56
    recording costs in, 152–55
    total production estimate, 153–55,
    172–73

vocal costs in, 148–52
Public service advertising, 6–7

Radio
    four-track splits for, 230
    in production budget, 137, 138, 149,
    151, 155, 172, 173
    stereo/mono mix for, 231-232
Recording session
    breaks in, 225, 227
    postproduction, 234–37
    preparing for, 217–21
    recording the :30, 224–25
    recording the :60, 223–24
    rehearsal, 221–23
    See also Mix; Overdubbing;
    Production budget
Reel
    copies of, 47
    length of, 45, 50–51
    mailing, 49
    musical style of, 45–46
    order and form of music on, 46–47
    originality of, 44
    presentation of, 49, 50
    vocal, 124–125
Remix, 235
Rep, 39–41, 53
Residuals
    musician, 13, 69–70, 158, 173
    origins of, 180–81
    status for jingle writers, 14–15, 181–82,
    185–86
    variations in payment, 182
    vocal, 13–14, 15, 20, 121–22, 186, 194
Rhythm section, in production budget,
    135
Right-to-work states, 36

SAG, 12, 15, 16, 17, 18, 19, 126, 127, 148,
    149, 150, 180, 212
Score, background, 21–22
Scoring
    creative fee for, 68–69
    reel, 46
Screen Actors Guild. See SAG
Sequencers, 41–42
Singer. See Jingle singer; Vocals
Slogan, lyric, 87
Stereo mix, 231–32
Stopwatch, 42
Strings

overdubbing, 227
in production budget, 136
Studio
    home/office, 43, 120, 157, 59, 172–73
    putting on hold, 131
    specialization of, 130–31
    See also Production budget;
        Recording session
Synthesist, 139, 149, 157–58
Synthesizer, 109–10, 120, 156–57

Tag, 20–21
Talent, hired, 109–32
    See also Jingle singer; Musician,
        studio; Payroll handling
Tape recorder, 42, 44
Tax guidelines, in payroll handling,
    177–78, 183
Television
    four-track splits for, 229–30
    mono mix for, 231–32
    in production budget, 137, 138, 148,
        150, 155, 172, 173

syndication, and performance rights,
    189–91

Union(s)
    bond, 179
    joining, 127–28
    and payment procedures, 179, 180
    signatory companies, 35–36
    wage scale
        musicians, 134–47
        singers, 148–49
    See also Residuals

Vocals
    overdubbing, 227–28
    residual, 13–14, 15, 20, 121–22, 186,
        194
    See also Jingle singer

Welfare payments, in production
    budget, 137–38
Woodwinds, in production budget, 136
Work-for-hire contract. *See* Contract